P9-BJB-739

ANIMALS IN RESEARCH
ISSUES AND CONFLICTS

ANIMALS in RESEARCH
Issues and Conflicts

J.J.McCoy

An Impact Book
Franklin Watts
New York   Chicago   London   Toronto   Sydney

179
m

Library of Congress Cataloging-in-Publication Data

McCoy, J. J. (Joseph J.), 1917–
    Animals in research : issues and conflicts / by J. J. McCoy.
        p.   cm.—(An Impact book)
    Includes bibliographical references and index.
    Summary: Examines the role of animals in testing for biological
research, medical purposes, and consumer products, and discusses
controversies raised over such practices.
    ISBN 0-531-13023-1
    1. Animal experimentation—United States.   2. Animal
experimentation—Canada.   3. Animal rights movement—United States.
4. Animal rights movement—Canada.   [1. Animal experimentation.
2. Animals—Treatment.]   I. Title.
    HV4930.M35   1993
    179'.4—dc20   92-21117 CIP AC

Franklin Watts 9-16-93 19,14

CONTENTS

INTRODUCTION

Animals and human beings have had a close relationship since prehistoric times. For the most part, it has been an association of symbiosis, with human beings receiving the lion's share of the benefits. It has also been a relationship in which animals have been exploited in various ways. None has engendered more emotion, censorship, and condemnation than the use of animals for experimentation.

Most of us accept the need to conduct research beneficial to human beings and animals. The conquest of human and animal diseases and the search for cures or treatments for others have involved the use of many animals of various species. The development of chemicals, food additives, pesticides, and other potentially harmful substances has also involved the use of many animals to test the safety of these substances.

But this use of animals is not without its opponents, some of whom have resorted to acts of violence and even terrorism. The opposition to the use of animals for experimentation is not new. Nineteenth-century English humanitarians, such as Richard Martin and Jeremy Bentham, led the opposition to animal experimentation and cruelty to animals in general. However, their crusade against the inhumane treatment and torture of animals was a passive one, as were the efforts of early twentieth-century humanitarians in America. It is a different story today. A new breed of animal protectionists has emerged. They are members of what is called the animal rights movement. They believe in and pursue an active approach to eliminating cruelty to animals, especially in research laboratories.

The older and traditional humane societies or animal welfare groups asked people to be kind to animals and to refrain from cruel acts. They circulated articles, handbills, leaflets, and other literature aimed at reducing cruelty to animals. And they have operated animal shelters for stray or unwanted animals.

Not so with the animal rights groups. They are more militant, more direct, and more aggressive in their campaign to free animals from exploitation. Their demands range from the reduction of the number of animals used in research to the wider use of alternatives to the total abolition of any form of animal exploitation. In backing up these demands, the animal rights advocates have resorted to demonstrations, boycotts, corporate shareholder resolutions, laboratory break-ins, theft of animals, destruction of equipment, violence, and even threats of bodily harm or death to researchers.

The growing strength of the animal rights groups and their well-filled treasuries are a matter of concern to the scientific community. So is the influence that animal rights activists have with the public and even with some politicians. Researchers have been put on the defensive and have been compelled to justify their studies and experiments. This they have done, but mainly to opponents who have only one objective in mind: the elimination of animal research and consumer product testing. Researchers have not only had to justify their research but to defend their laboratories and research facilities against vandalism.

Why has the use of animals in research and testing become a national issue, second, perhaps, only to the human abortion issue? What is there about dogs, cats, monkeys and other primates, guinea pigs, hamsters, rabbits, mice, and rats that evokes such emotional and violent response when they are used in research? What are the issues in this controversy, a controversy that has economic, ethical, moral, political, and social consequences?

The issue is of national importance because many Americans and Canadians feel deeply about it. Many do not believe we have the right to subject animals to pain and suffering in the laboratories. Others have not made up their minds, while still others believe that benefits to humanity are worth the sacrifice of animals. It is a complex issue, one that has no pat answers. At the core of the issue is whether animals have rights, an old concept that dates to the Middle Ages (the period in European history from about A.D. 476 to A.D. 1453). For centuries the Judeo-Christian concept of the separateness of human beings and animals dominated the treatment of animals.

People were told that animals had no souls; therefore they had no rights. Most philosophers went along with this church dictum. René Descartes, the seventeenth-century French mathematician and philosopher, wrote that animals were nothing more than "cleverly built machines." As such, they had no feelings or conscious responses. No animal, according to Descartes, could be compared to a human in any way.

Most of the early biologists and zoologists were more concerned with the classification and natural history of animals than with any ethical or moral questions concerning their treatment. Few, if any, attempts were made to establish a relationship between human beings and animals.

But this thinking changed in the nineteenth century. Charles Darwin, the English naturalist, dispelled some of the earlier beliefs and dogma regarding a relationship between human beings and animals. In his monumental work, *On the Origin of Species by Means of Natural Selection* published in 1859, Darwin proposed that all animals evolved from more primitive forms by a process he called "natural selection." That is, nature selected the most vigorous and best-suited animal forms for survival. And eventually, these primitive forms became more complex.

Darwin did not discuss human beings in *On the Origin of Species.* However, in 1871, he published a study of human evolution, *The Descent of Man*, in which he set forth the theory that humans also evolved from primitive forms. Thus, if Darwin's theories were correct, people and animals were part of an entity, a whole natural system. And if this was true, then it followed that human beings and animals were related, that there was a direct link between them. This thought caused as much controversy and consternation in America as it did in Europe. It established a physical, if not a spiritual, relationship between people and animals.

Modern scientific thought supposes, despite some missing links, that there is no break in the long chain of animal forms that have evolved over time. Complex animals forms, such as human beings, have evolved from simpler forms. While human beings have some different characteristics and behavior patterns, the overall difference is one of the degree of complexity when humans are compared to other animals.

Many people cling to the old Judeo-Christian concept of humans' preeminence or superiority over animals. Many others, including animal rights advocates, do not accept this concept. They reject the idea that there is a "superior" species. Since there is no superior species, human beings do not have the right to mistreat animals or exploit them in any way, including using them in research.

Various species and large numbers of animals are used in biomedical and behavioral research, product testing, and education every year. But among many people, the experimental use of cats and dogs causes more anguish and provokes more condemnation than does the similar use of other animals. There are some valid reasons for this. For one thing, cats and dogs are very popular pets. Millions of them are kept in homes in the United States and Canada, not to mention elsewhere in the world. But more than that, cats and dogs have a special bond with human beings. In many households they are accorded equal status with their human owners, and are looked upon as members of the family.

The bond between these two animals and human beings goes back thousands of years: more than twenty thousand years in the case of the dog and about five thousand years for the cat. The pact between human and dog, a pact that has lasted a long time, began when wild dogs and the cave people joined forces. There are several theories as to how the cave dwellers and wild dogs formed a pact of mutualism. Konrad Lorenz, the Austrian psychologist and animal behaviorist, gives an interesting account of this ancient pact in his book *Man Meets Dog*. Both man and dog benefitted from this alliance. The dog served the cave people as a hunting companion, pet, and guardian. The cave people, in turn, fed the dog and protected him from larger predators such as the saber-toothed tiger and dire wolf.

The contributions of the dog to modern society need no listing or elaboration; the proof is in the facts. Dog ownership is at an all-time high according to the Pet Industry Advisory Council, a lobbying group based in Washington, D.C. In recent years, the influence of dogs (and other pets) on the mental and physical health of human beings has been documented in numerous articles, papers, and reports. But it is the loyalty, devotion, and companionship of this unique animal that make it difficult for people to accept its use in biomedical research.

What records we have of the cat's early association with human beings are from ancient Egyptian tombs and mastabas (*mastabas* are rectangular structures with sloping sides and flat roofs; many of them contained paintings and likenesses of human beings and cats). Judging by the evidence found in these structures, cats were held in high esteem by the ancient Egyptians.

In fact, cats were even regarded as minor gods. Some Egyptian deities were supposed to have catlike features and traits. For example, Ra, the sun god, was closely identified with the male cat. Bast or Pasht, the cat goddess, was a very popular deity. Her popularity is substantiated by the large number of her images, ranging from life-size paintings to tiny cat earrings found in Egyptian tombs.

Cats became popular pets and rodent catchers in other countries. Herodotus, the fifth century B.C. historian and traveler, extolled the virtues and characteristics of Egyptian cats in Book II of his *Histories*. Eventually, the reputation of the cat as a pet and rodent hunter grew and this diminutive feline was in great demand. It soon became a popular pet in all parts of the world. Today, cats occupy a special niche in our society. While they differ from dogs in temperament and their attitudes toward people (some people say that cats are more selective in their association with human beings), most cats have a close relationship with their owners. This unique and interesting animal is also used in various types of experiments, the victim or subject of biomedical and behavioral research, depending on viewpoint.

The other animals commonly used in research—rabbits, hamsters, guinea pigs, mice, rats, monkeys, and other nonhuman primates—have lesser or no special bonds with human beings. Nevertheless, many people deplore their use in research. These animals, along with the dog and cat, are the protagonists, the principal figures, in the animals in research controversy.

This book is a synthesis of that controversy. It is an effort to present a balanced view or provide "both sides of the story," examining the main issues and conflicts of that controversy.

Why Use Animals in Research?

The use of animals for experimentation dates back to ancient times, when Greek and Roman philosophers and physicians explored the bodies of animals to learn more about anatomy and physiology. Galen, the Greek anatomist and physician, is credited with being the founder of experimental physiology. His studies were conducted on a variety of animals. Pliny the Elder, the Roman scholar; Andreas Vesalius, the Flemish physician; and Aristotle, the noted Greek philosopher, sated their curiosity about the workings of the animal body by studying the anatomy and physiology of different animals.

These early animal experiments were crude by the standards of modern biomedical research. Little was known about the mechanisms of the human and animal body. Aristotle, for example, believed the heart was the center of the nervous system. He is said to have experimented on as many as fifty species of animals in studies of the nervous and circulatory systems. In ancient Constantinople (now Istanbul, Turkey), Flavius Vegetius Renatus, a Roman physician, was a pioneer in the study of the animal digestive, circulatory, respiratory, nervous, and genitourinary systems. Vegetius, as he was known in ancient times, advocated careful surgical techniques when experimenting on animals.

Among the old civilizations, that of the Hindus came closest to having what might be called a systematic practice of animal or veterinary medicine. In this practice, various animals were dissected in efforts to learn about animal anatomy and physiology. Despite the experimenting on animals, the Hindus regarded all living creatures as brothers.

Scholars who have translated some of the ancient Sanskrit veterinary writings tell of special hospitals for animals operated by the Hindu state. Here, Hindu animal doctors studied and treated the diseases of animals. Among the animals listed in the Sanskrit writings were elephants, horses, cattle, poultry, and various cage birds.

The Hindu doctors had enough knowledge of animal anatomy to establish a system of animal medicine. They performed minor surgery, cauterized wounds (by burning or searing them), set broken bones, and resorted to bloodletting when all other methods failed. The Sanskrit writings also mention that Hindu animal doctors practiced obstetrics, taking special care of pregnant cattle and elephants.

In other ancient cultures, such as the Babylonian, Hebrew, and Arab, animal medicine and experimentation were closely linked with human medicine. Superstition, ritual, and magic were rampant. Anyone professing to know something about animals could set himself up as an animal doctor. Consequently, the field of animal medicine was staffed by farriers (horseshoers), livestock farmers, and stablemen.

After hundreds of years of quasi-scientific animal and human medical practices, true scientific thought emerged in Europe. Roger Bacon, the thirteenth-century English philosopher, proposed a system of natural history that was far superior to anything before. He called for new scientific experimentation, criticizing long-accepted theories and practices.

However, clerical opposition to scientific thought and experimentation, especially in the field of medicine, was very strong. Human and animal experimentation was taboo. The clergy believed that human and animal diseases were concrete evidence of divine wrath. Scientists and scholars had no right to interfere with these visitations, since that responsibility belonged to the church.

This position of the clergy was especially troublesome to physicians, for they were forbidden to dissect human cadavers. Physicians, artists, and sculptors wishing to study the anatomy of the human body or dissect it had to steal cadavers and work on them in secret, risking discovery and punishment by death. As a result of the restrictions on the use of human corpses, physicians turned to the use of animals to learn more about disease and its effects on the animal body.

Today, animals are used in research for a number of reasons, chief among them being the restriction, for ethical and moral reasons, on the use of human beings as research subjects. In 1964, the World Medical Association (WMA) stated at its international conference in Helsinki, Finland, "Clinical research must conform to the moral and scientific principles that justify medical research." The WMA statement emphasized the fact that "medical research should be based on laboratory and animal experiments or other scientifically established facts." This policy was, in effect, a repudiation of the medical and behavioral experiments performed on human beings by Nazi physicians and scientists during World War II.

Although there is some research and experimentation carried out on human beings today (psychiatric and psychological studies, drug therapy, and the like), animals form the bulk of biomedical research subjects. The National Academy of Sciences Natural Resource Council (NRC) spent three years studying the issue of the use of animals in research. In its assessment, the NRC stated that "animals are a critical part of human health care." Also cited in the report was a long list of medical advances and achievements due to the use of animals in research. The NRC committee that undertook the study admitted that laboratory animals have been mistreated by some members of the scientific community. However, they added that it was not to be supposed that abuse or neglect of laboratory animals was widespread.[1]

Which animals and how many of them are used annually in biomedical research? Laboratory animals include cats, dogs, rabbits, guinea pigs, hamsters, mice, rats, monkeys, and nonhuman primates such as chimpanzees, and, in the agricultural field, horses, cattle, sheep, goats, and swine. As for how many animals are used each year, estimates vary according to the source. Estimates in animal rights literature range from 20 to 70 million. However, the Office of Technology Assessment gives a figure of 17 to 22 million, of which 90 percent are rodents. The percentage of cats and dogs, according to this assessment, is 1 to 2 percent, or about 200,000 of these animals.[2]

The use of animals to test the safety of consumer products such as cosmetics, drugs, and food might be called a form of research. Mice, rats, and rabbits are commonly used for product testing, but other animals may be, depending on the particular test. Estimates on the number of animals used in product testing vary and range from several million to half of all the animals used in research. The number of animals used in education is smaller, somewhere in the area of 50,000 to 60,000 animals in use in medical and veterinary schools. (There are no figures for animals used in secondary education.)

THE VALUE OF ANIMALS
AS RESEARCH TOOLS _____

In general, animals are used in research to study living systems. Animals, with the exception of elephants, turtles and tortoises, and a few other species, have relatively short lives. For example, mice have a life span of about three years. The relatively short life span of laboratory animals enables researchers to conduct certain studies and experiments that would not be possible on human beings because of the longer life span of humans.

Some animal diseases are identical to or are closely related to human diseases, for example, rabies, tuberculosis, leptospirosis (infectious jaundice), and anthrax (a bacterial disease affecting animals and human beings). Animals susceptible to these diseases can be used as models for studying the disease.

Researchers use animals to learn more about common animal and human disorders. Animals contribute to the growing fund of knowledge about genetics, psychology, and neurology. They are proving valuable in their contributions to the fields of mental illness, drug addiction, and senility. On the other hand, these advances and achievements have caused pain and suffering to millions of animals, a fact that cannot be denied.

Opponents of biomedical research argue that the findings from animal research cannot be extrapolated to human beings. While this may be regarded more as an opinion than as a fact, it is circulated by antivivisectionists in their newsletters, pamphlets, and other literature. *Vivisection* is the act of cutting into or dissecting the body of a living animal, especially for the purpose of research. The word is derived from the Latin *vivas*, meaning alive, and *sectio*, the act of cutting. *Antivivisectionist*, then, is a broadened term that means anyone opposed to any form of experimentation on live animals.

It is true that some findings from animal experiments or tests may not be applicable to human beings. But there are enough similarities between human beings and animals to justify animal research. Dr. Maud Slye, an early twentieth-century cancer researcher, conducted studies on mice. Her studies involved spontaneous tumors in mice. Lung and other tumors that developed in her mice did so naturally; they were not implanted or otherwise artificially produced.

Dr. Slye's studies investigated the possibility that cancer could be inherited. One of her conclusions, based on the growth of spontaneous tumors in her mice, as well as autopsies performed on several thousand mice, was that a recessive gene was responsible for the inheritance of cancer. When she stated that her findings could be extrapolated to human beings, critics said she was wrong. Dr. Slye's response was "tissue is tissue." It must be added that Dr. Slye's recessive gene conclusion was also challenged. (She was conducting cancer research in the early 1930s, before the discovery of deoxyribonucleic acid [DNA], when her conclusion that cancer was caused by a recessive gene was disputed.) Dr. Slye was not quite right, but we know today that heredity does play a role in some forms of cancer. This explains why physicians taking a patient's history ask whether anyone in the family has had cancer.

Similarities between animals and human beings do exist. For instance, there is a biochemical connection between animals and human beings, an example being the serum albumin found in the blood of human beings and all other vertebrates. Hemoglobin is produced in all mammals, including human beings, and researchers have demonstrated that the hemoglobin of chimpanzees is identical to that of human beings. It has also been learned that there is some degree of similarity between the DNA (deoxyribonucleic acid, the hereditary material of organisms) recombination of human beings and that of animals.

Mice, hamsters, and guinea pigs have some physiological responses similar to those seen in human beings. And it is well known that cats, dogs, and other animals can be infected with certain human diseases, and vice versa.

Ethologists, or animal behaviorists, have pointed out that some animals have altruistic behavior similar to that of human beings. For example, dogs, cats, and nonhuman primates practice behavior patterns that indicate these animals care for each other. And wolves, baboons, chimpanzees, orangutans, and gorillas have social tendencies similar to those of human beings.

Many of the new insights and discoveries about human behavior have resulted from basic studies on animals. Since it is not always feasible to test new ideas or concepts about behavior on human beings, some animals have served as substitutes or surrogates. While certain animals are ideal for such research, there are some limitations. John Paul Scott, an American zoologist and ethologist, points out that "both the behavior of the experimental animal and the corresponding human activity must be so well known that we can be certain we are working with identical phenomena."[3]

There are dissimilarities, too. These can have a bearing on the value of using certain animals for biomedical research or product testing. For example, animals may have different responses to drugs or chemicals. A case in point is thalidomide, a sedative given to European women in the 1960s to prevent miscarriages. However, thalidomide turned out to be a chemical that resulted in thousands of deformed children. Yet the drug did not produce deformed young in the animals on which it was originally tested. Other dissimilarities involve the posture of animals versus that of human beings, the reasoning power of human beings, the special capacities of both animals and human beings, and the differences in characteristics and traits.

Are the similarities and dissimilarities the only basis

for judging whether animals can be used for research? Animal rights advocates say they are not, that there are also ethical and moral considerations. Some of them refer to the beliefs of Jeremy Bentham, the nineteenth-century English philosopher and humanitarian mentioned earlier. Bentham believed that all moral, social, or political action should be directed toward achieving the greatest good for the greatest number of people. He argued that only an animal's capacities to suffer or experience pleasure are morally relevant. He stated that the issue of animal welfare was not whether animals could "reason or talk, but can they suffer?" Other animal welfare advocates have stronger feelings and beliefs about the use of animals in research; their opposition is discussed in Chapter Six.

Various federal government agencies and departments use animals for biomedical research and product testing. The U.S. Department of Health and Human Services conducts such studies in four of its divisions: National Institutes of Health (NIH), Food and Drug Administration (FDA), National Institute on Drug Abuse (NIDA), and National Institute for Occupational Safety and Health (NIOSH). NIH is the largest of these agencies and uses many more animals than the other federal agencies. Other agencies or departments that use animals for research are the U.S. Department of the Interior, Department of Transportation, Consumer Product Safety Commission (CPSC), Environmental Protection Agency (EPA), National Aeronautics and Space Administration (NASA), and the Veterans Administration.

Animals are also used in experiments conducted by researchers in colleges and universities. They are also used in large numbers by manufacturers testing the safety of products such as cosmetics, chemicals, and pharmaceuticals. Some of the federal agencies, such as the FDA, EPA, CPSC, and NIOSH, often specify the use of animals in testing consumer products.

Animal rights advocates and antivivisectionists challenge the use of animals in research, arguing that besides being inhumane, it is unnecessary. In addition, they claim that laboratory animals are abused.

There are some notable examples in which opponents charged that animals were misused in research. One of these was a study known as the "maternal and sibling deprivation studies," conducted by Harvey Harlow and associates at the University of Wisconsin in the early 1960s. This research is still referred to by animal rights advocates and antivivisectionists as an example of cruelty to and misuse of animals in research.

In the Harlow study, infant rhesus monkeys were separated from their mothers shortly after birth and kept in isolation. However, they were given surrogate mothers. Some of the baby monkeys were given heated cloth dolls, while others were given nothing more than wire mesh structures. Some of the baby monkeys were isolated for three or four months, while others remained in isolation for a year.

The monkeys isolated for only a few months were, after being taken out of isolation, able to relate to people and other monkeys and to get along with their peers. But the monkeys isolated for a year were unable to form any kind of bond and had very poor social interaction.

When the Harlow experiments were publicized, there was an outcry of protest from antivivisectionists and humanitarians. The study was denounced as inhumane, high in suffering and unwarranted stress. Harlow and his associates were condemned and vilified. The usefulness of the study was also criticized.

Some aspects of the study merited criticism. It is doubtful that this use of animals would be accepted today, considering the standards now in existence for the care and use of laboratory animals. For example, the isolation of monkeys and nonhuman primates is prohibited under the regulations of the Federal Animal Welfare Act.

Was this use of animals wrong? Inhumane? Was the study of little value, as some critics charged? Humanitarians said yes; most scientists said no. The Harlow experiments, stressful though they may have been, contributed to the advancement of knowledge in the field of pediatrics. They showed that attachments to a single mother figure are not necessary for normal social development. This is considered an important contribution to the field of human development.

Another research study that allegedly involved the misuse and mistreatment of animals occurred at the American Museum of Natural History in New York City in the summer of 1976. The research was concerned with the sexual responses of desensitized cats. It was conducted by Lester R. Aaronson and associates. Aaronson was chairman and curator of the museum's Department of Animal Behavior. His project was funded by the National Institutes of Health and the National Institute of Child Health and Human Development.

Cats were chosen for this study because they are relatively complex animals. Considerable data on their brains and nervous systems, showing some similarities between their brains and those of human beings, were available to the researchers. After some nerve surgery, the cats in the study became disoriented and lost interest in sexual activity.

Henry Spira, a former student of Peter Singer, a professor of ethics and the author of *Animal Liberation*, led the attack on Aaronson and the American Museum of Natural History. Aaronson was accused of being a "pervert and sadist." His study was labeled as worthless as far as any relevancy to human beings was concerned. The experiments were attacked as cruel and inhumane.

The main purpose of Aaronson's study was to gain knowledge about low and high sexual activity that could be applied to human beings, with some side benefits for cats. Aaronson's laboratory and procedures were repeatedly monitored by the National Society for Medical Research, National Institutes of Health, the Animal and Plant Health Inspection Service of the United States Department of Agriculture (APHIS), the American Society for the Prevention of Cruelty to Animals, and other animal welfare organizations. His experiments were conducted in conformity with the regulations in the Animal Welfare Act. Were Aaronson's studies relevant to human sexual activity? The Division of Research Grants, National Institutes of Health, thought so when it approved funding for the project. So did other scientific organizations. Nevertheless, the opposition to Aaronson's experiments was so strong that the museum eventually cancelled the project. However, there were those who thought that the charges against Aaronson's research were out of proportion to the discomfort suffered by the cats.

There are more examples of the use of animals in research and testing that have been condemned by animal rights advocates as unnecessary, cruel, or needlessly painful or stressful. Some of them are discussed in the chapters on biomedical research and consumer product testing.

Despite the charges of animal rights advocates, the use of animals in research is regulated by law and by guidelines. Various public and private organizations have designed procedures for the care and use of research animals. The New York Academy of Science, Committee on Animal Research, issued guidelines on the treatment and use of animals in biomedical research, consumer product testing, and educational studies or experiments. The American Diabetes Association (ADA) issued a policy statement on the use of animals in diabetes research. The ADA policy statement emphasizes the humane care of animals used in any research or educational program concerned with diabetes. The National Academy of Sciences, Psychologists for the Ethical Treatment of Animals, American Medical Association, Physicians Committee for

Responsible Medicine, Canadian Council on Animal Care, and other organizations have issued position papers or have drawn up guidelines regarding the care and use of laboratory animals.

There is always some risk of abuse or mistreatment in the use of animals for research. The very nature or purpose of some animal experiments dictates that pain and stress will occur. An important question to ask is, When does an experiment produce pain and suffering to a point where it is unacceptable in human terms? The question of who makes this decision also arises. It is also debatable whether the results of an experiment justify the pain and suffering it causes. However, it is necessary to remember that not every experiment will yield results beneficial to human beings or animals. And regardless of the expected results of an experiment, some pain, discomfort, or stress will probably be present.

Researchers are well aware that the condition and well-being of their laboratory animals are crucial factors in the yield and validity of their experiments. The responses of unhealthy or stressed animals can greatly affect the results of a study or experiment. Researchers know that undue pain or distress can produce unwanted variables in their findings; these variables can interfere with the interpretation of the results. Only a negligent researcher would mistreat his or her laboratory animals.

New technology may have a marked effect on the use of animals in research. The developing field of biotechnology is having a definite influence on the kinds and numbers of animals used in certain types of experiments. One way in which biotechnology is reducing the number of animals used in research is in the development of new tests that will be acceptable to regulatory agencies such as the FDA, EPA, and NIOSH.

But biotechnology may require the use of more animals of different species; it is still too soon to tell. At the present time, it is estimated that biotechnology uses about 11 percent of all laboratory rodents (mice, rats, guinea pigs, and hamsters); about 5 percent of the pigs; and close to 2 percent of the rabbits and dogs available for research. This new field of research, however, uses very few nonhuman primates or cats.

An example of biotechnology is research being conducted on the rabies virus. Early rabies research conducted by the nineteenth-century French chemist Louis Pasteur involved the search for a vaccine. The rabies virus is transmitted through the bite of a rabid animal, such as a dog, fox, or raccoon. Pasteur's experiments revealed that the rabies virus localized in the animal brain in the form of what are called Negri bodies. He cultured viruses from the brain tissue of rabid dogs and injected them into rabbits. In every case, rabies appeared in the rabbits in about fourteen days.

From these experiments, Pasteur went on to develop a rabies vaccine that protected dogs and other animals. Once the vaccine was effective on dogs, Pasteur set out to develop one for humans. After considerable experimenting that included human subjects, he perfected a system of inoculations that prevented the development of rabies in a patient bitten by a rabid dog. This system of inoculations became known as the Pasteur treatment for rabies. It was not a cure; there is no known cure for rabies.

New diagnostic tests are using antibodies produced in cell cultures. From these cultures, vaccines can be developed without the use of live animals. Advances in determining molecular structure can be used to predict biochemical functions. Here again, a reduction in the use of animals can result. Scientists can employ such advances to determine the active sites of molecules and even the locations of viruses. Data obtained from such experiments can be used in the development of synthetic drugs in a more direct way. However, new drugs or compounds will still have to undergo safety tests on animals, and animals will still be needed for the validation of results.

The use of animals for research and product testing remains an emotional issue. It has precipitated a confrontation between animal rights activists and responsible scientists that has far-reaching effects, especially on the health and welfare of the public. The position of some scientists that the interests and welfare of animals must be secondary to those of human beings fans the flames of the controversy. Inflammatory rhetoric from both sides clouds the issues, often misleading and confusing the public.

In the long run, it might be said that the use of animals in research is a matter for conscience and values. There are many questions to be answered. Are the lives of human beings more important than those of animals? Were the lives of the rhesus monkeys used by Dr. Jonas Salk in developing the Salk polio vaccine more important than those of the millions of children now spared this crippling disease? If pain or serious risk to human health or life arises, is it not better—not to mention more morally correct—to experiment on animals rather than on human beings?

Animals, then, are used as substitutes for human beings in a wide variety of experiments and studies. They have served as organisms on which toxic chemicals and other harmful substances are tested. And they are used by students to learn about the anatomy and physiology of the animal body. All of these uses are condemned by animal rights activists and antivivisectionists.

BIOMEDICAL AND
BEHAVIORAL RESEARCH

Various species of animals are used in biomedical and behavioral research. Scientists in these fields conduct or perform experiments in many disciplines—bacteriology, cardiology, endocrinology, nutrition, neurology, immunology, nephrology, oncology, pathology, virology, and psychology. The use of animals in these research areas has produced medical advances, discoveries, and new techniques that researchers say could not otherwise have been achieved or developed.

SOME MEDICAL ADVANCES AND ACHIEVEMENTS

While animals have added to the store of medical knowledge in past centuries, the greatest advances have occurred in the twentieth century. An important discovery in the early part of the century was the identification and development of insulin. This major medical breakthrough resulted from research on diabetes in dogs conducted by the Canadian physician Frederick Banting and his associates. Although there were some treatments for diabetes at the time of Dr. Banting's research, none was effective.

Diabetes is marked by an insufficiency of insulin, which is manufactured in the pancreas. The pancreas is a long, thin gland situated crosswise behind the stomach. It has two functions: it produces enzymes to help digestion, and it produces insulin and glucagon.

Dr. Banting believed it possible to make an extract out of tissue from beef pancreas that could be used in the treatment of diabetes. In Banting's experiments, a number of dogs were used, some of which had undergone the removal of their pancreas. An extract of beef pancreas was eventually developed, and Banting called it "isletin." It was so named because the beef tissue used in making the extract came from that part of the pancreas known as the islets of Langerhans. This section of the pancreas was named after the nineteenth-century German pathologist Paul Langerhans. Later, the extract's name was changed to insulin, which is derived from the Latin word *insula*, or island.

Today, thousands of lives are saved every year by insulin. Children and adults with diabetes mellitus lead normal lives with injections or oral doses of insulin. Banting received world recognition for the research and development of insulin. He freely admitted that without his laboratory dogs he could not have produced it.

Another twentieth-century medical milestone was the development of a vaccine against poliomyelitis, a disease that cripples both children and adults. Dr. Jonas Salk, a microbiologist, developed the first polio vaccine in the 1950s. Salk's research was conducted on rhesus monkeys. Prior to the development of a vaccine, thousands of people, young and old alike, were stricken by the disease. Polio causes atrophy of the arms and legs, body paralysis, and in the more severe forms death, or life in an iron lung or respirator.

In more recent years, procedures for organ transplants were developed on dogs, nonhuman primates, and other animals. The transplantation of skin, cornea, and other organs could not, according to researchers, be made a safe procedure without the experience and knowledge gained from animal experiments.

Early in the development of human kidney transplantation procedures, surgeons faced a high rejection rate. Kidneys taken from an unrelated person and transplanted into another did not work. However, experiments on dogs using the drug 6-mercaptopurine (an immunosuppressant) after transplanting an organ prolonged the retention time of an organ from an unrelated animal.

The development of cyclosporin, an immunosuppressant used after human organ transplantations, proved to be a major advance in this field of medicine. After five years of testing on mice, rats, and other animals, cyclosporin was used in human trials. Since this immunosuppressant became available for use after heart transplantations, the survival rate of patients receiving new hearts dramatically increased.

OPEN-HEART SURGERY

Open-heart surgery is no longer headline news. But in the 1970s, such surgery on human beings had to await the results of experiments performed on cats and dogs. These experiments involved the design and use of heart/lung machines vital to open-heart surgery. Researchers working on this project in the early 1930s clamped off dog and cat arteries and routed the animal's blood through the forerunner of the present-day heart/lung machine.

Later, the early heart/lung machine was improved upon by a roller pump developed by Dr. Michael DeBakey, an American specialist in heart surgery. The roller pump changed the course of the blood from the vasculature into and through the heart/lung machine. In doing so, it added oxygen to the blood. This pump, first developed and used on animals, is now an essential part of the modern heart/lung machine.

THE RHESUS FACTOR

The rhesus, or Rh, factor was identified during tests on rhesus monkeys. The Rh factor involves the presence of very complicated substances on the surface of human red blood cells. Experiments on the monkeys revealed two types of Rh factor: Rh positive and Rh negative.

Rhesus factor incompatibility between a woman and a fetus she is carrying causes problems. This incompatibility can be described as an antagonism between the rhesus blood groups of a mother and a developing baby. Rhesus incompatibility, as researchers learned from their experiments on monkeys, only occurs if the mother has Rh negative blood and the baby has Rh positive blood by way of Rh positive genes from the father. However, researchers also learned that an offspring may inherit Rh negative genes from a father with Rh positive blood. The Rh factor research on monkeys and its application to human beings were significant breakthroughs in the understanding of the immunology of pregnancy.

HEPATITIS

Hepatitis, or inflammation of the liver, is a debilitating viral disease. There are several types of hepatitis. In acute hepatitis A, the liver becomes tender and enlarged. Bilirubin, a substance produced when the liver breaks down old red blood cells, collects in the bloodstream and causes jaundice. The virus may be present for several weeks before any signs or symptoms appear. Acute hepatitis A is highly infectious and can be transmitted through contaminated blood or feces. There is no specific treatment for this form of hepatitis. However, bed rest and a nutritious diet help speed recovery.

Acute hepatitis B is also highly contagious. The symptoms are the same as those seen in acute hepatitis A. The main difference between the two types of hepatitis is the duration and severity of the symptoms, which include weakness, loss of appetite, and abdominal discomfort. The symptoms of acute hepatitis B are more severe and last longer than those of acute hepatitis A.

Dogs are susceptible to a form of hepatitis. Infectious canine hepatitis is spread by contact with nasal discharge or urine. (It is not caused by the same hepatitis viruses that infect human beings.) A vaccine against infectious canine hepatitis was developed about thirty years ago. It is only recently that a vaccine effective against acute hepatitis B has been developed.

BURNS

The treatment of burn victims is a major concern. Hundreds of people are severely burned each year. Some are scarred for life by burns caused by fire or chemicals. Third-degree burns are the most devastating, since all layers of the skin are destroyed by prolonged contact with heat, flame, or chemicals.

In 1944, a British biologist, P. B. Medawar, experimented with skin transplants on cattle. His subject was a cow known as a "free martin," a sexually maldeveloped female calf born as a twin to a bull calf. Male hormones transferred to the female calf through the placenta while she is still in the womb render the female calf sterile. The bull calf is not sterile.

Medawar's experiments showed that skin and other tissue could be successfully transplanted between the bull calf and his free martin twin at any stage of their lives. In short, they tolerated each other's tissue and antigens (proteins). Medawar's pioneering work with cattle in this important area of medicine led to other advances in the treatment of burns in animals and human beings.

Another area of biomedicine in which animals play an important role is research on the nervous system. The human brain contains 200 billion neurons, or nerve cells. These neurons connect with up to several hundred thousand other neurons, as well as with muscles and glands. Animals are being used to study neuron development and function. While tissue cultures, brain slices, or simple vertebrate neuronal systems can be used for such studies, researchers in this field say there is no adequate substitute for living animals. An understanding of the very complex functions of the human and animal brain in health and disease still depends on the use of animals in this specialized field of research.

MEMORY RESEARCH
It is estimated that 5 percent of people over the age of sixty-five have severe memory problems or loss of memory and cognition. Another 10 percent are believed to have mild to moderate cognitive or awareness problems. Moreover, certain conditions or diseases, such as Alzheimer's disease and Korsakoff's syndrome, affect mental function and can cause extreme memory loss as well as bizarre behavior.

Alzheimer's disease is mental deterioration accompanied by memory loss. Korsakoff's syndrome, a group of signs and symptoms that indicate psychosis, occurs in those with severe alcoholism. The symptoms are disorientation, falsification of memory (lying), and hallucinations.

Animal research has added much to our understanding of these two diseases since Alois Alzheimer, a German neurologist, announced his findings on the disease, and Sergei Sergeyevich Korsakoff, a Russian physician, stated his theories on the disease bearing his name. Both of these scientists conducted their research in the late nineteenth century.

Most of the data on neurotransmitters involved in these two diseases have been obtained from studies on the brains and nervous systems of chimpanzees. These nonhuman primates are closer to human beings than other animals, which explains their value in neurological and other biomedical research. Chimpanzees have age-related losses in memory just as human beings do. An important finding in this field of research was that memory impairment with advancing age first appears as failure of *immediate* memory. That is, a person may not remember the day's date but may be able to recall an event that happened years ago.

Clonidine, a chemical used as a neurotransmitter (a substance that transmits nerve impulses), has improved the memories of macaques, short-tailed monkeys native to northern Africa, Japan, and southeastern Asia. The drug has also been effective in improving the memories of patients suffering from Korsakoff's syndrome. Researchers believe that memory studies on animals may offer an approach to the eventual treatment of Alzheimer's disease.

While tissue cultures, biochemical methods, and brain imaging in human beings provide some alternatives to the use of experiments with animals, animals are still necessary for this type of biomedical research. The promising field of neural transplantation for the treatment of Alzheimer's disease and Parkinson's disease requires the use of animals. Since this area of biomedical research also requires the use of a large number of animals, neuroscientists are especially targeted by antivivisectionists and animal rights advocates.

One of the issues in the use of animals in research is the pain caused by experiments. There is no question that many experiments cause pain to laboratory animals. In fact, the very purpose of some experiments is to induce pain to learn more about this phenomenon common to both animals and human beings.

Pain is a common symptom of disease and injury. Medical and veterinary researchers seek ways to reduce or minimize the pain and discomfort suffered by laboratory animals. Researchers have developed techniques that are as humane as possible within the context and goal of an experiment. For instance, they have learned that the slightest reflex movement of a rat's tail indicates discomfort or pain when something is done to the animal. Reflex behavior, such as the tail flick, is a useful tool in judging how effective a certain analgesic, or painkiller, is in managing pain.

Many experiments involving pain can be performed on anesthetized animals. However, these experiments are performed when anesthetics will not interfere with the objectives of the particular experiment.

Animals have benefitted from some pain experiments performed on human beings. For example, certain psychophysical studies conducted on human beings have been repeated in animals. These experiments have made it possible for neurology researchers to trace nerve fibers from the skin, muscles, and internal organs. Each of these nerve fibers is a specific carrier of pain signals. These studies enabled researchers to explore the passage and transformation of pain signals in anesthetized animals.

PSYCHIATRIC AND PSYCHOLOGICAL STUDIES

Monkeys, chimpanzees, and other nonhuman primates are important subjects for certain medical and behavioral studies, but their use has been condemned as cruel and inhumane. Especially censored are experiments in which the nonhuman primates are subjected to electric shocks and other trauma. This type of experiment is known as a "learned helplessness study." The state of helplessness in which this kind of experiment places a monkey or ape is, according to researchers, similar to the state of depression in which a human being feels helpless and hopeless.

Not so, say many opponents of these experiments. They do not accept the relationship between human depression and the collapse state in the monkeys or apes caused by electric shock or some other trauma. Besides, the animals undergoing such painful experiments do not show any symptoms associated with human depression. They do not suffer a loss of sleep, they do not have appetite problems, they do not have the suicidal tendencies associated with severe depression. Thus, according to animal rights activists, these experiments contribute little to an understanding of the complexities of human anxiety and depression. All these experiments achieve, according to opponents, is to produce reactions in terrified or tortured animals, symptoms reminiscent of what used to be called shell shock in combat soldiers.

Animals have been used in both biomedical and behavioral studies in American and Russian space programs. Monkeys, chimpanzees, dogs, rats, and mice preceded human astronauts into outer space. The first animal into outer space was Laika, a Russian dog, that orbited the earth in 1957. But she did not return to earth, for the space capsule in which she rode, *Sputnik II*, disintegrated five months later.

In 1960, two more Russian dogs, Belka and Strelka, were rocketed 200 miles above the earth in a space capsule. Russian scientists obtained important information from the animals in these early space flights. They learned much about the effects of acceleration, deceleration, weightlessness, and exposure to cosmic rays. An important question was whether exposure to cosmic rays would affect the breeding ability of an animal or human being. Another important question was whether such exposure would cause genetic mutations. Strelka's exposure to cosmic rays did not affect her reproductive ability. Five months after her memorable flight into outer space, she gave birth to a litter of normal puppies. Pushinska, one of the pups, was given to President John F. Kennedy as a pet for his daughter.

Seven chimpanzees were chosen to be the first non-human primates to be sent into space in the American space program. They were known as the "Astrochimps." Chimpanzees were selected for this project for several reasons: (1) they were intelligent and cooperative animals; (2) they were nearly human in size; and (3) they had a reflex action time close to that of humans, seven-tenths of a second for the chimps and five-tenths of a second for the average man.

The first chimp into space was Ham. He rocketed 155 miles above the Caribbean Sea on February 1, 1961. His capsule traveled on an arc to a point 420 miles from the launching pad. When Ham's capsule was recovered from the sea near the Bahama islands, he was found to be in good condition, none the worse for his exciting flight through outer space. Ham, a chimpanzee, age three years, eight months, born in the Cameroons in Africa, was the first primate to soar into outer space.

Acquired Immune Deficiency Syndrome (AIDS)

Chimpanzees have also been used in research on acquired immune deficiency syndrome, or AIDS. (A syndrome is a group of signs and symptoms that characterize a disease.) A disease somewhat like AIDS is simian acquired immune deficiency syndrome (SAIDS) seen in rhesus monkeys. It led researchers to believe that these monkeys could be used for AIDS research. The SAIDS virus was isolated, infection studies were done, and efforts to develop a vaccine began and are making progress.

But AIDS research is a different story. While chimpanzees have been infected with the human immunodeficiency virus (HIV), the virus that causes AIDS, they have not developed full-fledged AIDS. Instead, they develop flulike symptoms rather than the complications seen in AIDS. Researchers have other problems in using chimpanzees as models. First, these primates are becoming scarce; they are classified as an endangered species. AIDS-infected chimpanzees must be kept in isolation, which presents difficulties. These primates are very social animals and isolation is an extremely stressful experience for them. Furthermore, provisions of the Animal Welfare Act specify that nonhuman primates must be kept in an environment that will not cause them any physical or psychological harm.

Researchers say that the ability of HIV to undergo changes has interfered with the development of an AIDS vaccine. But progress has been made in developing a vaccine for the monkey immunodeficiency syndrome, SAIDS. About all that can be said for the AIDS animal research is that its methodology can be useful in human clinical trials. A presidential commission that studied the problem stated in its report, "The lack of appropriate animal models for HIV research makes the application of animal research to humans uncertain." The knowledge acquired about AIDS, its prevention and symptomatic treatment, comes from in vitro research (*in vitro* means outside the living body and in an artificial environment) and clinical trials with human patients. But animals are still being used in AIDS research.

A recently discovered virus, known as feline T-lymphotropic lentivirus, causes a disease in cats that has some similarity to AIDS. In its structure, the virus resembles HIV. However, there are some major differences, one being the fact that the virus cannot be analyzed genetically. Some researchers think that cats infected with this virus may provide useful models for research on certain aspects of AIDS.[1]

CANCER RESEARCH

Thousands of animals have been used in cancer research, with rodents playing an important role, but the value of animals in this field of research has been questioned. While human cancer is basically the same as that found in mice and rats, there are significant differences that warrant a different approach to research applicable to human beings.

Many cancer experiments involve the use of cell cultures, biochemical or other in vitro techniques, and computer models. Cancer research projects usually begin with in vitro studies that utilize either human or rodent cells. Later in the project, animal in vitro studies take over in the assessment of the causes of cancer, the biology of metastasis (the transfer of tumors from one organ or part of the body to another not directly connected to it), and the interaction of a tumor with the body's defense mechanisms.

Chemotherapy is a major treatment of cancer based on results of animal tests. A recent technique involves the use of human tumors kept in cell culture to screen drugs for safety and effectiveness. But the program for the frequency of use and the way to administer the drugs, such as orally or intravenously, are tested on animals. Animal studies are vital for determining the toxicity of a cancer drug. The evaluation of "methods for safely administering drugs directly into the central nervous system to treat certain brain tumors" is another important example of the use of animals in this field of biomedical research. Primates are used as animal models in the later stages of these experiments.[2]

Another important use of animals in cancer research is in the work done on chemotherapy for treating childhood leukemia. Untreated leukemia is usually fatal. Animals have been used in the development and testing of chemotherapeutic agents used in treating this disease.

Almost every facet of present cancer management

methods, as well as the advances made in this field, has somewhere along the line involved the use of animals. The data obtained from animal research are important for their application to cancer diagnostic tests and the treatment of both human beings and animals. But animal rights advocates, and some scientists, call for either restrictions on the use of animals in cancer research or their total elimination. Most cancer researchers say such measures would seriously disrupt or close down valuable cancer research. They argue that no currently available alternative can completely replace testing on animals in this important research field.

Animal research has produced benefits for various animals. Vaccines for canine distemper, feline panleukopenia (cat distemper), parvovirus, infectious canine hepatitis, leptospirosis (a bacterial disease that affects dogs and other animals and occurs in two forms: canicola fever and Weil's disease), tetanus, equine encephalitis, Bang's disease (brucellosis in human beings), and heartworm infestations have all been produced as a result of animal experiments. Millions of dogs, cats, and other animals have profited from these vaccines.

Especially important for both human beings and animals was the development of a vaccine against Bang's disease in dairy cattle and rabies in dogs. These two diseases are transmissible to human beings.

There are three types of brucella organisms: *Brucella abortus*, the cattle type; *B. melitensis*, affecting goats; and *B. suis*, found in swine. (Brucella organisms have also been found in deer, bison, and some other animals.) The brucella organisms were named after Dr. David Bruce, a British army surgeon who isolated *Brucella melitensis* in goat milk served to British soldiers on the island of Malta in 1887. (The disease in human beings is sometimes called Malta fever, or undulant fever.)

The development of a vaccine against this debilitating

disease was important for two reasons: (1) it prevented the loss of dairy calves and (2) it reduced the incidence of the transmission of this disease to farmers and others who drank raw milk.

Other research benefitting animals includes the development of vermicides for internal parasites, improvements in animal nutrition, invention or development of new surgical instruments and techniques (for example, use of staples in place of sutures for closing a surgical or other wound, which was demonstrated on dogs and other animals), and advances in the diagnosis and treatment of animal diseases.

In addition to the use of staples for closing wounds, an electrocautery hemostat has been invented for use on both animals and human beings. A hemostat is an instrument for constricting a blood vessel to check the flow or escape of blood during an operation. The hemostat is an old instrument, as is the electrocautery device, which has been in existence for about thirty-five years. Dr. Edward A. Lottick, a physician in Kingston, Pennsylvania, found a way to combine the two in his invention, the electrocautery hemostat.

Dr. Lottick's instrument was tried out on sheep obtained from the Animal Research Center in Hershey, Pennsylvania. The electrocautery hemostat proved to be quick and efficient. It enabled the surgeon to grasp and cauterize a bleeding vessel without changing hands or instruments, making the procedure much faster, and it was more efficient in diminishing blood loss. Both human beings and animals benefit from the use of this instrument.

It can be seen from this brief account that advances and achievements made in human and animal health have resulted from the use of animals in biomedical and behavioral research. More than eight hundred such advances and achievements depended on animal studies or experiments, according to an American Medical Association report.

The cast of animals used in research consists of numerous species and roles. Dogs, as noted earlier, were instrumental in the discovery and development of insulin. Procedures for the transplantation of organs involved dogs, primates, and other animals. A vaccine against acute hepatitis B was developed with the help of chimpanzees and other primates.

But these and other medical and veterinary advances are thrust aside by animal rights advocates and antivivisectionists. Even more moderate organizations, such as the Medical Research Modernization Committee (MRMC), cast a critical eye on the continued use of animals in biomedical research. They advocate the substitution of alternatives. While the MRMC admits that in vitro techniques are no substitutes for use of whole animals, alternatives "can be powerful tools for studies at the cellular level, particularly when human tissues are used."[3]

The charges against the use of animals in research range from the infliction of pain and suffering to performance of unnecessary experiments to irrelevancy to human beings. Consequently, researchers have been forced to defend their work against a strong and well-financed animal rights movement.

The National Association for Biomedical Research reported that animal rights groups, such as the People for the Ethical Treatment of Animals (PETA) and the Animal Liberation Front (ALF), have severely hampered biomedical research through theft of animals, destruction of valuable research equipment and records, fire bombing, and threats of bodily harm and even death to researchers. (The philosophy, policies, and tactics of animal rights organizations are covered in a later chapter.)

Physicians say there is justification for the use of animals in biomedical research. In the paper, *Use of Animals in Biomedical Research: The Challenge and Response*, the American Medical Association stated that animal research is essential for the improvement of the health and welfare of the American people. The AMA opposes any legislation or social action that will limit or restrict such use of animals.[4]

According to the AMA, the use of animals in biomedical research is supported by most Americans. However, they want assurances that laboratory animals are treated humanely and are used only when necessary. The AMA believes that animal rights advocates have exploited this public concern and have used it to impede, degrade, or eliminate important biomedical research. Many distinguished scientists and physicians think that the tactics and rhetoric of PETA, ALF, and the antivivisection societies will seriously compromise the future of biomedical research if these organizations are allowed to continue with their harassment and obstructive actions.

The contributions to human health and welfare made by animal research have not been exaggerated or overstated, according to the AMA. These contributions have received world recognition. Fifty-four of the seventy-six Nobel Prizes in medicine and physiology since 1901 have been awarded to scientists for discoveries that involved the use of animals. These discoveries included breakthroughs in the diagnosis, treatment, and prevention of both human and animal diseases.

The National Association for Biomedical Research (NABR) has more than three hundred institutional members. Seventy percent are universities with medical or veterinary schools or substantial biomedical research programs. The NABR insists that its members are concerned about the proper treatment of animals used in research programs. It has charged the animal rights movement with resorting to "visceral images with spoken half-truths, lies, and emotional invectives." According to the NABR, animal rights advocates try to portray biomedical researchers as uncaring or unfeeling people who are motivated solely by research grants, the need to publish, and profits.

The use of animals in biomedical and behavioral research has opponents in both the animal rights movement and the scientific community. Some call for the total use of alternatives, while others say that the use of animals should be reduced or limited. The same is true in the next category of the animals in research controversy: the testing of consumer products on animals.

CONSUMER PRODUCT TESTING

Animals are widely used to test the safety and efficiency of chemicals and other consumer products. Tests are conducted on products such as floor wax, detergents, pesticides, soaps, shoe polish, shampoos, and drugs.

CONSUMER PRODUCT TESTS

Acute toxicity tests are tests that usually consist of administering a single dose of the product or chemical in a concentration high enough to produce toxic responses or death. One such test is the LD/50 (lethal dose/50) test, in which one-half of the test animals can be expected to die.

Eye and skin irritation tests involve a single exposure to a substance or product. They are aimed at providing warnings to users of the product for the handling of the product or lists of harmful effects in case of misuse or accidental exposure. The most common procedure to test for irritation is the Draize test, one that has been targeted for elimination by PETA and other animal rights groups.

Repeated, or long-term chronic, toxicity tests consist

of exposing an animal to a product or substance for periods of two weeks to more than a year. These tests are aimed at determining the effects of long-term exposure to drugs or other products that may be used for months or years by a consumer. Rodents are used for these tests.

Carcinogenicity tests consist of exposing an animal to chemicals or substances for most of the animal's lifetime. The purpose is to detect any carcinogens in the substance or product. Mice and rats are used in these tests.

Reproductive toxicity tests involve a variety of procedures aimed at determining the presence of substances that might cause infertility, miscarriages, or birth defects. Rabbits and rats are used in these tests.

Neurotoxicity tests involve a variety of doses and exposures to a substance or product. The purpose is to determine any toxic effects on the nervous system, such as changes in behavior, lack of coordination, motor disorders, and learning disabilities in the test animals.

Mutagenicity tests are aimed at learning whether specific substances can cause any changes in the genetic material of cells. (In the case of the drug thalidomide, the drug did not cause any mutations or deformities in test animals; the reverse was true when the drug was given to pregnant women.)

Most of these tests require the use of large numbers of animals. There are different estimates as to the total used on a yearly basis. Since the use of mice and rats in biomedical research and testing is not regulated by the Federal Animal Welfare Act, the number used is not reported. Thus, the figures given by various organizations may be considered to be "guesstimates" rather than true estimates. They range from several million animals per year to as many as 10 million.

The cosmetic industry, in particular, has been attacked by animal rights organizations for its use of large numbers of animals, mostly rabbits, to test cosmetics.

These consumer products, as well as food and drugs, are regulated under the provisions of the federal Food, Drug and Cosmetic Act and its amendments. While the law does not specify what tests a manufacturer must conduct on its products, it does require proof of the safety of a product and its ingredients. The FDA, EPA, and Consumer Product Safety Commission may require animal testing of a consumer product.

Manufacturers have relied on animals to test the safety of their products for what they believe to be valid reasons. One is, of course, safety. Another is protection of the manufacturer from lawsuits. If no testing was performed, a manufacturer would be compelled by law to print this warning on the product label: WARNING: THE SAFETY OF THIS PRODUCT HAS NOT BEEN DETERMINED.

Obviously, no manufacturer wants to have such a label on its products. The product would self-destruct, for only a few people might buy it, mainly those who could not read the label or those who ignore labels.

In defending themselves against attacks by PETA and other animal rights groups, cosmetic manufacturers argue that the safety of consumers is a prime concern and the main reason for the use of live animals to test products. Consumers should believe they can use cosmetics without experiencing any harmful effects, say the manufacturers. Also, employees handling cosmetic materials should be able to do so with safety. Some manufacturers maintain that animal testing is the most effective way to ensure the safety of a product and to comply with FDA regulations. While some alternatives are available, they are not yet reliable enough to eliminate the use of animals completely.

On the other hand, PETA and other animal rights groups say the use of animals for testing consumer products is not only cruel but unnecessary. They point to new technologies that have provided alternatives to animal testing, techniques that not only are humane but are cheaper and more exact. They cite in vitro studies, computer assays, simulated tissue and body fluid level measurements, mass spectrometry, and gas chromatography as alternatives. (PETA was responsible for ending the use of the Draize test by some major cosmetic and consumer products manufacturers.)

THE DRAIZE TEST

The Draize test, which tests for eye and skin irritation, was named after Dr. John Draize, an English researcher and senior author of a paper describing the test. This controversial test was originally developed for use in England but soon became a standard test in the United States, Canada, and other countries. It was sanctioned but not ordered by the FDA as a test that would meet a requirement of the Food, Drug and Cosmetic Act, which states that cosmetics "be free of deleterious or poisonous substances."

Rabbits are used in the Draize test because their eyes are especially sensitive. Also, they have no tear ducts; they cannot wash test materials out of their eyes. In performing the test, a rabbit's head is placed in a stock to prevent the animal from scratching or pawing at the eye in which a substance has been placed. The lower lid of one eye is pulled down and away from the eye. Then the test substance, such as nail polish remover, shampoo, or mascara, is dropped into or smeared on the eye. The other eye acts as a control. Testers look for redness in the affected eye, edema (swelling), hemorrhage, and other signs of irritation. Corneal ulcers and blindness are often the result of the Draize test, depending on the materials used. The rabbits may be killed after a test or may be used in some other test.

In 1989, because of pressure by PETA, two major cosmetic manufacturers, Revlon and Avon, agreed to stop all testing of their products on animals. PETA's tactics consisted of organizing boycotts, promoting shareholder resolutions, and alerting the general public to the use and cruelty of the Draize test.

Other consumer product manufacturers were attacked by PETA and other animal rights groups. They included Procter and Gamble, American Home Products, Bristol-Myers-Squibb, and Colgate-Palmolive corporations. Procter and Gamble manufactures soaps and other household products. American Home Products makes Pam cooking spray, Black Flag pesticide, Sani-flush, and other products. Bristol-Myers-Squibb manufactures pharmaceuticals and over-the-counter drugs and medicines. Colgate-Palmolive makes toothpaste, soaps, detergents, and other products. All of these corporations relied on animals to test the safety of their products.

While some manufacturers have halted the use of animals for testing their products—or have at least reduced the number of animals used—others say they have no alternative but to continue animal testing. If they cannot prove the safety of their products, the FDA will resort to regulatory actions. Such action would also take place if there were a complaint about a product. The FDA has the authority to inspect manufacturing plants and the power to seize adulterated or mislabeled products. The Food, Drug and Cosmetic Act defines an adulterated product as one that "contains a substance which may make it harmful to consumers under customary conditions of use."

Opponents of the Draize test have charged that it not only is cruel and inhumane but is outdated and unreliable. But the acting director of the FDA's Center for Veterinary Medicine disagreed with this charge at a congressional hearing in 1986. The congressional committee was inquiring into the use of animals for product testing. The acting director testified that the Draize test was still the most reliable method of determining the potential "harmfulness or safety of a product instilled in the eye, such as ophthalmic drugs, devices or cosmetic products." He stated that alternatives could not replace the Draize test.[1]

Later, Dr. Frank Young, at that time the FDA commissioner, stated that "the responses and results of tissue or cell culture tests alone cannot, at the present time, be the basis for determining the safety of a substance." He added that certain tests should never be carried out on human beings. Therefore, and since at the present time no adequate alternatives exist, whole animal testing remains unavoidable.

FDA TESTING GUIDELINES

The FDA, like some other federal agencies, has issued guidelines for the use of animals in product testing. The agency believes that the proper use of in vitro tests can reduce the number of animals used for the development of a product. Manufacturers should thus develop and use in vitro tests. However, there may never be a total replacement for the Draize test because of the limitations of in vitro tests.

The agency believes that a quick and inexpensive test, despite its inability to detect everything, can be used early on in the developmental phase of a product. Such use can eliminate chemicals that fail to pass in vitro tests. This early detection could reduce the number of chemicals needed to be tested on animals.

In vitro techniques, based partially on prior animal tests, could also be used as the final safety test for a product. However, in vitro tests would be limited so that only a minor change in an active product ingredient needed to be made. But previous experience would be needed for a tester to draw the conclusion that a specific in vitro test was capable of detecting any likely changes caused by reformulations. Since the FDA has no testing requirements for the premarketing of cosmetics, the agency has not developed plans for that purpose.

In issuing these statements, the FDA pointed out that they were not to be regarded as regulations, but as scientific opinions.

The Consumer Product Safety Commission (CPSC) The federal Consumer Product Safety Commission has jurisdiction over all nonmedical household products. It is the only federal agency that has any regulations dealing with tests for irritation caused by a product. In May 1980, the CPSC placed an embargo on the use of the Draize test, pending the results of a study on the use of anesthetics for the animals used in this test. The study revealed that a double dose of tetracaine administered to rabbits reduced the pain produced by the test material. The anesthetic did not affect the irritancy scores or results.

The CPSC has issued guidelines for the use of animals for product testing:

- No testing for eye irritancy if the substance is a known primary skin irritant.
- An ophthalmic anesthetic, such as tetracaine, should be used *before* placing any substance in a rabbit's eye.
- It is recommended that a tier-testing approach to reduce the number of animals be used. The gradual increase in the dose for animals until irritation is determined, instead of initial use of a larger number of animals for tests, is the goal of this approach. Also, rabbits used in skin irritation tests should not be placed in stocks. They should have access to water and food while a substance is on their skin.

The CPSC issued a statement in March 1988: "We believe that an adequate non-animal replacement exists either for the Draize eye irritancy test or other acute toxicity tests." The agency added that "non-animal tests presently under development are not yet at a stage where they can be validated prior to their incorporation into regulatory protocols."

In general, the CPSC position on the use of animals in product testing is that manufacturers are not required to conduct animal tests. All they have to do is label their products in such a way that a consumer is alerted to any hazards posed by the product. While animal testing may be necessary in some cases, such testing should be limited to the *lowest feasible number of animals.* All precautions should be taken to eliminate or reduce pain and discomfort in the animals.

Animal rights advocates were quick to point out a discrepancy in the CPSC position. The agency stated that it does not require testing for nonmedical consumer products. It further stated that nonanimal alternatives were not yet an acceptable measure of consumer safety. Then what is? asked the animal rights advocates. Further confusing the public and manufacturers, the CPSC more or less admitted that the only safety standard it will accept is that demonstrated by animal testing.

More suggestions and recommendations regarding the troublesome Draize test have been put forth. The Interagency Regulatory Liaison Group issued the following:

- Substances known to be corrosive may be assumed to be eye irritants and therefore should not be used in the manufacture of consumer eye products.
- Only three rabbits should be used in the Draize test instead of the usual six to ten animals. However, if the test results are equivocal, more rabbits may be used.
- Anesthetics should not be used in most tests. But if the substance is likely to cause intense pain, local anesthetics may be used prior to the application of the substance.

None of the limitations, recommendations, or guidelines for the Draize test is acceptable to PETA and other animal rights groups. They want total elimination of the Draize test and the use of animals for any test. For them, there is no compromise on this issue.

Manufacturers continue to defend their use of the Draize test. They are still fearful of lawsuits in the absence of animal tests. This defensive position began in 1974, when a woman accidentally spilled some shampoo in her eyes while bathing. The shampoo caused burning and pain and the destruction of her corneal epithelium.

The FDA brought suit against the manufacturer on behalf of the victim. But the court ruled in favor of the manufacturer because the FDA failed to show that the shampoo was any more dangerous than others on the market. Also, under normal use, that is, in a diluted form, the shampoo would not have caused the damage it did in concentrated form. Since the woman dropped the container of shampoo, the use was not "normal." The court also ruled that test results obtained from rabbits could be extrapolated to human beings.

The pressures and tactics used by PETA have been successful in forcing some large product manufacturers to stop using the Draize test. Revlon, Avon, Fabergé, Mary Kay Cosmetics, and Amway Corporation all declared a moratorium on the use of animals for product safety testing. These corporations realized that if they did not stop using animals in their product testing, the animal rights activists would increase their pressures and engage in more demonstrations, boycotts, and possible violent actions.

In a letter to the author, the manager of Avon's Consumer Information Center stated that the corporation has ended all animal testing. The new testing program uses nonanimal laboratory tests, clinical tests on human beings, and a large data base of ingredients and products that had been previously tested. (It is assumed that the data base was assembled with findings from animal tests.) The letter writer pointed out that Avon was the "first major cosmetic company in the world to eliminate product testing on animals."

In another letter to the author, the senior product information specialist at Amway Corporation stated, "Future product safety evaluations will proceed through a multi-tiered process." This process involves the analysis of raw material safety from suppliers and the scientific literature. The letter went on to state that "as they are evaluated and validated for Amway's line of products, non-animal in vitro techniques will be incorporated into our overall safety review program."

Not all of the major corporations that have curtailed or ceased animal testing have widely advertised that fact. Liability is still a major fear. There could be backlash from consumers because cosmetics or other products were not tested on animals. The point has been brought up that consumers suffering from a reaction or injury from the use of a product would have a relatively easy time proving negligence in court because of the absence of animal tests.

Small companies are especially vulnerable to censorship for testing their products on animals because their products are often nonessential items. Some small companies have stopped using animal tests; others have not. Yet it is alleged that the products of some of these small manufacturers contain more dangerous substances than those found in cosmetics and other products made by large corporations.

What about the corporations that supply the cosmetic and other manufacturers with raw materials? Do they test their materials? If so, how? Many of them do test their raw materials and on animals.

Some manufacturers have lashed back at the animal rights activists. They say they are dealing with irrational opponents. A spokesman for the Cosmetic, Toiletry and Fragrance Association, a trade organization, charged that the industry was forced to deal with "zealots who cannot comprehend that a child's life is more important than a dog's—who see nothing wrong with making a child the ultimate guinea pig."

In a way, the manufacturers are faced with a dilemma: Appease the animal rights activists and prevent boycotts and loss of sales or continue animal testing and avoid liability, but face more harassment from the animal rights movement.

Some industry leaders believe that Avon and the other corporations that gave up animal testing acted too hastily in capitulating to PETA and the other animal rights groups. Others think it wrong to allow well-organized and well-funded groups to use scare tactics and, in some cases, such as the actions of the Animal Liberation Front, terrorism to force business people to forego their responsibilities to the public and their respective industries.

The animal rights movement continues its crusade for the elimination of the Draize and other product tests. They campaign for state laws that will end or at least limit the use of animals for product testing. Some states are considering such laws. Maryland was the first to consider a law of this type. However, it was defeated in 1988 after heavy lobbying by the cosmetic industry. A pending Pennsylvania bill has a section entitled "Prohibited Tests." Under the provisions of this law, "A person may not subject a live animal to an eye irritancy test, including the Draize test, or to use a live animal in an acute toxicity test, including the LD/50 test, for the purpose of testing cosmetics or household products." Other states considering similar legislation are California, Connecticut, Illinois, and Massachusetts.

LD/50 Test

Another animal test that has been condemned by the animal rights advocates is the LD/50 test. It provides an estimate of the amount of a toxic substance that causes the death of 50 percent of a group of laboratory animals. It has been criticized as cumbersome, unreliable, and cruel. This test was developed in England in 1927 by a mathematician. Its original application was to estimate the toxicity level of very potent drugs, such as digitalis, diphtheria toxin, and insulin. Its opponents say it has outlived its use.

As many as 200 animals may be used in a single LD/50 test, most commonly for the oral testing of a substance or product. Rats or other laboratory animals are force-fed the substance via a stomach tube. Then the animals are observed for two weeks or until death. Animals that survive the test are usually killed later.

Other procedures utilizing the LD/50 test include the inhalation of a chemical or substance. Animals are forced to breathe the vapor or powder of a chemical or substance. Chemicals may also be applied to the skin of an animal in the test. Finally, there is a procedure in which a chemical or substance is injected into an animal's body. In all the tests, observers look for signs of poisoning: for example, bleeding from the eyes, nose, or mouth; difficulty in breathing; tremors; convulsions; paralysis; and coma.

Critics of the test say that it concentrates on *when* an animal dies and not so much on *why*. They maintain that knowing the lethal dose and nature of a chemical or substance that can be obtained from human studies is of greater value than the LD/50 test results, especially when treating poison victims. According to opponents of this test, it does not predict a lethal dose in human beings very accurately because of the difference between the human and animal species. Critics also say that the general idea of applying the toxic effects of a substance or product from animal tests to human beings is open to question. According to an FDA survey, use of the LD/50 test has declined by 96 percent since the 1970s.

More animals are used in the long-term, or chronic, toxicity tests than in the acute toxicity tests. Chronic tests may take up to five years and require the use of hundreds of animals. The decision to use the long-term test depends on the substance. Long-term tests are mainly used to test the toxicity of pharmaceuticals and chemicals on an extended exposure basis. Animals used in all forms of the LD/50 test are dogs, rats, hamsters, and guinea pigs.

TESTING SUBSTANCES FOR CARCINOGENICITY
There is disagreement as to the value of using animals to test chemicals and other substances for carcinogenicity, or the ability to produce tumors. Some scientists believe that cancer tests on animals actually provoke or induce unnaturally high levels of cell division. Such cell division is known to increase the risk of mutations leading to cancer. Some believe that the idea that there is no safe dose of a carcinogen should be reexamined. Many chemicals that cause cell division, and ultimately cancer, may be safe at lower dosages.

But these beliefs or opinions are challenged. The points raised are important, but some scientists say it is too early to change testing methods. More studies are needed. Also, when something works, let it alone. They allude to the fact that the present product testing system has adequately protected the public.

The debate about the value of testing chemicals and other substances on animals for carcinogenicity goes on. Some health authorities maintain that even if there is a difference between human and animal mechanisms or tissues, the fact remains that if a chemical causes cancer in an animal, there is a good chance it will do so in human beings. Animals have to be used for acute and chronic toxicity studies because it is unethical to expose human beings to potential carcinogens for twenty or thirty years. A case in point was the long-range exposure of workers to asbestos, a carcinogen.

The Humane Society of the United States, in condemning the use of the LD/50 test, stated that its results are of little value in diagnosis and treatment. This society argues that animal tests do not yield enough data on the following:

The poisonous dose of a chemical or substance
The prediction of poisoning signs and symptoms
The prevention or correction of overdose
The lethal or nonlethal dose of a chemical or substance
The poisoning risks to newborn babies and infants
The long-term, or cumulative, effect of a chemical or substance on the human body
The specific cause of death in laboratory animals
The specific organs affected by the chemical or substance [2]

The use of animals to test the safety of consumer products is one of the prime targets of animal rights advocates. They say the Draize and LD/50 tests must be stopped. They argue that alternatives are now available. But proponents of animal testing disagree. True, there are some in vitro techniques that are promising but not at the stage to totally replace animals. Therefore, the end of the use of animals in consumer product testing is not yet in sight. Much depends on the speed at which scientists discover, develop, and validate alternative methods to the Draize and LD/50 tests.

Considerable progress has been made in developing alternatives for animal testing and reducing the number and kinds of animals used in biomedical and behavioral research. But there is another field in which animals are used for experimentation that has attracted the attention of animal rights activists and antivivisectionists. It is the use of animals in schools, colleges, and universities. Especially under attack is the dissecting of animals in biology classes.

ANIMAL EXPERIMENTATION IN EDUCATION

Animal studies and experiments have been a part of biology courses for many years. The dissection of frogs, cats, and other animals has been a popular or unpopular learning tool, depending on the student, in high schools, colleges, and universities. Some students dissect an assigned animal, whether a frog, cat, or fetal pig, with interest and perhaps curiosity. Others do so reluctantly, even with strong feelings of revulsion or disgust. Still others refuse to dissect any animal.

The Federal Animal Welfare Act, discussed in the next chapter, requires that colleges and universities conducting animal studies or experiments register with the Department of Agriculture. But elementary and high schools are exempt from such registration. They are not monitored or inspected by any agents of the Department of Agriculture, the agency responsible for the enforcement of the Animal Welfare Act. This lack of monitoring has been the focus of animal welfare group campaigns against the use of animals in classrooms for a number of years.

While there is no federal control of the use of animals

in the classroom, the dissection of animals by students is condemned by humanitarians and antivivisectionists. Some years ago, the Animal Welfare Institute, Humane Society of the United States, and Canadian Council on Animal Care collaborated in drawing up the following guidelines for the use of animals in elementary and high schools:

- In biological procedures involving live organisms, species such as plants, bacteria, fungi, protozoa, worms, snails, or insects should be used whenever possible. Their wide variety and availability in large numbers, the simplicity of their maintenance, and relatively humane ways of disposing of them make them especially suitable for student work.
- No procedure shall be performed on any warm-blooded animal that might cause it pain, suffering or discomfort or otherwise interfere with its normal health. Warm-blooded animals include, besides man, all mammals and birds.
- No surgery shall be performed on any living vertebrate animal: i.e., mammal, bird, amphibian, reptile, and fish.
- No lesson or experiment shall be performed on a vertebrate animal that employs microorganisms that can cause disease in animals or human beings. No ionizing radiation, cancer-producing agents, toxic chemicals, drugs producing pain or deformity, extremes in temperatures, electric or other shock, excessive noise, noxious fumes, exercise to the point of exhaustion, overcrowding or other distressing stimuli shall be used on any animal.
- The study or observation of classroom animals must be directly supervised by a competent biology teacher who shall approve a project plan before a student begins work. The supervisor shall oversee all experimental procedures, be responsible for their non-hazardous nature (to animals and students), and shall

personally inspect experimental animals during the course of the project to ensure that their health and comfort are fully sustained.

- Vertebrate studies shall be conducted only in locations where proper supervision is available. This means either in a school or institution of research or higher learning. No vertebrate animal studies shall be conducted at home, other than observations of normal animal behavior, for example, how a pet dog or cat behaves.
- In vertebrate studies, palatable food shall be provided in sufficient quantity to maintain normal growth of the animal. Diets deficient in essential foods are prohibited. Food shall not be withdrawn from an animal for periods longer than twelve hours, and clean drinking water shall be available at all times and should not be replaced with alcohol or drugs.
- Bird eggs subjected to experimental manipulation shall not be allowed to hatch. The embryos shall be killed humanely no later than the nineteenth day of incubation. If normal egg embryos are to be hatched, then satisfactory arrangements must be made for the humane disposal of the chicks.
- In those rare instances where the killing of a vertebrate animal is deemed necessary, it shall be performed in an approved humane manner (rapidly and painlessly) by an adult experienced in such techniques.
- Projects involving vertebrate animals will normally be restricted to measuring and studying normal physiological functions, for example, normal growth, activity cycle, metabolism, blood circulation, learning processes, normal behavior, reproduction, communication or isolated organ techniques. None of these studies requires the infliction of pain.
- The comfort of the animal shall receive first consideration. All animals shall be housed in appropriate spacious, comfortable and sanitary quarters. Adequate provision shall be made for the care of the animals at all times, including weekends and vacation periods.

And all animals shall be handled gently and humanely at all times.

These guidelines, while restricting the use of animals in the classroom and calling for their humane treatment, do not rule out animal experimentation. They and others like them have been followed in American and Canadian elementary and secondary schools. In the absence of federal control and inspections, schools more or less police themselves. While animals still play an important role in school biology courses, the trend is to study alternative topics such as molecular biology and ecology.

Despite these and other guidelines for the use of animals in elementary and high school classrooms and biology laboratories, animal rights advocates and antivivisectionists want to eliminate the use of animals in education. The more moderate animal welfare organizations, such as the Humane Society of the United States and the Animal Welfare Institute, tolerate the use of animals for instruction in schools, subject, of course, to guidelines that emphasize the humane treatment of animals. But these organizations, along with the more militant groups, want to see the end of dissection in the classroom.

The dissection of animals in high schools attracted national attention in 1987 when a California high school student, Jenifer Graham, refused to dissect a frog. She objected to the dissecting on moral grounds. Jenifer was told that she would fail the biology course if she did not dissect a frog. (She had an A grade in the course up to this time.) She persisted in her refusal to dissect a frog and her grade was lowered to D (later, it was raised to a C). This low grade was unacceptable to Jenifer and her parents. She brought suit against the local school board for failing to offer an alternative to dissection.

The lawsuit dragged on for months at great cost to the Grahams. Finally, a federal judge issued a ruling on August 1, 1988. His ruling: dismissal of the charge against the school board and a compromise for Jenifer. Since a frog's anatomy and physiology were part of the biology course, her knowledge of these systems could and had to be tested. But, according to the judge, since Jenifer did not like the idea of killing frogs for dissection, she need not dissect a frog provided by the school. She could dissect a frog that had died of natural causes, rather than a healthy one that had been killed for the purpose of dissection.

The judge's compromise for Jenifer was not much help. It meant that someone would have to go hunt for a frog that had died of natural causes. Few people have ever found such a frog. Most frogs die from predation or pollution or some other unnatural cause. The judge failed to realize that finding a frog dead from natural causes would be no easy task. In fact, it would be a matter of pure luck.

In the end, Jenifer's right to refuse to dissect a frog was upheld. So was the school's right to test a student's knowledge of a frog's anatomy and physiology on a real frog. An important result of the case was the enactment of a state law—the first of its kind—that upholds the right of a student under eighteen years of age to conscientiously object to dissecting an animal. This law specifically refers to educational projects "involving the harmful or destructive use of animals." Under the provisions of this law, a biology teacher and student may cooperate in developing an alternative to dissection.

Since Jenifer's case, more students have refused to dissect an animal, and there have been demonstrations against dissection. Students have been supported in their cause by parents and various animal rights organizations eager to see the end of dissection in schools.

In October 1991, PETA launched a full-scale, month-long antidissection campaign in schools across the country. PETA encouraged students to protest the dissection of animals in biology class units or laboratories. More than that, students were urged to let their school boards know that they did not want any "animal-based studies" in their classrooms.[1]

The revolt of students over the issue of dissection has caused school administrators and biology teachers to reevaluate this instructional tool. Some cogent questions are posed. While the dissecting of frogs in high schools dates to the early part of the twentieth century, is it really necessary today? Can't students learn just as much about animal anatomy and physiology from videotapes, take-apart models, and computer simulations?

It is true that there are some students who might profit from dissecting a frog or other animal. These are students who plan to become human or veterinary surgeons or pathologists, careers in which manual dexterity and dissecting techniques are of value. But opponents say it is not necessary for a student to acquire manual skills by dissecting; such skills, they say, can be obtained by performing surgery under the eye of an expert surgeon.

Millions of frogs are dissected every year in high school biology courses. Leopard frogs, *Rana pipiens pipiens*, are the species mainly used for dissection. They are a widely distributed species in North America, with a range that includes most of the United States (except the Pacific Coast) and areas extending deep into Canada and Mexico. This frog often lives some distance from water, mostly in meadows. It is in great demand, not only for dissecting but as fish bait. At one time, this frog played an important role in testing for human pregnancy, as did rabbits. The development of special pregnancy kits now precludes the use of frogs and rabbits for this purpose.

Undoubtedly the demand for leopard frogs for dissection has contributed to a decrease in their populations in some regions of the country. But there are other reasons for such losses—pollution, pesticides, drainage of swamplands, and prolonged droughts.

Frogs are not the only animals used for dissection,

although they are probably the most popular subjects. A bit down the popularity scale is the fetal pig; the cat is used more sparingly. Also dissected in schools are crayfish, grasshoppers, starfish, and other invertebrates.

The fetal pig is also used in college biology courses. Students use laboratory manuals to guide them in dissecting the pig. These exercises contain detailed descriptions and illustrations of the various systems of the fetal pig and step-by-step procedures for dissection. For instance, in the exercise on the urogenital system of the fetal pig, the biology student is given this advice: "Although you will dissect the reproductive system of only one sex, you should use another student's specimen to study the opposite sex."[2]

Many biology teachers and other educators believe that dissection is an important learning tool. They have what they consider to be valid reasons for including this controversial teaching technique in biology courses. One of their contentions is that dissecting gives a student firsthand knowledge of the internal structure of an animal. By dissecting a frog or fetal pig, for example, a student can see the relationship between various tissues; he or she can also feel the texture of animal tissue. Computer models and other alternatives cannot provide this experience. In dissection, a student learns about the relationship between the structure of an animal's body and its function. Finally, dissection allows a holistic approach to the study of animal anatomy and physiology.

But antivivisectionists and animal rights advocates are not impressed by these assertions. They feel that dissecting animals in schools must stop. Some opponents, such as PETA, say that animals should not be used for any purpose in the classroom. Others point out that dissecting an animal can be a very traumatic experience for a young student. Junior and senior high school students have been observed to run a gamut of emotions when faced with the assignment of dissecting a frog, pig, or other animal. They have shown fear, distaste, revulsion, and even horror. When these facts are taken into consideration, some opponents of dissection say it has no place in the modern school program. There is no valid reason to subject students to what, for many, is a disgusting or upsetting experience. Furthermore, according to opponents of dissection, modern technology has provided adequate substitutes for this outmoded and unwanted technique.

The pressure to abandon dissection and animal experimentation in colleges and universities, especially medical and veterinary schools, is gaining in strength. College students and animal rights groups protest the use of animals in education. A number of colleges and universities, as well as medical and veterinary schools, have reassessed their animal use programs.

A charge brought against college biology programs and medical and veterinary courses in which animal experiments are performed is that many of the experiments are "mindless duplications." They are unnecessary, they cause pain and suffering to animals, and they turn off students.

The American Antivivisection Society charges that a number of colleges and universities are guilty of violating provisions of the federal Animal Welfare Act. Such violations result in pain and discomfort to animals used in research or experimental programs in these institutions.

Included on the AAVS proscribed list are the University of Pennsylvania (this university's research laboratories were broken into by agents of the Animal Liberation Front and researchers threatened with bodily harm), University of California at Berkeley, Harvard University, Columbia University, Medical College of Wisconsin, University of Utah, University of Hawaii, Yale University, and University of Georgia.[3]

Many medical students are now using alternatives. The American Medical Student Association (AMSA) has taken the position that medical students who object to experimenting on animals be allowed to use alternatives. An AMSA argument is that students who object to human abortions would never be forced to undergo or perform such operations. Similarly, a student who is opposed to the use of animals for experimentation should not be forced to perform animal experiments. Today, some medical schools are allowing students to choose between animal experiments and suitable alternatives.

Some veterinary students also object to animal experiments. They are in a field in which animals may be not only subjects, but patients as well. Most veterinary schools operate hospitals or clinics. Nevertheless, they have been affected by the demands to limit or eliminate animal experiments as teaching tools in their physiology, pharmacology, and surgery courses. Veterinary educators are reassessing their curricula and teaching techniques as a result of pressures brought by students, antivivisectionists, and animal rights advocates. There are a number of alternatives now available for use by veterinary students. But can they totally replace animals in these specialized schools?

In most veterinary schools, according to a survey, students spend from four to seven hours a day in what has been described as "excessive mind-numbing lectures," physiology laboratories, and in practice surgery. Dr. Roy Pollock, director of the Center for Medical Information, New York State College of Veterinary Medicine, recommended a reduction in the amount of time that a student must spend in listening to lectures. According to Dr. Pollock, students need to use information, rather than merely commit it to memory.

More medical and veterinary educators now believe that substituting other procedures for the use of animals in research and experimentation will not dilute the quality and effectiveness of education. In fact, they point to some distinct advantages in the use of alternatives to traditional animal methods and techniques. The efficiency of alternative methods reduces the time required to set up an experiment, and those methods are easier to supervise. Most animal experiments take a lot of time and require more supervision.[4]

Can the use of animals as teaching tools be replaced by alternatives? As in the case of biomedical and behavioral research, this is a disputed point. Animal rights groups, antivivisectionists, and some educators say yes, and such alternative techniques are now available. Others say that alternatives cannot totally replace the use of animals in medical education, especially in veterinary medicine, because animals are the obvious models in this specialized field of education.

If animals are used for teaching purposes in the foreseeable future, they will not be unprotected. Animal studies and experiments in colleges and universities, as in other research facilities, are regulated by provisions of the Federal Animal Welfare Act. If colleges and universities violate these provisions, as charged by the American Antivivisection Society, then they are subject to penalties. Important provisions of this laboratory animal protection law, as well as other guidelines for the humane treatment and use of experimental animals, are presented in the next chapter.

ANIMAL PROTECTION
LAWS AND GUIDELINES

Prior to 1966, federal law did not protect laboratory animals. Most states had anticruelty laws, but they varied in the kind of protection offered, as well as in the penalties for violations. When the Federal Animal Welfare Act was passed by Congress in 1966, laboratory animals were given the protection humanitarians had been demanding for a long time. The use and treatment of laboratory animals were now regulated.

This important legislation was not whisked through Congress. There was considerable opposition to its form, phrasing, and provisions. Like Thomas Jefferson's Declaration of Independence, the Animal Welfare Act underwent many changes, deletions, and additions. It had a stormy passage through the Senate and House of Representatives. There were months of heated debate and compromise involving humanitarians, antivivisectionists, scientists, politicians, and government officials before the law was finally enacted, and it has since been amended several times.

ANIMAL WELFARE ACT (AWA) _____

This important federal animal protection law is administered and enforced by the United States Department of Agriculture's Animal and Plant Health Inspection Service (APHIS). In enacting this law, Congress pointed out that the use of animals was important to certain kinds of research intended to advance "knowledge of diseases, their treatment and cure, and injuries that can be sustained by both human beings and animals." Congress also noted that methods for testing substances were being developed that were expected to be faster, less expensive, and more accurate than some traditional animal tests. The reference in 1966 was to the development of alternatives still under investigation.

The AWA defines an animal as "any live or dead dog, cat, monkey (or other nonhuman primate), guinea pig, hamster, rabbit or such other warm-blooded animal, as the Secretary of Agriculture may determine is being used or is intended for use for research, testing or experimentation."

TYPES OF RESEARCH FACILITIES _____

A research facility is defined as any school (except elementary and high schools), institution, organization, laboratory, or person that uses or intends to use live animals for research or testing products. Also included in this definition is any person or organization or institution that receives funds under a grant, award, loan, or contract from a department or agency of the United States government for the purpose of research or product testing.[1] These research facilities fall into categories:

- *Federal and state facilities:* These include public institutions administered or funded by a state or federal agency.

- *Pharmaceutical manufacturers*: Research facilities of these manufacturers must be registered with APHIS, even if they are already registered under the federal Virus-Serum-Toxin Act.
- *Diagnostic laboratories or any facility performing laboratory functions*: These must register with the U.S. Department of Agriculture.
- *Educational research facilities above the secondary school level*: These must register and include colleges, universities, medical and veterinary schools, and biology classes conducting animal research or experimentation.
- *Marine mammal research facilities*: Facilities using seals, whales, or other marine mammals for behavioral, biomedical, or related studies must register with the USDA. Furthermore, if the marine mammal facility also exhibits marine mammals, it must obtain an exhibitor's license. The same standards of animal care and treatment apply to an exhibitor as to a research facility.
- *Federal research centers*: These do not have to register. However, they must comply with all the animal care and use standards of the Animal Welfare Act.
- *All schools below the college level*: These are exempt from registering with the USDA. However, the USDA discourages animal research or experimentation in elementary and secondary schools.
- *Small-scale diagnostic laboratories conducting studies on nonregulated animals, such as mice and rats*: These may apply for exemption from registering with the USDA.
- *Agricultural research stations conducting studies or tests or agricultural practices involving horses, cattle, sheep, or other livestock*: These are not required to register.
- *Research facilities using biologic specimens alone*: Facilities using dead animals or parts or organs thereof need not register with the USDA.
- *Institutions using nonregulated animals such as birds, domestic mice, and rats*: These are exempt, but they

must register if they use wild rodents, such as the field mouse or wood rat.

Registered research facilities are required to maintain accurate records on animal use. They must keep track of the purchase, sale, and identification of previous ownership of dogs and cats. (Monkeys, guinea pigs, hamsters, and rabbits are not included in this requirement.) No animal researcher or facility may purchase any dog or cat from anyone other than a licensed laboratory animal dealer. This important provision protects dog and cat owners from the unlawful use of their pets in a laboratory should a pet be stolen, lost, or turned over to a research facility by a publicly funded pound or animal shelter. According to PETA, each year 200,000 cats and dogs end up in laboratories under "pound seizure" laws.

THE CARE AND TREATMENT OF LABORATORY ANIMALS

Animal Welfare Act provisions are very specific about the care, treatment, and use of experimental animals. Under provisions of the law, the secretary of agriculture is authorized to formulate and put into effect standards for the humane care of laboratory animals. Among the standards now in force are minimum requirements for handling, housing, feeding, watering, sanitation, and protection from extremes in weather and temperatures.

Adequate veterinary care must be provided to all experimental animals. Animals must be separated by species when necessary for their safety. A research facility using primates must provide a physical environment conducive to the well-being of monkeys, chimpanzees, and other nonhuman primates. The Harlow experiments discussed in Chapter One were severely criticized because of the isolation of baby monkeys.

All experiments must be performed with a minimum

of pain. Animals must be given anesthetics, tranquilizers, or euthanasia as determined by a veterinarian. The person in charge of an experiment is responsible for considering the use of alternatives when an experiment is likely to cause intense pain or distress.

In those experiments likely to cause severe pain and distress, a veterinarian must be consulted in the planning of the procedure. In the planning stages, attention should be paid to the appropriate use of anesthetics or other painkillers. If it is necessary to withhold pain relievers for the validity of an experiment, then such withholding shall continue only for the minimum time it takes for the experiment. That is, once a result has been obtained, the animal should not be denied pain or stress relievers.

The secretary of agriculture may issue rules or regulations regarding the design and performance of an experiment or study. This means that a halt can be called to any experiment or research project by a federal inspector for the purpose of determining whether the standards set forth by the AWA are being followed. Animal rights advocates claim that the standards are not always enforced or that inspections are too infrequent.

An important amendment to the AWA requires all research facilities to establish an institutional animal committee. This committee is to be appointed by the director or chief executive officer of the research facility. The committee must have at least three members, and members must have the knowledge and ability to assess the quality of the care and treatment of laboratory animals being used in the facility. They must also be able to evaluate scientific practices as determined by the needs of the particular research facility.

One member of the committee must be a veterinarian. At least one member may not be affiliated in any way with the research facility other than as a member of the animal care committee. No member of the committee can be a member of the immediate family of a person affiliated with the research facility. A quorum is necessary for all formal actions and deliberations of the committee, including inspections of laboratory animals, facilities, and experiments.

This animal care committee is required to inspect—at least twice a year—all animal study areas and animal facilities. It must inspect and evaluate all experiments involving pain and stress. The condition of the laboratory animals must be noted to ensure compliance with the standards mandated in the AWA. Exceptions to the inspection requirements may be made by the secretary of agriculture if animals are studied or observed in their natural environment or if the study area is difficult to assess.

The committee is required to file a report with APHIS, certifying that such inspections have been conducted. The report must be signed by a majority of the committee members conducting the inspections. The report must include any violations of the AWA standards, with special attention paid to any deficient conditions in the care and treatment of animals. And any committee minority or dissident views of a committee member must be included in the report.

The committee notifies the research facility of any deficiencies or violations of the AWA standards. If, after receiving such notification, and given an opportunity to correct any deficiencies or violations, a research facility fails to comply with the committee's recommendations, the committee notifies the Animal and Plant Health Inspection Service of the violations.

Federal research facilities, such as the Centers for Disease Control in Atlanta, Georgia, must also establish an animal care committee. However, a federal research facility committee reports any deficiencies or violations to the head of the research facility rather than to APHIS.

Each federal research facility must provide for the training of scientists, animal technicians, and other personnel involved in the care, treatment, or use of laboratory animals. The training must include what constitutes humane practices of animal care and experimentation, and what research or testing methods minimize or eliminate the use of animals or reduce pain and distress.

If a federally funded research facility fails to comply with the AWA standards and regulations, it is put on notice by the Department of Agriculture. The facility must then bring its practices and animal care into compliance with the AWA standards. If a federal research facility fails to correct deficiencies and violations, federal support will be suspended or revoked, depending on the circumstances and nature of the violations.

The Animal Welfare Act carries penalties for anyone who interferes with someone performing his or her duties under the provisions of the law. Anyone who assaults, resists, opposes, impedes, intimidates, or interferes with anyone performing his or her duties under the AWA provisions is liable to a fine of a maximum of $5,000 or imprisonment for not more than three years or both. Whoever kills any person performing duties under the provisions of the AWA will be prosecuted under United States Code 18, the code that deals with murder.

The Animal Welfare Act has been amended several times. The latest amendment, enacted in 1990, is concerned with the welfare of guinea pigs, hamsters, and rabbits. It covers the humane handling, care, treatment, and transportation of these small laboratory animals.

The 1990 amendment revises the space requirements for these animals in cargo areas of aircraft. It also regulates ventilation and temperature control in those compartments. When too many animals have been packed into cages or spaces while being transported to research facilities, they have suffered from cramping, heat, cold, or poor stowage. The lack of adequate ventilation and extremes in temperatures, in particular, cause the deaths of guinea pigs, hamsters, and rabbits on their way to research laboratories.

However, the transportation industry has objected to the ventilation and temperature control requirements specified in the AWA amendment. Transportation officials maintain that full compliance is not possible because aircraft used in the transportation of small animals do not have mechanical ventilation or cooling systems in their cargo holds. Despite the objections, no changes were made in the 1990 amendment.

POUND SEIZURE LAWS

A number of states have enacted pound seizure laws that require publicly funded animal shelters or municipal pounds to turn unwanted dogs and cats over to research laboratories. A pound is a building or enclosure where stray or lost animals are kept. The term comes from an English word, *impound*, which means to hold or contain. Animals in municipal pounds, if not claimed within a specified time, may be put to sleep or turned over to a research facility.

Pound seizure laws are very controversial and have been condemned by animal rights groups, antivivisectionists, and animal welfare organizations. Campaigns are under way in various states to repeal such laws. New York State has repealed its pound seizure law, known as the Hatch-Metcalf Act (named after two New York state legislators), which was enacted in the 1950s. This law required the American SPCA to turn unwanted dogs and cats over to laboratories. It was repealed in 1987 when the New York legislature enacted a law protecting shelter or pound animals. This new law prohibits any dog pound, animal shelter, SPCA facility, dog protective association, dog control officer, peace officer, or employee of these organizations from releasing any dog or cat to a research laboratory.

Massachusetts has also repealed a law that required

municipal pounds and publicly funded animal shelters to turn animals over to research facilities. The Massachusetts State legislature also ordered its Public Health Department to establish regulations for the licensing of research facilities using cats and dogs for experiments or educational purposes. This provision includes research facilities exempt from registration with the USDA.

The new Massachusetts animal protection law also authorizes the Massachusetts SPCA and the Animal Rescue League to conduct a minimum of four annual inspections of research facilities. This law, unwelcome to researchers, has far-reaching effects for the protection of all animals in the state of Massachusetts.

Canada's Animals for Research Act, passed in 1969, has caused as much consternation and anger in that country as have pound seizure laws in the United States. Under this Canadian law, municipalities can provide animals for research purposes, providing the animals are strays or are unclaimed. In the fall of 1990, Canadian animal rights groups met with the Canadian minister of agriculture to discuss changes in the law. What the animal rights advocates want is the elimination of the provisions requiring municipal pounds to turn unwanted animals over to laboratories.

But Canadian researchers oppose such elimination. Some researchers at the University of Toronto argue that important research would be jeopardized by a lack of animals if they were not provided by municipal pounds; animals sold by laboratory animal breeders or dealers are expensive. The University of Toronto researchers conduct important research on cardiovascular diseases and diabetes, as well as organ transplants, on animals obtained from pounds. A spokesperson for the university researchers stated that it "was easy to say go to an alternative. But certain types of research and training are impossible without the real thing."

Various medical, veterinary, scientific, and animal welfare organizations in the United States and Canada have established guidelines for the humane care and use of laboratory animals. One is the *Guide for the Care and Use of Laboratory Animals,* published by the United States National Institutes of Health (NIH). The NIH guide has been approved by the governing board of the National Research Council, whose members are drawn from the National Academy of Sciences, National Academy of Engineering, and Institute of Medicine.

The stated purpose of the NIH guide is to "assist institutions in caring for and using laboratory animals in ways judged to be professionally and humanely appropriate."[2] The guide acknowledges the fact that researchers have both a scientific and an ethical responsibility for the humane treatment of laboratory animals. Also, according to the guide, the intent of research should be to provide information or data that will advance knowledge of immediate or potential benefit to human beings and animals. Scientists should, however, continue to seek and develop valid alternatives to animals. This guide is a primary reference put to use in both public and private research facilities and institutions.

The NIH guide presents a range of recommendations for the humane care and treatment of laboratory animals. These include veterinary care, housing, bedding, food, water, sanitation, surgery, postsurgical care, social environment for primates, restraints, and euthanasia.

In the matter of restraint, the guide advises that animals should be introduced to the restraint equipment (stocks or squeeze cages) before the experiment to prevent undue stress. The period of restraint should be the minimum needed for the purpose of the experiment. Prolonged restraint must be approved by the facility animal committee. Researchers must be alert to any lesions or illnesses that may develop during restraint. If these or other conditions occur, the animal must be treated by a veterinarian. If necessary, the animal should be temporarily or permanently removed from the stock or squeeze cage or other restraint device.

An important recommendation is the one concerning restricted activity of experimental animals. There are no hard-and-fast rules. Animals confined to a cage or restraint device may be somewhat limited in their activity. The NIH guide admits that "there are no unequivocal data relating the quality or quantity of an animal's activity to its physical or psychological well-being." According to the guide, restricting an animal to a cage does not necessarily limit the amount of activity it has. A mouse can get enough exercise running around a cage or walking or running on an exercise wheel. Larger animals, though, do need to be exercised.

The NIH guide provides the responsible researcher with important recommendations for the care, treatment, and use of laboratory animals. The emphasis is on reducing the pain, distress, and discomfort of animals, while recognizing that these factors may be the focus of some experiments.

THE CANADIAN COUNCIL ON ANIMAL CARE (CCAC)

Most Canadians are as concerned as Americans about the welfare of laboratory animals. The Canadian Council on Animal Care was established in 1968. Its stated purpose is to improve the care and treatment of laboratory animals. The CCAC works in cooperation with both scientific and humanitarian organizations. It recognizes the changes that have taken place in the scientific community and among animal welfare advocates, especially the growth of the animal rights movement.

The CCAC approach to the issue of animal research

has merited the support of the Canadian scientific community, research granting agencies, government agencies, colleges, universities, and the Canadian Federation of Humane Societies. This organization also has the approval and cooperation of the Canadian Medical Research Council and the Natural Sciences and Engineering Research Council for its rational approach to the use and treatment of animals in research.

With assistance from the Canadian Federation of Humane Societies, the CCAC established standards for animal care and experimentation. These standards and recommendations are presented in a two-volume work: *Guide to the Care and Use of Experimental Animals*.[3] Canadian researchers, like their American counterparts, must conduct their research according to specified standards and regulations.

According to the CCAC, researchers must conform to the principles and guidelines set down in the *Guide*. The use of animals should only be considered after researchers have sought and failed to find suitable alternatives. Researchers need to use the best methods on the fewest possible animals. Proposed research projects or experiments should be justified in terms of the declared objectives. Furthermore, the design or plan of a research project or experiment must provide every practicable safeguard for the animals.

CCAC principles of animal research require that there be a reasonable expectation that the results will make significant contributions to human and animal health. Moreover, Canadian researchers have the moral obligation to abide by the humanitarian concept that experimental animals are not to be subjected to needless pain or suffering.

The CCAC principles, like those set forth in the American Animal Welfare Act, dictate that if pain and suffering are necessary aspects of an experiment or study, then they should be held to an absolute minimum, in both intensity and duration. Also, any animal observed to be in intense pain or distress that cannot be eased after an experiment should be humanely and immediately destroyed.

Experiments involving the withholding of food and water should be of short duration, and they should have no lasting effect on the health of an animal. Prolonged restraint should be used only after alternative methods have been considered and found impractical for the specific experiment. The method of restraint must provide an animal with the opportunity to assume normal positions such as standing, sitting, or lying down. An animal must not be forced to lie or stand or crouch in one position without relief or rest periods. In general, there must be a minimum of physical and mental discomfort.

The CCAC guidelines discourage painful experiments or multiple surgical procedures aimed solely at instructing students or demonstrating some established scientific fact or principle—in short, no repetitive or unnecessary experiments. Such experiments are unjustified, according to the CCAC, because there are alternatives, such as use of audiovisual aids and computer models.

Contrary to what the public is led to believe by the allegations of animal rights advocates and the emotional literature disseminated by antivivisectionists, researchers are required to adhere to the standards of the Animal Welfare Act or, in the case of Canadian researchers, recommendations and rules set forth by the Canadian Council on Animal Care.

Animal rights advocates and antivivisectionists are not satisfied with the protection offered by the Animal Welfare Act and the Canadian Council on Animal Care guidelines. According to opponents, the guidelines and standards do not go far enough—they allow for too much pain and distress. Furthermore, according to animal rights activists, the provisions of the Animal Welfare Act are not followed in every case, and inspections by agents are too infrequent. Opponents maintain that, all in all, the animal protection system is not all that researchers and government agencies would like the public to believe; it has flaws that cause pain and suffering to animals.

Accordingly, animal rights advocates want more stringent laws on the federal, state, and local levels. Efforts to obtain such laws are under way. In 1990, for example, animal rights activists in Cambridge, Massachusetts, demanded the enactment of a local ordinance that would further regulate animal research beyond that mandated in the Animal Welfare Act.

The proposed ordinance establishes an advisory committee that regulates all animal experiments within the Cambridge city limits. This law could affect more than 50,000 animals used at Harvard University, the Massachusetts Institute of Technology, and some local companies conducting research.

Animal rights advocates and antivivisectionists who favor this ordinance—and others like it—believe it makes up for deficiencies they claim exist in the Federal Animal Welfare Act, the NIH guidelines, and other animal care and use guidelines. As an example, domestic mice and rats, which constitute about 90 percent of the laboratory animals used in the Cambridge area, are not protected by the AWA or any other law.

The Massachusetts SPCA maintains that most of the monitoring and inspecting of animal research facilities by state and federal inspectors is inadequate. The inspections deal mainly with a research facility's physical plant and housing of animals, rather than with their pain and suffering.

There is opposition to the Cambridge ordinance and laws like it. First of all, opponents point out that the 1985 amendment to the Animal Welfare Act requires research facilities or institutions to establish "watchdog" committees to monitor experiments and the care and treatment of animals. The opponents argue that all registered research facilities do have such committees and are complying with the standards set down in the act. Therefore, laws like the Cambridge ordinance are unnecessary.

The pressures and actions of animal rights activists are of concern to politicians. The issue is double-edged. Stronger laboratory animal protection laws can have a direct effect on the availability of animals for important research. They can also affect psychological and pharmaceutical tests and studies. In such cases, the public would be the loser.

The animal rights movement is steadily growing in membership and influence, as well as funding. Many members of animal rights groups are articulate voters; politicians realize that the fight to influence the public's attitude toward the use of animals in research is a serious one. Politicians can no longer dismiss the animal rights advocates as do-gooders or fanatics. A wrong move by a politician regarding the animals in research issue can be fatal in an election.

Nevertheless, bills dealing with one phase or another of the issue have been introduced into state legislatures and Congress. Senator Howell Hefflin, a Democrat from Alabama, introduced into Congress the Animal Research Facility Protection Act of 1990. Hefflin's bill would amend the Animal Welfare Act, making it a federal crime for anyone stealing or causing the loss of any animal from a research laboratory. The bill would also outlaw the destruction of property and equipment, vandalism or theft, and entry into a laboratory with the intent to destroy equipment or research records.

Since the actions mentioned in the Hefflin bill would be federal crimes, the FBI could employ its vast resources against those persons or organizations breaking the law. The bill also provides that the secretary of agriculture and the United States attorney general could conduct a study of the "extent and effects of domestic and international terrorism on animal research, production and processing facilities."

Researchers endorse Hefflin's bill. After more than a decade of demonstrations, laboratory break-ins, vandalism, destruction of equipment and valuable records, and threats of bodily harm and even death, researchers feel that it is time they received some relief and protection.

Animal rights advocates welcome House of Representatives Bill 1389, introduced into the House by Robert Torricelli, Democrat from New Jersey, and endorsed by more than thirty members of Congress. Torricelli's bill is designed to "promote the dissemination of biomedical information through modern methods of science and technology, and to prevent the duplication of experiments on live animals, and for other purposes."

HR 1389 states that "overwhelming numbers of animals are used in duplicate research because of the research community's inability to determine what research has been performed."[4] This situation, according to the bill, has resulted from an inefficient system of storage and dissemination of medical information. The bill recommends the establishment of a National Center for Research Accountability. This center, along with a "comprehensive literature search before approval of federal funding," would spare millions of animals from pain and suffering caused by duplication of experiments.

Regardless of the Animal Welfare Act, NIH and other animal care and use guidelines, and various proposed state laboratory animal protection laws, animal rights activists and antivivisectionists continue to pressure and harass researchers. The major organizations that oppose the use of animals in biomedical research, product testing, and education are examined in the next chapter.

The Opposition
to Animal
Experimentation
in Research

The appearance of animal rights and animal liberation groups in the 1970s precipitated a drastic change in the arguments and tactics in the crusade to eliminate cruelty to animals. These new animal welfare organizations took over the leadership of the movement, which began in the nineteenth century. The passive policies of the traditional humane societies were jettisoned, and a more militant and aggressive approach emerged.

It is generally agreed that the rapid rise and expansion of the modern animal rights movement received their impetus from the arguments of three books. These were *Animals, Man and Morals* by Godlovitch, Godlovitch, and Harris; *Victims of Science* by Richard Ryder; and *Animal Liberation* by Peter Singer. These books served as a call to action and attracted hundreds of recruits to the new animal rights movement.

Singer's book was the bible of many of the animal rights activists, providing them with philosophical arguments and guidelines for the liberation of animals. At the time, Peter Singer was professor of philosophy and bioethics at Monash University in Melbourne, Australia. *Bioethics* is the study of the ethical and moral questions involved in the application of new biological and medical findings, for example, genetic engineering and drug research.

People's misuse of animals, according to Singer, causes pain and suffering comparable to that inflicted on blacks by antebellum Southerners. In his book, *Animal Liberation*, he charges that human beings are "specieists." He claims that the mistreatment of animals is condoned by human beings because it promotes the "trivial interests of their own species." He maintains that the cruelties inflicted on animals in research continue because of the general acceptance of this "specieism." Because of this acceptance, cruelties to animals are practiced that would not be tolerated if inflicted on human beings.[1]

Singer also questions other uses of animals, such as for food and fiber. His book was important to the developing animal rights movement for two reasons. First, he presented the cause of animal exploitation on a more intellectual plane than did the older, more traditional, animal welfare groups. He zeroed in on the ethical and moral aspects of the exploitation and mistreatment of animals. And second, his book attracted the attention of activists seeking a new cause. These are people who bring to the animal rights movement the same dedication, commitment, and aggressiveness that served other causes.

Another animal rights book that was a call to action was Tom Regan's *The Case for Animal Rights*. Regan argues that if "it is wrong to treat weaker human beings, especially those who are lacking in normal human intelligence, as tools or renewable resources or models or commodities, then it cannot be right, therefore, to treat other animals as tools, models and the like."[2]

In implementing their philosophy, animal rights organizations use more aggressive tactics than do the traditional humane societies. And sometimes the tactics border on terrorism.

PEOPLE FOR THE ETHICAL TREATMENT OF ANIMALS (PETA)

PETA was founded in 1980 by Alex Pacheco and Ingrid Newkirk. At the time, Pacheco was a student who had taken a course in bioethics taught by Peter Singer. Newkirk was an animal disease control officer in Washington, D.C. Starting with eighteen members, PETA quickly grew; by 1983, it claimed a membership of 12,000. Equally important, PETA's income was in the millions. The organization now has more than 250,000 members and a multimillion-dollar budget.

PETA's rather meteoric rise in strength, funding, and influence can be attributed to superior organization and dedicated membership. Although some of its philosophy is difficult for the average person to understand, especially the concepts of specieism and racism as applied to animals, the organization continues to attract recruits.

In an interview, Ingrid Newkirk stated her animal rights philosophy in no uncertain terms. She announced that human beings do not have the "right to life." In a parody of Gertrude Stein, the American author whose famous line "A rose is a rose is a rose" has often been quoted, Newkirk said, "A rat is a pig is a dog is a boy."[3]

In a 1983 *Washington Post* interview, Newkirk stated, "Six million Jews died in concentration camps, but six billion chickens will die this year in slaughterhouses." She added that animal liberationists consider meat eating "primitive, barbaric and arrogant." Pet ownership, according to Newkirk, is fascism.

PETA has achieved what it considers major victories in the crusade to liberate animals. Early on, it exposed the United States Department of Defense's planned experiments on gunshot wounds involving the use of cats and dogs. In the experiments, the animals would be shot with bullets for the purpose of studying tissue damage. However, the investigation by PETA agents and their public reports eventually forced Caspar Weinberger, then secretary of defense, to cancel the experiments.

PETA scored what animal rights activists believed to be another major victory for animal liberation when Alex Pacheco exposed the alleged neglect and inhumane treatment of monkeys. In 1981, Edward Taub, a psychologist, was conducting research at the Institute for Behavioral Research in Silver Spring, Maryland. The research involved tests to show how numbness in an arm or leg could impair its use. Taub severed the sensory nerves in one arm of experimental monkeys, a procedure known as *deafferentation*.

Pacheco posed as a college student interested in research. Under this cover, he obtained a position as an intern in the Institute for Behavioral Research, where he monitored Taub's research procedures and the treatment of the monkeys.

While on the night shift, Pacheco and another member of PETA took a photo of a monkey named Domitian (apparently named after the Roman emperor who ruled during A.D. 81–96). The photo was supposed to show the monkey's suffering while undergoing an experiment. Pacheco and his associate took Domitian out of his cage and restrained his arms and legs with straps attached to a chairlike apparatus. The photo was snapped before Domitian relaxed in the chair as he usually did before an experiment.

The restraining apparatus used by Pacheco to take his staged photo was one used by Dr. Taub for a one-hour period only. But it was never used in the way Pacheco used it for the photo. In experiments using this equipment—simulating human spinal cord injuries—a monkey was seated on a Plexiglas board with arms and legs held motionless. In this type of restraint, precise measurements of sensation loss could be made on a nerve-shattered arm or leg.

Pacheco also took photos of what were supposed to be conditions of neglect and poor sanitation in Dr. Taub's laboratory. Pacheco's evidence was enough for the police to raid Taub's laboratory. Taub was arrested and charged with 119 counts of cruelty to animals. One of the charges against him was that he failed to provide veterinary care for six monkeys; specifically, no bandages were placed on the nerve-severed arms and legs of the monkeys.

Seven veterinarians who testified at Taub's trial on the need for such bandaging failed to agree. But two other veterinarians—who were not familiar with the kind of injuries received by the monkeys—thought Taub was negligent in not bandaging them. The court agreed with these two veterinarians and found Taub guilty of cruelty to animals.

Pacheco, when questioned at the trial of Taub, admitted that when Dr. Taub was away on vacation, he—Pacheco—allowed conditions in the laboratory to go downhill and become unsanitary. He then took the photo of the deplorable conditions.[4]

Taub's arrest was the first time any researcher had been legally called to account for cruelty to animals. Eventually, the 119 charges brought against him were reduced to a single charge: failure to provide veterinary care for the monkeys as mandated in the Animal Welfare Act. But his conviction on this charge was overturned. He later went to the University of Alabama, where he applied the important information learned from the Silver Spring monkeys (as they became known) to human stroke victims.

Pacheco opened a Pandora's box of evils when he reported the alleged cruelty to animals at the Institute of Behavioral Research (IBR). Following the raid on the laboratory, the IBR wanted to transfer the monkeys to the National Institutes of Health, the agency that had approved Dr. Taub's research project. But the NIH refused to take the monkeys, stating that it had no projects, ongoing or contemplated, that could use them.

PETA wanted possession of the monkeys. After the raid, the police placed them in the care of three PETA members. They drove the monkeys to Florida in a truck. Later, when the court turned over the monkeys to the Institute for Behavioral Research, they were not in good condition. Their white blood cell counts were elevated, which indicated the primates were under severe stress; in addition, they showed signs of depression and withdrawal.

PETA and some other animal rights groups, among them the International Primate Protection League, sought custody of the monkeys. But some scientific organizations called for the completion of Dr. Taub's research since, in their opinion, it was important. They were also concerned that a precedent might be set. If a court allowed animal rights groups to bring suit over the disposition of the Silver Spring monkeys, then animal rights groups had legal standing and could sue over the use of animals in any research. This would lead to a situation that could have drastic effects on biomedical research.

Since neither the Institute for Behavioral Research nor the NIH wanted the Silver Spring monkeys, they were kept in limbo, generating bad publicity for both organizations. But something had to be done about the monkeys, and the story of their plight eventually reached Congress. Several hundred members appealed to the NIH for the transfer of the monkeys to a primate sanctuary; the NIH rejected the request. Instead of going to a sanctuary, the monkeys were hauled to the Delta Regional Primate Research Center in Covington, Louisiana. However, five monkeys that had not been operated on in Taub's laboratory were sent to the San Diego Zoo. A female monkey named Sarah, used as a control for Taub's experiments, was kept by the NIH for breeding purposes at the Delta Primate Center. Researchers there found that Sarah's ovaries had been removed, thus making her useless for breeding.

Exposure of the conditions in Taub's laboratory was regarded as a major victory by the animal rights movement. It was a black mark for biomedical research, but it was an isolated case, not an everyday occurrence in research laboratories.

In 1991, Supreme Court Justice Anthony M. Kennedy barred the NIH from killing two Silver Spring monkeys in the Delta Primate Center. The two monkeys, Allan and Titus, had been used in brain experiments under what was called "terminal anesthesia." That is, they would die after the experiments.

Justice Kennedy acted on a petition presented by PETA and other animal rights groups. The petition was an attempt to block the killing of Allan and Titus. After review, the Supreme Court overturned Justice Kennedy's order and denied the petition.

Consequently, Titus was put to sleep. But Allan was first used in a four-hour experiment that measured signals to his brain. When this study was completed, Allan died without coming out of the anesthesia. The information obtained from the experiment with Allan has been important to spinal cord research and the study of strokes.

In a 1991 mailing, which it entitled *National Referendum*, PETA stated, "Six to eight million animals will die every month in our nation's commercial, military, and federally funded university laboratories." It reaffirmed its efforts to eliminate the use of animals for product testing and stop the dissecting of animals in schools and universities.

ANIMAL LIBERATION FRONT (ALF)

ALF is an international animal rights organization with a direct action approach to the liberation of animals. It is believed that an ALF cell, or unit, was created or imported into the United States in the early 1980s. Both the FBI and Scotland Yard have labeled ALF as a terrorist organization. ALF has expanded its activities quickly, mainly because its organization and tactics had been tested in England.

ALF came to the public's notice when members broke into research laboratories, damaged equipment, destroyed records, and stole research animals. ALF claimed credit for break-ins at Howard University's Medical School and the United States Naval Research Institute located in a suburb of Washington, D.C.

ALF STRIKES AGAIN! This slogan is written on the walls of laboratories vandalized by this terrorist organization. ALF's destructive activities have resulted in higher costs for biomedical research at some colleges and universities. More than a hundred medical schools were included in a survey made by the Association of American Medical Colleges. Seventy-six reported losing more than 30,000 working hours because of break-ins, vandalism, and destruction of research records. The medical schools reported over 3,000 incidents involving faculty or staff, including harassment, bomb scares, threats of bodily harm, and even death threats.

ALF has more or less abandoned its avowed interest in eliminating inhumane treatment of animals in research laboratories. In a note left behind in an October 1986 raid on a University of Oregon laboratory, ALF agents proclaimed: "We openly concede we found few instances of noncompliance with guidelines of the Federal Animal Welfare Act governing humane care and treatment of animals."

But ALF's new approach is one of destruction instead of exposure of cruelty to animals. Breaking valuable equipment, destroying or stealing research records, releasing laboratory animals, and committing other acts of vandalism—not to mention threatening researchers—are the tactics employed by this terrorist organization.

In keeping with this approach, ALF agents destroyed a $10,000 microscope in a raid on a laboratory at the University of Oregon. In the note left behind, the ALF agents bragged that the microscope had been "destroyed in about ten seconds with a steel wrecking bar purchased for less than five dollars." The note went on to say that any monetary damage they could do represents "money unavailable for the purchase, mutilation and slaughter of living animals."

Six months after the University of Oregon break-in, ALF agents set fire to an animal diagnostic laboratory being built at the University of California at Davis. The fire caused more than $4 million in damages. The California Attorney General's Office called ALF one of California's most dangerous organizations. Later, the FBI added ALF to its list of domestic terrorist organizations.

So far, with one exception, ALF agents have managed to avoid capture and arrest. The exception was Roger Troen, an agent who was involved in the University of Oregon laboratory raid. He was arrested, tried, and convicted of theft and burglary. PETA went to his rescue, paying $27,000 of his legal fees; the animal rights groups also paid his fine of $34,000.

ALF is very efficient in its plans and tactics. In 1989, its agents broke into a laboratory at the University of Arizona and made off with 11,000 experimental mice and rats. In addition to the theft of the rodents, the agents set off a bomb that damaged two buildings, causing an estimated $250,000 in damages.

In January 1990, ALF agents forced their way into the office of Adrian R. Morrison, a researcher at the University of Pennsylvania investigating patterns and effects of sleep on animals. The ALF agents stole films, videotapes, slides, and computer disks. They left behind their calling card: ALF—FIRST STRIKE! Morrison later received a telephone call in which the caller warned him that the break-in was a "gentle warning."

The ALF struck again in February of 1992 with a raid on two research facilities at Michigan State University in East Lansing. One facility was set on fire, which destroyed more than thirty years of animal science research. Equipment and property valued at more than $75,000 were also destroyed, according to the chairman of the university's animal science department. The raid was aimed at the work of Richard J. Aulerich, an animal science professor who had been conducting research on toxins and their effects on animals. His research involved feeding food containing toxic material to mink. Mink are very susceptible to toxic chemicals, such as PCB, found in contaminated fish. Professor Aulerich's research would have benefited both humans and animals.

Members of the ALF broke into Professor Aulerich's office, rifled the files, and started a fire that gutted the office. Smoke from the fire damaged two other offices, a reception area, and a conference room. The mink cages were opened, but the mink were not removed. The ALF agents spray-painted their message on the walls: AULERICH TORTURES MINKS and FUR IS MURDER.

The seriousness of the research laboratory break-ins and the damage caused by ALF agents have prompted Congress to consider some "research protection" bills. One would make it a felony to break into any research facility operating under the provisions of the Animal Welfare Act. Another would offer protection to federally funded health research facilities and primate centers. In the case of the felony bill, the Department of Agriculture would be the enforcement agency. The bill that offers protection to the health research facilities and primate centers would be enforced by the FBI. However, opinion is divided over making laboratory break-ins and vandalism federal crimes. But James Mason, a deputy assistant secretary in the Department of Health and Human Services, warned: "The people who broke into the lab [Morrison's] are terrorists. The nation must not tolerate this kind of criminal activity."

ANIMAL WELFARE INSTITUTE (AWI)

The Animal Welfare Institute, a moderate animal protection organization, is based in Washington, D.C. Its stated purpose is to "reduce the sum total of pain and fear inflicted on animals by man." The organization is involved in a broad range of activities aimed at reducing cruelty to animals. It offers numerous books, pamphlets, and articles on humane education, wildlife conservation, trapping, attitudes toward animals, and the use of animals for research.

The AWI is active in the area of animal research. It is concerned with the humane treatment of laboratory animals, proper nutrition, housing, and development of alternatives to animal testing and research. Agents of the AWI monitor animal experimentation by research facilities to ensure that they adhere to Animal Welfare Act standards.

An officer of the AWI served on a National Resource Committee that recommended that research facilities receiving public funds reduce the number of vertebrates used in experiments and consider the use of alternatives. Christine Stevens, a founder of the Animal Welfare Institute, did not sign the committee's report. She complained that the NRC refused to acknowledge the widespread problem of the unnecessary suffering that has been inflicted on laboratory animals. Nothing in the NRC report, according to Stevens, "even hinted at the long drawn-out pain and suffering undergone by many laboratory animals."

AMERICAN ANTIVIVISECTION SOCIETY (AAVS)

The American Antivivisection Society, located in Jenkintown, Pennsylvania, defines vivisection as the "cutting, burning, freezing, poisoning, crushing, starving, internally or externally mutilating, shocking or subjecting to every conceivable kind of stress—any animal that can be handled in a laboratory." With this lengthy definition, the AAVS has stretched the original definition of vivisection, cutting into the body, to one that includes any action against or experiment on an animal.

Vivisection continues, according to the AAVS, because of grants from public and private agencies such as the National Institutes of Health on the public side and the Ford and Rockefeller foundations in the private sector. The AAVS charges that much of the biomedical research using animals is worthless in terms of relevancy to human beings.

The AAVS offers brochures, books, audiovisual aids, and other material dealing with vivisection and suffering of laboratory animals. It distributes buttons that state, ANIMAL EXPERIMENTS ARE CRUEL: STOP THEM. An AAVS poster states: HELP STOP VIVISECTION.

The AAVS, like the Animal Welfare Institute, does not engage in or condone violence or vandalism in spreading its message. Instead, it publishes articles and reports in a monthly publication, *The AV Magazine*.

AMERICAN HUMANE ASSOCIATION (AHA)

The AHA, a federation of American humane societies, was founded in the latter part of the nineteenth century. Its main purpose then was to campaign for the protection of the diminishing bison and livestock being shipped on railroads. In the twentieth century, the AHA has broadened its scope of activities on behalf of animals, including addressing the issue of animals in research.

This older animal protection organization offers an educational program that covers various areas in which animals are exploited or abused. And like other moderate organizations, the AHA does not condone violence or vandalism in efforts to protect animals from abuse and misuse. It maintains a staff of investigators who look into situations involving animal abuse, from research to use of animals in films and television.

HUMANE SOCIETY OF THE UNITED STATES (HSUS)

The HSUS is another federation of humane societies in the United States, with functions similar to those of the AHA. It maintains an educational division, a group of investigators, and a cadre of legislative experts.

On the matter of the use of animals in research, a HSUS fact sheet states, "Although animal research may have scientific merit in some cases, it is often painful and stressful to animals; costly; time-consuming; and unlikely to improve human health." The HSUS believes that the evaluation of animal research projects should address the following questions:

Can the use of animals in an experiment be replaced by nonanimal methods that would yield comparable or superior results? If not, can the proposed number of animals for use in an experiment be reduced to a minimum without compromising results?

Can the proposed procedures be refined so that any pain, suffering, or deprivation experienced by the animals be minimized without compromising results?

With these questions, the HSUS emphasizes the three R's of a more humane approach to animal experimentation:

that is, *replacement* by other methods or alternatives, *reduction* in the number of animals used per experiment, and *refinement* of experiment procedures. Many researchers are using this approach in their experiments or studies.

AMERICAN SPCA (ASPCA)

Another leading moderate animal welfare organization is the American SPCA, founded in New York City by the humanitarian Henry Bergh in 1866. The ASPCA does not demand the total abolition of animal research, but it does take the position that animal experimentation should be allowed only when there is no known or feasible alternative. Even then, any experiment should be expected to produce new and substantive information; there should be no repetitive experiments. Furthermore, experiments should be designed to use the minimum number of the most suitable species. The animals should be maintained in a sanitary environment and treated humanely during and after an experiment. All efforts should be made to reduce pain and suffering.

This humane society—the first in the United States—does not approve of violence or terrorism in pursuing its policy of eliminating cruelty to animals. It has an extensive education program, including a videotape, "A Question of Respect," which explores the subject of animal research. The tape stresses the need to develop alternatives and advocates a balance between the rights of animals and the requirements of ethical scientific research.

The foregoing animal rights and welfare organizations might be considered the leaders in the animal rights movement since they receive the most public attention. However, many more organizations are involved in the crusade to reduce cruelty to animals, both in research and in other areas of animal exploitation. They include many

SPCAs, such as the Massachusetts SPCA and the Pennsylvania SPCA, two older and moderate animal welfare organizations; newer groups composed of physicians, veterinarians, and psychologists; and smaller but militant animal rights groups.

Their positions range from reforms in the use of animals in research to the abolition of animal research to the liberation of animals from all forms of exploitation. While these organizations do not receive the notice or headlines that PETA, ALF, or the other leading animal rights groups do, they are active in the movement. Here are some of them.

MEDICAL RESEARCH MODERNIZATION COMMITTEE (MRMC)

The MRMC organization suggests in a report, "A Critical Look at Animal Research," that the use of animals in research continues for several reasons. One is that in the academic world, scientists must "publish or perish." Animal research, according to the MRMC, provides a route to the publication of articles and books. It is easy, states the MRMC, to change a few variables in an experiment and come up with new or interesting results suitable for publication. Another reason for the continued use of animals in research is that experiments on animals can be completed sooner than those on human beings because of the shorter life spans of laboratory animals.

More scientists, according to the MRMC report, have been trained in the use of animals for research. It is difficult for them to switch to alternatives such as tissue cultures and computer simulations. Also, the report continues, scientists can prove nearly anything with animals. That is, by using various animal species, researchers can confirm almost any theory they select. Researchers deny these charges.

PHYSICIANS COMMITTEE FOR RESPONSIBLE MEDICINE (PCRM) _____

The PCRM is a Washington, D.C., based organization that lists physicians, scientists, and medical students among its members. Its approach to the animals in research issue is one of promoting the development and use of alternatives. Members are active in various fields of medicine and science; one member, Dr. Ruy Tchao, developed an alternative to the controversial Draize test. The PCRM advocates a balance between the rights of animals and the requirements of ethical scientific research.

ASSOCIATION OF VETERINARIANS FOR ANIMAL RIGHTS (AVAR) _____

In a position paper, the AVAR stated that the "issue is highly complex partly because of the prevailing perception that the use of nonhuman animals in research is the key to improving our health and increasing our longevity and comfort."

While the AVAR recognizes that there are some benefits from using animals in research, it does not believe that the end justifies the means. It calls for an end to the dependence on animals for research, especially when such research "leads to their harm." This organization of veterinarians calls for more legislation to control and monitor all animal experiments.

The AVAR recommends the creation of a national or international data base of information for researchers to eliminate duplication of experiments. While making its demands and recommendations, the AVAR recognizes that the use of animals in research will continue "into the foreseeable future." It does not advocate violence or terrorism.

* * *

Researchers in Canada have also had their share of animal rights accusations, charges, and obstructive tactics. Especially singled out by the animal rights activists is the University of Toronto, which activists claim is the largest user of experimental animals in Canada. They charge the university's medical science, dentistry, zoology, and psychology departments with the use of more than 90,000 animals annually in research projects.

Targeted by the animal rights activists were experiments performed in the university's dentistry department. They charged that cats from local pounds, along with some monkeys, were used in painful experiments. The purpose of the experiments was to chart the pathways in the brain that are responsible for the perceptions of pain. It was alleged that dentistry researchers did not use any anesthesia or analgesics. One University of Toronto alumnus had this to say about these experiments: "The pain we undergo voluntarily at the dentist is acceptable; the incomprehensible pain and helpless terror suffered by an animal at the hands of 'dental scientists' is not."

When the animal rights advocates raised the issue of the use of animals in research to a national controversy in the 1970s and 1980s, they caught the scientific community more or less flat-footed. Researchers were unprepared for the intensity of the assault by the animal rights movement. But they have recovered and defend their research with rational arguments and scientific facts.

"The current animal rights movement threatens the future of health science far more than many physicians recognize." This statement appeared in an article in *The New England Journal of Medicine*.[5] The authors went on to say that the "movement is no fringe group of fanatics who cannot have a serious effect on the real world." The article pointed out that by impugning the motives of researchers (the need to publish, the competition for grant money, and so on) and giving an inaccurate picture of the conditions under which most animal experiments are performed, the leaders of the movement have won the support of "well-intentioned but misguided followers."

David T. Hardy, an attorney in the Washington Legal Foundation, also had something to say about the animal rights movement. In his booklet, *America's New Extremists: What You Need to Know about the Animal Rights Movement*, he wrote, "Animal rights activists might be regarded as harmless eccentrics, were it not for the fact that others are willing to take them quite seriously and put them into action, often violent action."[6]

Finally, Susan Sperking, a cultural anthropologist and the author of *Animal Liberators: Research and Morality*, argues that animal rights activists "relate to animals as people." They anthropomorphize animals; that is, they attribute human traits and motivations to animals. But, according to Sperking, pets are the only animals most animal rights activists come into contact with on a daily basis.

Regardless of how animal rights advocates are viewed, collectively they are a strong and influential force in the animal protection field. Scientists are concerned about the growing strength of the animal rights movement. They are worried about the future of their research, important for both human beings and animals. They resent the charges made by the animal rights activists and antivivisectionists. They realize they cannot retreat or ignore the controversy. And so they have answered the charges of the animal rights advocates and antivivisectionists with refinements of experiments, reduction in the use of animals, and a continuous search for alternatives to the use of animals in research.

ALTERNATIVES TO THE USE OF ANIMALS

A number of alternatives to the use of animals in research, product testing, and education have been developed since the rise of the animal rights movement. However, their availability does not mean an immediate end to the use of animals; there are some drawbacks in their general application to biomedical research and product testing.

What is an alternative? A standard definition is "one of two or more things that may be chosen." In the research field it amounts to animal versus nonanimal use. But the word has different meanings in the animals in research controversy. For some people, it means a technique or method that totally replaces animals in research or product testing, such as a substitute for the controversial LD/50 test. Another meaning of alternative as applied to biomedical research or testing is a technique that reduces the need for animals.

A number of public and private research centers are at work in developing alternatives. A leader in this important field is the Center for Alternatives to Animal Testing (CAAT) at Johns Hopkins University in Baltimore, Maryland. This center—the largest of its kind in the world—fosters and funds research aimed at developing in vitro and other techniques not using whole animals. (*Whole animal* is a term used in research. It differentiates between a whole live or dead animal and its organs or parts as used in research or product testing.)

The center has managed to avoid taking sides in the animals in research controversy. Its director, Alan M. Goldberg, puts it this way: "For a long time CAAT stayed out of the politics and focused on science and testing. However, we have not been allowed to be silent. We have become vocal about the appropriate use of animals in testing and research, and try to provide factual information on the status and reality of alternatives."[1]

Some alternatives now use cell and tissue cultures in vitro; microorganisms and other species believed to have limited or no feeling for pain or suffering, such as invertebrates like protozoa; computer models that can provide answers or guidance in research procedures or techniques; fewer animals per experiment or study; fewer techniques that cause pain and discomfort.

A number of manufacturers are developing alternatives for testing the safety of their products. For instance, Colgate-Palmolive, one of the major corporations that reduced its use of animals as a result of the actions and pressures of PETA and other animal rights organizations, has developed an alternative known as the chorioallantoic membrane assay, or CAM, and uses fetal membrane material. The test is used to prescreen new formulas and ingredients for safety. According to Colgate-Palmolive, the corporation research facility's use of animals for experiments and testing products has been reduced by as much as 90 percent.

Another large corporation, Hoffman-LaRoche, a pharmaceutical manufacturer in New Jersey, has also reduced its use of animals by more than 60 percent. It has done so by computer-assisted modeling, a technique that allows researchers to see the shape and structure of a chemical or substance in a three-dimensional image on a computer screen. However, computer modeling may not totally replace the use of animals; rather, it fits into the reduction and refinement category of animal research.

Researchers using in vitro tests obtain specific cells— human or animal—depending on the specific study or experiment. In product testing, a chemical or substance is applied to the cells and monitored for reactions or responses. There are some disadvantages to cell culture. One is that some cells change character when cultured; another is that the supply of specific cells may be limited from time to time.

In vitro methodology, while promising to replace, reduce, and refine animal experiments, has not progressed as rapidly as expected because of some difficulties and technicalities. One is that federal regulations require specific tests of a chemical or product before it can be approved for release to the public. For example, the United States Environmental Protection Agency (EPA) can require toxicology testing under two of its statutes, the Federal Insecticide, Fungicide and Rodenticide Act and the Toxic Substance Act.

The EPA evaluates chemicals and other potentially harmful substances for their toxicity as shown by short- and long-term animal exposure tests, that is, acute and chronic toxicity tests, on animals. The EPA considers animal tests to be critical elements in toxicity evaluations.

Another barrier to progress in the use of in vitro and other alternatives is that manufacturers are still fearful of lawsuits. Should a consumer or user of a product have an adverse reaction to a product or substance that has been tested on alternatives, rather than by the standard animal tests, a lawsuit might easily go against a manufacturer. Thus there is resistance to the use of alternatives among some manufacturers. Another factor in the reluctant use of alternatives by some manufacturers is that they are new and have not been time-tested as have the standard animal tests. Equally important, in vitro and other nonanimal methods need to be standardized and validated.

The development of cell culture tests is proceeding slowly because of certain considerations. One is that a single cell in culture cannot produce exactly the same responses or interactions that take place in all other cells in a human or animal body. The reactions and responses in cells in vitro may not always be exact copies of the ones that actually occur in the body.

THE VALIDATION OF ALTERNATIVES _____

The validation of in vitro tests and other nonanimal methods is crucial for their acceptance by industry and federal regulatory agencies. Progress in validating nonanimal tests or methods has been slow, a major impediment being the lack of coordination among testing laboratories.

There are some other problems, one of which concerns the Ames test developed by Dr. Bruce Ames. This test employs bacterial cultures as an alternative to the use of animals in identifying cancer-causing agents in a chemical or substance. The test picks out carcinogens by their ability to produce mutations in a special strain of *Salmonella* bacteria. But this test has what some critics call a weakness—a chemical that passes the Ames test could, in human beings, be metabolized into a carcinogen or could cause the formation of cancer-causing tumors.

For an alternative test to be validated, it must undergo two major steps or stages: (1) the test must be standardized—it must be described or defined in a form that can be duplicated by other researchers in other laboratories; (2) the laboratory that develops the alternative test or method must perform what is known as a "blind study." The purpose of this study is to make sure there are no built-in irregularities in the test results.

After an alternative has passed through these stages, it is subjected to duplication in different laboratories. (This procedure is known as macrovalidation.) Once an in vitro or other alternative test has passed through these important stages, a nucleus of a data base has been established. This data base can be used to evaluate the accuracy and reliability of an alternative test or technique.

Since alternative tests are relatively new and not widely used at the present time, they have not provided a substantial backlog of data, nor is their data base comparable to that accumulated by animal tests over many years. Animal tests and experiments have offered a method of assessing and quantifying the risks in a chemical or other substance. Although condemned by animal rights advocates and antivivisectionists, animal testing has undoubtedly protected the public from the hazards of toxic chemicals and substances, such as food additives and pesticides.

RISK ASSESSMENT

What is the risk involved in the use of a cosmetic? Of a detergent? Of consumption of a certain food with various additives? The answers lie in the evaluation of a chemical or substance on a short- or long-term exposure basis. Information obtained from in vitro and other studies and tests involving animals is used to evaluate the risk in consuming or using food or products containing potentially harmful chemicals or substances. Some critics say that no single in vitro test has yet reached the stage where it is unconditionally validated. They believe that a battery of tests will be required for risk evaluation for any given chemical or substance.

Researchers at the Center for Alternatives to Animal Testing believe that results of the search for and development of new alternatives will be a "tier system of testing." That is, it will consist of a series, or rows, of tests. In a tier system, chemicals and products will be tested first by computer simulations, then by a nonanimal test such as the Ames test. Ultimately, by passing through these tiers or stages, only safe products or substances will reach the final tier: testing on animals. The tier system is expected to reduce the number of animals required for testing a specific product.

The end of animal testing is some distance away. The National Research Council is of the opinion that alternatives will never completely replace use of animals in product testing and certainly not in biomedical and behavioral research. The NRC also believes that to abandon the use of animals in biomedical research would be counterproductive because important health benefits to both human beings and animals would be lost. Also, the total abandonment of the use of animals in biomedical research could lead to unethical research and more testing on human beings than is being performed at the present time.[2] (As an example, some AIDS patients are more or less human "guinea pigs" since they are taking unproven drugs as a last resort because of desperation.)

ALTERNATIVES TO ANIMALS IN BIOMEDICAL RESEARCH

Despite the efforts of researchers to practice the three R's of humane research, animal rights advocates and antivivisectionists clamor for the abolition of the use of animals in biomedical and behavioral research. Some scientists believe that people do not understand or appreciate the importance of both types of research. Nor do they seem to realize, according to researchers, that animals are indispensable in biomedical and behavioral research. Certain experiments and studies cannot be performed or conducted with in vitro or other nonanimal techniques. Alternatives are not, as yet, total substitutes for use of animals

110

in biomedical and behavioral research, research that yields benefits for both human beings and animals.

There is no question that having substitutes for animals in biomedical and behavioral research is highly desirable. Progress has been made in developing and using some alternatives, although scientists say there are no realistic substitutes for living organisms.

Animals are still a valuable part of research into disease. Rhesus monkeys may play an important role in producing data on Parkinson's disease, a neurological disorder that destroys brain cells and afflicts older persons with palsy (loss of feeling or control of movement of some part of the body, such as head, hands, and feet) and muscle rigidity. The experimental monkeys are given a drug that destroys specific cells in the same area of the brain affected by Parkinson's disease, and the monkeys exhibit all of the symptoms seen in human patients afflicted with it. The monkeys used in the Parkinson's disease research responded well to levodopa, a drug now used to treat the disease in humans. So far, no alternatives have been developed to take the place of animals in this field of biomedical research.

Tissue cultures are now being used as alternatives in some areas of biomedical research. Certain human and animal tissues continue to live after having been removed from the original organism, but they must be maintained in a culture dish. Using this technique, a wide range of in vitro methods have been developed, including subcellular refraction, use of tissue biopsies, and study of tissue slices.

Two types of tissue culture are in use: cell culture and organ culture. In cell culture, the cells are kept under conditions that allow them to survive and multiply. Researchers obtain cells for culturing from several sources— autopsies, fetuses, human and animal placenta, and animals that have been humanely destroyed.

Since the abortion issue is still very controversial, the

use of human aborted fetuses for research has been challenged. At the present time, only fetuses from tubular pregnancies and miscarriages may be used for research. In the spring of 1992, Congress passed a bill that would permit the use of aborted fetuses. President Bush said he would veto the bill unless it limited the use of human fetuses to miscarriages and tubular pregnancies. Researchers say these sources are not satisfactory, since such fetuses may be infected or otherwise unsuitable for research in such areas as Parkinson's and Alzheimer's diseases.

The approach to organ culture is different. Here the emphasis is on preserving the tissue structure and function of an organ such as a kidney or liver. Organ culture is a short-term technique, one that usually requires the sacrifice of an animal after an organ culture is established. A main advantage of organ culture is that a number of cultures can be established from a single donor animal.

There are some advantages in using in vitro systems as opposed to whole animals. One is the greater sensitivity of an in vitro technique. Another is that the experimental conditions of an in vitro experiment are more easily controlled than those of an animal experiment. Still another is the greater speed at which an in vitro experiment can be performed. Important, too, is the relatively lower cost of in vitro techniques compared to most animal experiments. But in vitro techniques may have some limitations, for example, a lack of neurological, hormonal, and immunological controls.[3]

Computer modeling is another alternative that can be used in some forms of biomedical research. This technique can provide mathematical models of human systems such as the circulatory and central nervous systems. It is possible to design mathematical and computer-assisted models of biochemical processes, but there are some limitations to this alternative. For one thing, the development of such models depends largely on the amount and quality of the data used in making them. Furthermore, researchers may include data obtained from whole animal studies or experiments. Another point is that an animal study may be needed for validating a computer model.

In vitro techniques are being used to obtain a new understanding of the action of the HIV (the virus that causes AIDS) on cells. In another research area, tissue cultures are being used to investigate certain aspects of diabetes, cancer, glaucoma, cystic fibrosis, muscular dystrophy, and certain other diseases.

A new and potentially controversial alternative is the use of transgenic animals. A transgenic animal is one that has new genes put into place by the microinjection of purified DNA. The insertion is made into the pronucleus of a fertilized egg. This transference of genetic material (it is possible to microinject human genetic material into mice)[4] leads to its integration into the DNA chromosomes of the chosen animal. It is later transmitted as a trait that can be inherited by succeeding generations.

Where do transgenic animals fit into the alternative category? After all, a transgenic animal is still an animal. Researchers using transgenic animals can be accused of furthering the use of animals in biomedical research, and, more than that, there are ethical considerations in "creating" such creatures.

There are a number of cases in which transgenic technology, or "genetic engineering," has resulted in the creation of some unusual animal models, for example, hepatitis B transgenic mice. Investigators have shown that the "expression of hepatitis B surface antigen in transgenic mouse liver can induce a disease state that resembles chronic hepatitis."[5] Chimpanzees have been the main models for hepatitis studies, but transgenic mice can now replace these costly and endangered animals.

Transgenic mice can be used as models in certain HIV studies. Mice, like chimpanzees and other animals, do not develop AIDS. This would be another area of biomedical research in which study of transgenic rodents could reduce dependence on the use of larger and rarer species.

Another important biomedical research area in which transgenic animals can be used is in investigations on Alzheimer's disease. Prior to the creation of transgenic animals, only a few animals, such as the chimpanzee and rhesus monkey, were involved in studies on Alzheimer's disease. Alzheimer's-like symptoms have been observed in old primates, but rodents have not displayed any evidence of this disease. However, researchers have demonstrated that by inserting a portion of an amyloid precursor (APP) (found in Alzheimer's disease) into transgenic mice, Alzheimer's-like symptoms occur.

The use of transgenic mice and rats can reduce the use of larger animals. But is it a true alternative? All these "new" animals do is shift the emphasis of certain animal use in biomedical research from larger animals to smaller ones. Use of transgenic rodents as an alternative is questionable as far as getting approval from animal rights advocates and antivivisectionists, especially since they are actively campaigning to obtain protection for mice, rats, and rabbits.

ALTERNATIVES TO THE USE OF ANIMALS IN EDUCATION

As in biomedical research and animal testing, there is a demand for the use of alternatives in schools, colleges, and universities. The National Association of Biology Teachers (NABT) supports the use of alternatives in the classroom whenever feasible. According to the NABT, alternatives must "satisfy the objectives of teaching scientific methodology and fundamental biology concepts."[6] The NABT emphasizes that the continued but modified use of living animals cannot be avoided in some areas of biology instruction and learning. This would include experiments on invertebrates and behavioral studies on vertebrates. Regardless of how animals will be used in the classroom or biology laboratory, the NABT recommends their responsible use, with special attention to their humane treatment and care.

There is a wide range of alternatives for high school and college use. They include X rays of animal and human anatomy and systems; heart imaging; computer models; films and film strips; audiovisual aids; computed tomography (CT) scans; magnetic resonance imaging; pyelograms of kidneys; and take-apart animal and human models. Medical and veterinary students have special alternatives, such as videotapes, manual skills simulators, clinical problem solving kits, and computer simulations.

Will alternatives ultimately replace animals in biomedical and behavioral research product testing and education as antivivisectionists and animal rights activists say they should?

The Committee on the Use of Laboratory Animals in Biomedical and Behavioral Research was appointed by the National Research Council in 1985. It was composed of representatives of a number of colleges and universities, a pharmaceutical manufacturer, a state health department, a cancer research center, and a humane society. No animal rights activist was appointed to the committee; the lone animal protection representative was Christine Stevens of the Animal Welfare Institute.

After a long study, the committee published its findings and conclusions. Among them were the following:

In many instances, a specific animal procedure or experiment is the best or only system for conducting research on a particular biological process. However, alternative methods may allow researchers to reduce the number of animals used in an experiment or a study. Some nonanimal models can replace animals in certain research areas. And some alternatives can refine experimental procedures so as to minimize pain and suffering (the three R's of humane research).

The committee recommended that researchers consider alternatives *before* using animals in an experiment or study, and that data bases be further developed and made available to researchers seeking appropriate experimental alternatives.

The tactics of the animal rights groups are not acceptable to everyone. Nevertheless, they have achieved a major victory: They took the issue of the use of animals in research out of the laboratories and into the open. The welfare of laboratory animals has improved through the efforts of both the animal rights movement and the scientific community. More manufacturers have stopped using animals to test their products or are using fewer animals for that purpose. The three *R*'s are now the condition under which biomedical research is being conducted. High school, university, and medical and veterinary students are using alternatives to animal experiments. More laboratory animal protection laws are being considered by state and local legislators. And the search for more alternatives goes on.

But there are problems still to be solved. The main one involves the human element. Antagonisms, emotions, confrontations, name-calling, threats of vandalism, and violence—all of these still cast shadows over the future of scientific research.

More rational people believe that what will be needed in the years ahead are compromise, better communication, less disinformation and misinformation, and appeals to reason rather than emotion. Both sides—the animal rights movement and the scientific community—must bend, must strive to reach an accord that will benefit animals and people. There must be accountability to the public for both sides, for it is the public that funds a great deal of research and the animal rights movement. The public must understand that animals may never be totally replaced in research, but that through the consistent use of the three *R*'s of humane research, much pain and suffering can be reduced and even eliminated.

116

Source Notes

Chapter One

1. National Academy of Sciences, Research Council Report, *Use of Laboratory Animals in Biomedical and Behavioral Research* (Washington, D.C.: National Academy Press, 1988).
2. Office of Technology Assessment, *Alternatives to Animal Use in Research and Testing and Education* (Washington, D.C.: U.S. Government Printing Office, 1986).
3. John Paul Scott, *Animal Behavior* (Chicago: University of Chicago Press, 1958).

Chapter Two

1. N. C. Pederson et al., "Isolation of a Lymphotropic Lentivirus from Domestic Cats with Immuno-Deficiency-Like Syndrome" *Science* 1987 235: 790–793.
2. Charles M. Balch et al., "The Vital Role of Animal Research in Advancing Cancer Diagnosis and Treatment" *Cancer Bulletin*, University of Texas, M. D.

Anderson Cancer Center, 42 (4) July–August 1990, 266–269.
3. Medical Research Modernization Committee, *A Critical Look at Animal Research* (New York: The Committee, 1990), 10.
4. American Medical Association, *Use of Animals in Biomedical Research: The Challenge and Response* (Chicago: AMA, 1989).

CHAPTER THREE
1. U.S. Senate Subcommittee on Science, Research and Technology Hearing, May 6, 1986 *Congressional Record* (Washington, D.C.: U.S. Government Printing Office, 1986), 10.
2. Humane Society of the United States, *Classical LD/50 Acute Toxicity Test* (Washington, D.C.: The Society, 1984).

CHAPTER FOUR
1. "Tactics Turn Rabid in Dissection War," *Insight* (Sept. 23, 1991), 21.
2. Warren F. Walker, "Anatomy and Dissection of the Fetal Pig," *Laboratory Exercise 5* (New York: W. H. Foreman and Company, 1988), 4.
3. American Antivivisection Society, *What Do All These Institutions Have in Common?* (Jenkintown, Pa.: The Society, 1990).
4. N. D. Barnard et al., "Use of and Alternatives to Animals in Laboratory Courses in U.S. Medical Schools" *Journal of Medical Education* 1988 63 (9) 720–722.

CHAPTER FIVE
1. Animal Welfare Act (as amended) 7 U.S.C. 2131–2157 Digest Section 2 e.
2. U.S. Department of Health and Human Services, National Institutes of Health, *Guide for the Care and Use of Laboratory Animals*, Publication No 86–23

(Washington, D.C.: U.S. Government Printing Office, 1985).

3. Canadian Council on Animal Care, *Guide to the Care and Use of Experimental Animals*, 2 vols. (Ottawa, Ontario: The Council, 1984).

4. House of Representatives Bill 1389, "To promote the dissemination of biomedical information through modern methods of science and technology and to prevent the duplication of experiments on live animals."

CHAPTER SIX

1. Peter Singer, *Animal Liberation* (New York: Random House, 1980).

2. Tom Regan, *The Case for Animal Rights* (Berkeley: University of California Press, 1983).

3. Katie McCabe, "Beyond Cruelty," reprint from *The Washingtonian* February 1990 25 (5).

4. Ibid.

5. Herbert Pardes et al., "Physicians and the Animal Rights Movement" *New England Journal of Medicine* June 6, 1991 124 (23) 1640–1643.

6. David T. Hardy, *America's New Extremists: What You Need to Know about the Animal Rights Movement* (Washington, D.C.: Washington Legal Foundation, 1990).

CHAPTER SEVEN

1. Alan M. Goldberg, Johns Hopkins Center for Alternatives to Animal Testing, Newsletter, Baltimore, Spring 1991, 4.

2. National Research Council, *Use of Laboratory Animals in Biomedical and Behavioral Research* (Washington, D.C.: National Academy Press, 1988).

3. National Research Council, *Use of Laboratory Animals in Biomedical and Behavioral Research* (Washington, D.C.: National Academy Press, 1988).

4. Jon Gordon, "Transgenic Animals as Alternatives to Animal Testing," Johns Hopkins Center for Alternatives to Animal Testing *Newsletter* Fall 1991 9 (2), 8–9.

5. Ibid.

6. National Association of Biology Teachers, *Policy Statement* (Reston, Va.: The Association, 1989).

FOR FURTHER READING

Fox, Michael Allen. *The Case for Animal Experimentation: An Evolutionary and Ethical Perspective.* Berkeley: University of California Press, 1986.

Langley, Gill, ed. *Animal Experimentation: The Consensus Changes.* New York: Chapman and Hall, 1989.

National Research Council. *The Future of Animals, Cells, Models and Systems in Research, Development and Testing.* Washington, D.C.: National Academy of Sciences Press, 1977.

Regan, Tom. *The Case for Animal Rights.* Berkeley: University of California Press, 1983.

Rowan, Andrew N. *Of Mice, Models and Men.* Albany: State University of New York Press, 1984.

Singer, Peter. *Animal Liberation.* New York: Random House, 1980.

INDEX

Humane Society of the United States (HSUS), 59, 62, 64, 99–100

In vitro studies, 50, 52, 107–9, 112–13

Insecticide, Fungicide and Rodenticide Act, 107

Institute for Behavioral Research (IBR), 90–93

Interagency Regulatory Liaison Group, 54

International Primate Protection League, 92

Irritation tests, eye/skin, 47, 50, 53

Kennedy, Justice Anthony M., 93

Korsakoff's syndrome, 34–35

Laboratory animals, care of, 26, 74–78, 80–83

Law and legislation, 57, 78–79, 84, 96

Lawsuits, 55–56, 64–65, 107–8

LD/50 (lethal dose/50) test, 47, 57–59, 105

Learned helplessness study, 36–37

Liability, product, 55–56, 107–8

Lorenz, Konrad, 11

Lottick, Dr. Edward A., 42

Macrovalidation, defined, 109

Man Meets Dog, 11

Martin, Richard, 8

Mary Kay Cosmetics, 55

Mason, James, 97

Mass spectrometry, 50

Maternal/sibling deprivation studies, 23–24

Medawar, P.B., 33

Medical Research Modernization Committee (MRMC), 43, 101

Memory research, 34–36

Monkeys, 28, 30, 90–93

Morrison, Adrian R., 95–96

Mutagenicity tests, 48

National Academy of Sciences, 18, 25

National Aeronautics and Space Administration (NASA), 22

National Association for Biomedical Research (NABR), 43, 44

National Association of Biology Teachers (NABT), 114–15

National Center for Research Accountability, 86

National Institute for Occupational Safety

DREAM SEASON

DREAM SEASON

A Professor Joins America's Oldest Semi-Pro Football Team

Bob Cowser, Jr.

Atlantic Monthly Press
New York

Published simultaneously in Canada
Printed in the United States of America

FIRST EDITION

Library of Congress Cataloging-in-Publication Data

Cowser, Bob.
Dream season : a professor joins America's oldest semi-pro
football team / Bob Cowser, Jr.
p. cm.
ISBN 0-87113-923-5
1. Coswer, Bob.   2. Football players—United States—Biography.
3. Watertown Red & Black (Football team)   4. Football—
New York—Watertown.   I. Title.
GV939.C67A3 2004
796.332'092—dc22
[B]   2004049510

Atlantic Monthly Press
841 Broadway
New York, NY 10003

04   05   06   07   08   10   9   8   7   6   5   4   3   2   1

For Jimmy, who shares my love of this game.
And for Jackson, who may someday.

Contents

It would be difficult to describe the subtle brotherhood of men that was here established on the seas. No one said that it was so. No one mentioned it. But it dwelt in the boat, and each man felt it warm him.... There was surely in it a quality that was personal and heartfelt.... [T]here was this comradeship that the correspondent, for instance, who had been taught to be cynical of men, knew even at the time was the best experience of his life. But no one said that it was so. No one mentioned it.

—Stephen Crane, "The Open Boat"

A Note on the Text

Modesty requires that I apologize for the violence, profanity, and statistics included in these pages. But it *is* the story of a football team, comprised of flesh-and-blood men of the biggest, hairiest kind, and I feel more allegiance to the truth of their story than to decorum. In my defense, you'll find that most of the violence herein is emotional, that most rough language is launched from the mouths of others (Don't kill the messenger!), and that the statistics really do help me to tell this story. At least I can say no animals were injured in the making of this book.

In an attempt to balance things, I have included between the chapters short, italicized scenes snatched from time, small windows into the mind of a man cruising the grooves of memory in his Subaru wagon. They were meant to let a little light and air in, yet now, rereading them, I see all manner of grief has crept in as well. What can I tell you?

In any case, my hope is every writer's hope, framed by Wallace Stevens in "The Planet on the Table": that you will find in the poverty of these words "some affluence . . . some lineament or character . . . of the planet of which they were part."

DREAM SEASON

Permission: An Introduction

Why did football bring me so to life? I can't say precisely. Part of it was my feeling that football was an island of directness in a world of circumspection. In football a man was asked to go out and do a difficult and brutal job, and he either did it or got out. There was nothing rhetorical or vague about it. . . . Whatever it was, I gave myself up to [it] utterly. The recompense I gained was the feeling of being alive.

> —Frederick Exley, Watertown, New York, native
> from *A Fan's Notes: A Fictional Memoir*

The chartered motor coach chortles and lurches through the blue-black Vermont summer night toward home, winding down rural two-lane highways, from Colchester up one side of Lake Champlain to the Vermont Bridge at Rouses Point, New York, then across and back down the other. Five hours to travel one hundred and fifty miles. In my reverie I hardly feel a thing, even when somewhere along lonely U.S. Highway 11 the clock strikes twelve and I turn thirty-one years old.

Before piling back into the bus, the team had gulped down what was left of our lunch—cold cuts, corn chips, and soda— and loaded our equipment, face masks pulled snugly through our shoulder pads, into the enormous luggage bays in the bus's belly. Then we made a beer stop before heading back in earnest. Some guys called home from the bank of pay phones outside, but I thought I'd keep the daydream going awhile longer.

I had obtained my wife Candace's permission to join the Watertown Red and Black semi-pro football team, America's oldest, several months before. Though football would have me out of town three nights a week between May and October, commuting to and from practice and games, I assured her I'd do my best to pull my weight around the house and with our infant son. At the time, she said she actually thought the whole thing was kind of courageous—a college professor going back to football after all these years. She said I needed to play, had to do it, that I would regret not giving it a try. She certainly didn't want to be the one to say no to the enterprise. Besides, she said, she was hoping it might help me get some closure where football was concerned. (It was not uncommon for me to watch four college football games of an autumn Saturday afternoon, then three more pro games on Sunday and one more Monday night.) Our season was six weeks old by then and I often got the impression she had no idea what she'd agreed to back in January. I was paying more attention to football, not less.

In the convenience store, I agreed to split a twelve-pack of Honey Brown with offensive tackle Mark Bowman, who graduated from Saint Lawrence University, a small private school on New York's northern tier, the same year I joined the faculty. Someone made a crack about the two Saint Lawrence guys drinking the pricey stuff. Now, back on the bus, 290-pound Bowman and I fill our pair of seats pretty well, so that I am almost relieved when Dave McNeil calls from his seat back by the toilet for me to come and do my "rookie chugs." He's threatened me with this since I got on the bus in the morning.

I take a longneck bottle back where he sits with Al Countryman and Bruce Gonseth and Jesse Lamora. McNeil wears sunglasses, wind pants, and a University of Kansas sweatshirt he got during his time in the army. He still wears the army crew cut too.

"Professor," he says with much relish.

"I went to college for, like, ten years," I tell him. "I know how to drink a beer."

"I went to college for a year," Al Countryman says absently from a couple rows back. "I decided it wasn't for me."

"No, Al," says Bruce Gonseth. "*They* decided it wasn't for you. That's what academic probation means."

Gonseth and Countryman work as New York State correctional officers at the Cape Vincent, New York, facility, McNeil at the county jail. Jesse Lamora drives a grain truck but he has an application in with the correctional officer academy in Albany. In *New Jack,* Ted Conover's account of his experience as a guard at Sing Sing prison downstate, Conover calls corrections New York State's "growth" industry, something particularly true in and around Watertown, a small, dying industrial city on the Black River, ten miles from Lake Ontario.

"Come on, Professor," McNeil says impatiently. "You gotta chug that motherfucker, every drop, without stopping. Jesse's gonna check it for you when you're done." Lamora holds a clear trash bag in the seat beside him, full of dead soldiers.

All of this strikes me as juvenile and inasmuch as it's a hazing ritual I'm opposed to it, but I like beer and I'm in a good humor and I don't expect this will be a problem. Seems a small price to pay. I turn the bottle up and let the beer flow down the back of my throat. As I drink, McNeil sings the theme from *Gilligan's Island,* adding emphasis when the lyrics mention "the Professor and Marianne." When I'm sure I've finished, I chug one more time then turn the bottle over to Jesse. But when he turns it upside down there's a drip.

McNeil erupts. "It's not empty!" He's yelling.

There's much war whooping and stomping of feet. It's just foam, I almost say.

"You've got to do it till you get it right, Professor," Lamora tells me.

"Five minutes, then you have to try again," says McNeil. "Send back another rookie! Come on, Bow."

I let Bowman slide past me down the aisle toward the back of the bus and slip into my seat. No sweat, I'm thinking, get it next time. Bowman downs the beer, no problem, and on my second trip I chug like a pro, without incident.

When I reach my seat the second time, Bowman and I talk awhile about acquaintances we share from S.L.U. I down the rest of my beers almost as quickly as the first two. One by one, McNeil initiates each of the ten or so rookies on the bus. Forty players are on board, the other dozen having caught rides home with friends and family.

Now Bowman takes a snooze against the enormous window. I have my Walkman on, Van Morrison's "Sweet Thing" rolling into "The Road" by Nick Drake. Up ahead I see Coach Ashcraft in a row by himself near the driver. He's what I imagine I'll look like when I'm forty-eight—the white ring of hair buzzed short, the neat white goatee. He's short and still barrel-chested, but he's let the drawstring in his Adidas wind pants all the way out.

The showers in our locker room hadn't worked but I don't mind sitting in my stink awhile. My only assignment tonight had been as a wedge buster on the kickoff team, but because we hung 58 points on the expansion Vermont Ice Storm I got to cover eight kicks and played a little offense late in the game. I'm feeling it, in my thighs and calves and in my head, and it feels good. I feel the beer too. What I don't feel is my thirty-one years.

🏈 🏈 🏈

My little brother started high school the year after I graduated and his homeroom teacher that first year had been my football coach, a snuff-dipping hot-rod enthusiast named Don Coady. Coady was an assistant coach in those days in charge of the offensive and defensive lines, along which I had played. The first day of school that year, as Coach Coady read aloud from the class roster to check attendance, he paused at my brother's name.

"Jimmy Cowser," he said. "You Bobby Cowser's brother?"

My brother smiled and nodded. Coady leaked some tobacco spit into an empty soda can on his desk.

"Son," Coady finally said, "ain't nothing to be proud of."

I'm sure there were many factors contributing to—moments culminating in—my decision to play competitive tackle football again past age thirty, but I imagine my wish to do so extends at least back to that moment in Coady's homeroom. The high school football coaches in Weakley County, Tennessee, used to meet at the Hearth restaurant on Saturday mornings to breakfast and discuss the previous night's games live on the radio—"Coaches' Corner" the show was called—and I used to believe my life began in earnest when at fifteen I first heard my name mentioned on that broadcast. Did that mean it had ended with Coady's dismissal?

By puberty, says *New York Times* columnist Robert Lipsyte, most American males have already become failed athletes. We are left to watch and cheer those who made "the cut" we didn't make, who always can do on the field, to paraphrase Hemingway, what we could do only sometimes. A tinge of envy always accompanies our admiration of these athletes and each of us must work through his own grief over this failure.

Of course it happens to athletes in every sport. Somehow, though, giving up tackle football seems hardest. You have to do it cold turkey. My brother-in-law, for example, was a scholarship college tennis player and when he finds the time he can still scrounge a pretty competitive tournament or a recreational match with a co-worker or one of his tennis-playing brothers. The 10K road races I ran through college and graduate school were full of very competitive former high school and college runners now competing in the "masters" class. The university where I now teach even has a sanctioned faculty/staff intramural ice hockey league. But nothing for ex-football players.

Maybe I started to feel too settled, too placed. Maybe, at thirty, with a mortgage and a baby, I felt too strongly the onset of my adulthood. Later that summer when I went to trade in my modest sports car for a more father-friendly Subaru station wagon, I talked with the car salesman for more than an hour about the trade-in we'd just finalized as one of many thresholds we cross in our adult lives. The first great disappointment in his life, he told me, the first of those thresholds, was when he realized that once his two years of junior college football were up, he wasn't athletic enough to make the jump to Division I football that many of his teammates would make. He figured a lot of men could tell that story. It was certainly true of me and maybe I sensed this football idea was my last chance to do something about it.

Or was it just the opposite? Maybe it was the security I felt in my new job, my new marriage, my new home that allowed me to resurrect the crazy idea that I could play football again. It was probably fifteen years of reasons. I see now that the hardest permission obtained would be that which I could only give myself, and would have to give myself over and over that season. I had to put aside my idea that a man could be an egghead or a meathead but not both and admit openly that though I loved learning and wisdom I also loved this game.

After all, of those I polled only my mother had given me grief about playing and that was because she believed, like Pascal, that humanity's unhappiness stemmed solely from the fact that we were incapable of staying quietly in our rooms, where it was safe.

Professors and football players are natural enemies; a Rutgers University English professor recently organized a group of students and faculty there, known as the Rutgers 1000, to campaign the administration for the abolition of the university's football program. But Saint Lawrence colleagues hadn't bristled. The department poet once played on the faculty hockey team and another colleague played football for Princeton in his day. Perhaps my egghead/meathead idea was only the corrosive residue of my own hopelessly rigid concepts of identity. Certainly conventional wisdom may hold that an English professor can't play football, but according to poet and erstwhile Yale center Archibald MacLeish, "conventional wisdom notwithstanding, there is no reason in football or in poetry why the two should not meet in a man's life if he has the weight and cares about the words." After all, Edgar Allan Poe's nephew and namesake was a turn-of-the-century All-American at Princeton, Robert Frost had been, like me, a high school defensive end, and James Dickey played football at Clemson.

My students laughed at news of my playing. One young woman said she knew a guy on the Watertown team, that he also took part in the Ultimate Fighting Championships when they passed through town. I'll admit that scared me; I wasn't looking to be part of a circus sideshow, and feared humiliation perhaps most of all. I slipped the idea that I would play football and write about it into a self-evaluation I had to compose and submit to my colleagues for my midpoint tenure review. At that point I was probably only half serious, desperate for an idea that might convince the department that I actually had a research plan. Of course I didn't attend the review meeting, but a friend tells me the only eyebrows raised were those out of concern for my physical health. Like my brother, my friends at work thought I stood the chance of being killed.

I had to face the fact that perhaps no one looked askance at my idea because I actually look like a football player (a short one, mind you; I look like a linebacker the way a Shetland pony looks like a horse). I had to deal with this fact each time I bought clothes from the J.Crew catalog—shirts or sweaters that hung from the shoulders of slender male models did not fit me in that way. When I go to be fitted for a suit, clothiers always fetch me the "athletic cut" jacket, also called the "portly cut," or they have to match the jacket from one suit with the pants from another. When I introduced myself to my next-door neighbor as a professor at the university, he asked if I was also a coach.

The COs having claimed the rear of the bus, the Fort Drum contingent, soldiers from the U.S. Army's Tenth Mountain Division, took the seats up front and are glued to the end of *Gladiator,* which plays on the bus's consoles as we roll home. Predictably, we'd watched *Any Given Sunday* and *Remember the Titans* on the way to the game, but *Gladiator* is the last video anyone brought. By the time we reach Potsdam, all the others— grocers, exterminators, and phys-ed teachers—are asleep anyway. I move up closer to Ashcraft to remind him he needs to drop me at the McDonald's in Canton ten miles ahead, where

I parked my car that morning. The bus will have sixty more miles to go to reach Watertown.

The driver parallel-parks the bus across the street from the McDonald's, but I don't see my car. Ashcraft climbs down from the bus with me and opens one of the bay doors. I find my bag right away but I'm drunk and sleepy and can't locate my equipment. I'm the first to unload and several players have wedged theirs on top of mine. After a few minutes I yank out a face mask that looks just like mine; it's actually Jesse Lamora's but I don't figure that out until the next day. I thank the coach. I could gush but am able to restrain myself, which surprises me considering the occasion, such as it is, and the beer. "Thank *you*, Cowz," he says, and he's back in the bus.

Once across the street I stand in the parking space where I know I left my car, hoping it will materialize. I see the PATRON PARKING ONLY sign but I'd bought a meal before getting on the bus, which I thought qualified me as a patron. Any other night and I'd be beside myself—it's past three A.M. But it's my birthday and I feel kind of bionic.

I walk into the municipal building and up to the police dispatcher's window. I calmly explain my dilemma. "Yes," she says, "we got a call about that. Let me get an officer."

Kevin Mousaw, who lives a few houses down from me, emerges from an office. He's always been exceedingly nice and he talks with me a minute about the football team.

"They noticed your car when they were closing up around eleven," he explains. "I ran the plates and vouched for you, told 'em they could just leave it there, but they have some regulation about not leaving until the lot was empty and this little girl really wanted to get home so Eric Johnson came and towed it."

My wife cuts Eric Johnson's wife's hair, or used to. Knowing exactly where the car is relaxes me even further and I tell

Kevin I don't need a ride, happy just to walk home. I lug my helmet and pads the three quarters of a mile to our house on Riverside Drive, past the Gray Lanes bowling alley, Pike's Auto, Canton Tire, and the high-rise retirement complex, replaying the whole night in my mind as I go: the small Colchester High School field amid the pines, the cool air.

When I reach the house I place my pads down on the porch. The Grasse River across the street is high and runs loud tonight. The night we moved in my wife, Candace, had thought the rushing river was a running toilet and tried to rouse me out of bed to check on it. Once I get upstairs I sit on the bed and jostle her shoulder.

"We won fifty-eight to seven," I say.

"That's nice. What time is it?"

"Late. After three."

"Go sleep down the hall," she tells me. "You smell like shoulder pads and beer."

This is fine with me. I'll tell her about the car in the morning. And I'll call my brother and tell him the whole story. I stand before the mirror to brush my teeth and examine the bruises forming on my upper shoulders just below where my shoulder pads extend, the yellowed bruises of an old man. I finger them as if to pinch myself and see if I'm dreaming.

Then I walk down the hallway toward the back of the house to the guest room where my nine-month-old son, Jackson, sleeps in his crib and I collapse on the nearby bed. When he wakes crying a little while later I pull him into the bed with me, holding him in the crook of my arm the way you'd cradle the pigskin. We sleep like babies.

My stepson, Jake, and I are sitting on the couch watching the 2000 Titans/Ravens AFC divisional playoff game from snowy Nashville, folding a week's worth of laundry and laying it carefully in the three or four baskets Candace has arranged at our feet. Okay, relatively carefully—we throw balls of paired socks into the farthest baskets, tallying hits and misses. He's winning.

Before Jake lived with me Candace says he never watched football—his father is a hunter and former track star, an ATV enthusiast. But since Jake and I became stepfather and son, the gridiron has been a kind of common ground. We play catch in the yard after he's home from school and I videotape his middle school games on Thursday afternoons. I don't know if teenage boys make such gestures, but I get the feeling his sitting down to watch this game is his attempt at understanding.

It's even colder here in Canton than in Nashville, just north of zero, the kind of day where we scheme not to leave the house. Candace is in the laundry room sorting the last dirty load while tiny Jackson, three months old, sleeps on the rumbling dryer. Sunday is the family's only morning home together since she's gone back to work and Candace likes to treat her boys with a big brunch of eggs, turkey bacon, and homemade waffles. I've tried with no *luck to drag her out to watch the Titans—she digs coach Jeff Fisher's haircut.*

Jake also likes the Titans, but I'm rooting for the Ravens. I like defense and a solid ground game, even ferocious linebacker Ray Lewis and his murder scandal. When I complain about a Titan player's celebration after a first-down catch, Jake says that's what he likes about football.

"The teams you like are boring," he says.

"We'll see if 'boring' wins this game," I say in good fun.

Then the Ravens start to pull away, toward the Super Bowl, and Jake gets up to leave the couch.

"The difference between you and me," he says, headed upstairs to his bedroom, "is that you only watch football, but I actually play."

Coming Out of the Stands

Dead coaches live in the air, son,
Live in the ear
Like fathers, and urge and urge.
        —James Dickey, "The Bee"

I phoned the Red and Black head coach and team president George Ashcraft on a snowy mid-January Saturday afternoon. My wife was downstairs on the couch giving four-month-old son Jackson a bottle in hopes he'd take a nap and I was sitting upstairs at the computer in the bedroom we had converted to an office, daydreaming about football. It was that terrible week between the NFL conference championship games and the Super Bowl, that quiet week when football-crazed people like me get a foretaste of what seven or eight months without football on television will be like once the anticlimactic Super Bowl has been played. I'm sure the panic prodded me to call.

I had gotten Ashcraft's number from the team Web site, which I had begun to visit frequently since committing to the idea of playing. I checked out the photo archive and the team calendar but focused mainly on the roster in order to reassure myself that the guys playing defensive end (where I thought I'd play) wouldn't make me, at five-foot-nine and 230 pounds, seem puny. I *was* puny when compared to NFL defensive ends, most of whom stood six-four and moved their 260 pounds through space with stunning rapidity. But this was not the NFL, as my wife reminded me many times over the course of the season, and I was pleasantly surprised that though there were enormous men on the roster they did not play defensive end. As a matter of fact, none of the ends were listed at more than six feet tall and none weighed more than I did.

When I dialed the team number a young man answered (Ashcraft's twenty-something son Adrian, I later deduced).

"Hello?"

"Hello, yes," I began. "I'm trying to reach Coach George Ashcraft, of the Red and Black."

"Yeah. Hang on." Adrian placed the phone down or held it away from his face. "Dad," I heard him yell, "it's somebody about the football team." He didn't seem annoyed really, though not really interested either. I guess I thought I would reach team headquarters, maybe an answering machine. Not his home.

Then Ashcraft was on the line.

"Hello. George Ashcraft."

"Hi Coach. This is Bob Cowser, calling you from up in Canton. How are you?"

"Fine."

"I'm calling about trying out for the Red and Black."

"Great, buddy," Ashcraft said. The enthusiasm seemed genuine.

"What do I need to know?" I asked him.

"We're going to have some meetings—organizational meetings—here in April, but don't worry about those. Just show up Friday, May fifth, ready to play."

"What about the practice schedule?"

"We practice twice a week, Tuesdays and Thursdays seven to nine P.M., and we play Saturday nights from July through September, into October if we're lucky enough to make the playoffs. But for the month of May, we're just going to practice on Fridays, until we loosen up."

"Sounds great," I said. And it did. Too great almost. May 5, the night of the first practice, happened to be the last day of my spring semester at S.L.U. I don't know what I had expected in terms of the practice schedule but commuting back and forth to Watertown only twice a week for practice seemed reasonable, something I could actually sell to my wife. I was out of class by two-thirty on Tuesday and Thursday, which left me plenty of time to get down to Watertown for practice by seven. And I liked the idea that my thirty-year-old body would have at least a day between practices to recover from the pounding I knew I'd take. Yes, it was all too convenient and left me no ready excuse to bail on the project.

"How big are you?" Ashcraft asked me.

"Five-nine and two hundred thirty," I told him.

"Mmm," he said. Had he hoped for bigger?

"I've been in the gym a few weeks now getting ready. I don't know what my forty time would be," I said. The gym bit was a lie; I planned to go, absolutely. I was still running daily but in truth I hadn't been in the gym since college. It was all part of my identity issue. I wanted to look like a professor, so I avoided weights altogether.

I really didn't know my forty-yard-dash time. I hadn't been clocked since high school, when I weighed 190 and ran a 5.01—a respectable time for a giant pro lineman, like Chad Clifton from my high school, but not nearly fast enough for someone as small as me.

"If you're in the gym, you're already ahead of the game—keep it up," Ashcraft told me. "And you know, we don't do time trials around here. If you can't take a hit, it doesn't matter how fast you are."

I said good-bye and hung up the phone. Yes, it was entirely too convenient, too possible. Practically a fait accompli. I was playing football. When I got downstairs, Candace had the baby asleep in her arms, and I decided to wait awhile before breaking the news.

*   *   *

I married Candace in my second year in New York, acquiring in the deal a minivan, a tired old dog, and an athletic fourteen-year-old stepson, Jake, who split time between his father's house and ours. I was a bit adrift when Candace and I met, new to town and recently divorced, and I can see now there was an element of mercy to the love she offered me. An ex-girlfriend had recommended Candace as the only hairstylist in town with whom I could trust my thinning hair and almost immediately after meeting her I forgot the promise I had made to myself never to marry again. Home-schooled by her mother since the seventh grade, she had skipped entirely the soul-killing American high school experience that had wrecked my own self-esteem, and I found her confidence intoxicating.

Candace brought our lives together with the force and foresight of a military commander and within the year we bought a house to make room for the baby she was carrying. Having been burned by a daughter-in-law already, two if you counted my brother's first wife, my parents were wary of Candace in the beginning, a divorced hairstylist with a teen-age son and a possessive prison guard for an ex-husband. (Candace's father, Bill, a heavy-machinery operator and charismatic minister, had had a few things to say himself about our moving in together and conceiving baby Jackson before we were married. "Seems to me you have a couple of carts before your horse," he said to me.) But she won the folks over straight-away. Her clients always say how surprised they are, getting up from the salon chair, that she isn't even five feet tall—her presence so fills the building. "She's the only person I've ever known you to be afraid of," my brother-in-law Frank tells me.

I started to take the local daily paper, the *Watertown Daily Times,* when we moved into the new house in June, a Harry Homeowner thing I did kind of ceremonially. (I took to wear-ing a bathrobe and slippers too.) The semi-pro season started in July, just as we'd moved in, and the paper introduced me to the football team via weekly Red and Black player profiles and game recaps in the sports section. Around the same time, dur-ing a pre-baby shopping trip to Watertown, Candace found the Red and Black Hall of Fame and Museum down a long hall-way off the food court at the Salmon Run Mall. Located im-mediately opposite the public restrooms, the place looked like the in-school suspension room back at my alma mater West-view High: painted cinder-block walls, industrial carpet. Tro-phy cases on the walls resembled those you find in a high school lobby, full of yellowing team photos and news clippings and old footballs commemorating great victories, the date and score painted on the pigskin in white but barely legible now.

Football historian Marc Maltby writes that as America became increasingly modernized and industrialized at the dawn of the twentieth century and as small, independent com-munities like Watertown began to disintegrate, supporting local professional football teams provided those communi-ties a means to retain a rapidly fading identity and to combat "the trend of bigness and impersonality." Larger cities like Syracuse and Scranton faced no real threat, but in towns like Watertown and Latrobe, Pennsylvania, local teams have been a source of great civic pride, an anchor to civic identity.

Watertown, now a city of some 26,000, had been settled early in the nineteenth century along the Black River, between the mighty St. Lawrence and Lake Ontario, the only real New York destination, some would say, north of Syracuse. Historically, Watertown men have worked industrial jobs (lumber primarily), made possible by the region's embarrassment of natural riches, though now, as the riches dwindle (serious embarrassment), it seems as many work in area prisons or drive a truck.

In their spare time, these men have always played football, the Red and Black having been around in one form or another since 1895, longer than any other of the more than five hundred semi-pro football franchises currently playing across the country. There are spans of time since 1895 when Watertown fielded no semi-pro team—the years of the world wars, most of the tumultuous sixties, the early seventies when debts and waning public interest threatened the team—but they are mere hiccups. The franchise owns all-time national semi-pro or minor league team records for wins (492 as of the 2001 season), games played (764), and losses (226), and ranks eighteenth all time with a .672 winning percentage.

While NFL fans are saturated with statistics, up-close and personal interviews, reels of classic game footage, semi-pro fans still deal mostly in legend, and the Red and Black's is fearsome. Football was an outlaw sport in its early days—the "red meat era," historians call the period—played by ringers or "tramp athletes" under assumed names, and working-class Watertown was just the place for such a game. Frederick Exley, son of 1930s' Red and Black star Earl Exley and the man who put Watertown football on the map in the 1968 novel *A Fan's Notes,* published an *Inside Sports* piece in 1983 about a Hawaii bartender who knew the Red and Black legend. "Have I ever heard of Watertown?" the bartender says to Exley. *"That's where the goddamn animals are."*

Originally fielded in 1895 by the Watertown Athletic Association, a group organized in the same year to promote local sport, Watertown's football team was known in its earliest incarnation as the Collegians and played civic teams from other northern New York cities like Carthage and Ogdensburg. Former Watertown mayor and chief team booster J. B. Wise beefed up his lineup of locals with former college stars from Syracuse and Cornell, classic ringers. Then in 1900, enamored of an old college uniform Watertown player/coach Harry Lamon wore regularly to practice, Wise announced that he was changing the team's name to the Watertown Red and Black, the name they've had ever since.

The new century brought changes to the team's profile as well. Thousands turned out to see home games in those days, arriving by bicycle and horse-drawn wagon, one department store even providing shuttle service to and from the contests. Legendary baseball manager Connie Mack brought his Philadelphia Athletics football club to Watertown to face the Red and Black early in the 1903 season, and later in that year the club played in a four-team world championship football tournament in New York City, organized in part by J. B.Wise, finishing second to a tough Franklin, Pennsylvania, team. Wise is said to have lost $10,000 in bets he took on the championship game, which the Red and Black lost 12–0.

That world championship tournament was held indoors at Madison Square Garden, played on a pinched gridiron only 80 yards long and 140 feet wide—a punt is said to have smashed a Garden light fixture and sent it crashing to the floor. According to the *New York Times* reports of the game, a member of the Asbury Park, New Jersey, Oreos, angered by a Red and

Black trick play that game officials allowed to stand and which had the Watertown boys poised for eventual victory, punched a Watertown player so hard the Watertownian lay unconscious on the Madison Square Garden turf for five minutes.

Legend has it that Green Bay Packer coach and stadium namesake Curly Lambeau offered the Red and Black a shot at the big time in the 1920s, a spot in the fledgling NFL, but was turned away. Nothing in my meager research confirms this, though chamber of commerce types still hail Watertown as the "Green Bay of the East." The team enjoyed an undisputed heyday in the middle 1950s, going 26–1–2 between 1954 and 1957 and recording twenty-one shutouts over that span. Coached by "Boots" Gaffney and later Nelson Sholette, then by both in '57, the Red and Black players of that era were mostly local Watertown boys, graduates of Watertown High and Immaculate Heart Academy, smallish players who relied on speed and the misdirection of the "T" formation to defeat bigger clubs from Syracuse, Rochester, Toledo, Niagara Falls, and Buffalo. But as the NFL and television emerged hand in hand in the later fifties and early sixties (think of the Alan Ameche touchdown in that muddy NFL Championship), interest in the hometown team waned until the team fell entirely from view in 1961.

Former and would-be players resurrected the team in 1969, headed by All-America Syracuse University center Pat Killorin. The feeling was, you couldn't stand idly by as tradition disappeared. In an interview with the *Watertown Daily Times* prior to the 1977 season, when debt and low numbers again threatened the club, current offensive coordinator and former star running back Mike Britton made a plea for community support based on the Red and Black's legacy. The names have changed, he said, but we're still here, living history.

It would seem those tough years are behind the Red and Black organization in the full morning of its third century. Interest generated by the team's 1996 centennial lingers, and that combined with the influx of talent from the now-booming army base on the city's outskirts, not to mention Coach Ashcraft's considerable business and promotional acumen, assure the team's solvency in the foreseeable future. On the field success may be another matter: current Red and Black players are painfully aware of the organization's illustrious history, and though the 2001 roster boasts players on the verge of all-time records in rushing, receiving, and passing, the team has not won a title since the 1980 squad beat the Troy Uncle Sammies 30–10 to claim the Empire Football League Championship. Individual records aside, Ashcraft's men cannot hope to be considered with Gaffney's or Sholette's among the all-time great teams until they win another.

It was hard for me to say how good current players on this team really were, or how my skills compared, I had been so long away from the game. From what I could gather from the newspaper—the *Watertown Daily Times* featured a Red and Black player in every Saturday edition during the season—these were guys who'd had Division II or III football scholarships but had flunked out of college, say, or had quit school to get married and support a family and ended up at a plant or a paper mill or with the U.S. Army at Fort Drum and now found themselves on the Red and Black roster.

The previous October, the baby only a month old, I had snuck down to Watertown to watch the Red and Black play. I decided to drive down only after I realized the college football game I had planned to watch on television would be preempted by a New York Rangers hockey game (hockey is king in the North Country). I left my house at kickoff time, seven-thirty, missing most of the first half, and the Watertown team already trailed its archrival the Syracuse Vipers when I arrived. This playoff game would decide the championship of the North Division of the Empire Football League, determining which team would play the Scranton Eagles in the EFL Championship the following week.

Players from both teams looked enormous standing at the crown of the field at Alex Duffy Stadium, which lay at the heart of the Jefferson County Fairgrounds in Watertown. The field's namesake, a local stonemason, had also been a Red and Black player, coach, and team president and was considered until his death in his late nineties its greatest ambassador. The facility was only adequate (the Red and Black board lobbied the city for new digs, something befitting a team with this kind of history), bordered by wooden posts run through with nylon cord. The city had erected two stands of aluminum bleachers, one on the home sideline and another, smaller one across the field, and they were full that October night. Many other fans set up lawn chairs behind the end zones, next to coolers full of beer. I stalked the sidelines trying to find a comfortable place to stand. I felt the restlessness I often felt at football games since my playing career had ended.

That October night at the fairgrounds the Syracuse Vipers' smallish but swift receiver Rashaad Porche took advantage of the Watertown secondary throughout the second half and gradually the Syracuse team pulled away, first down by first down. Porche wore number 6 and late in the fourth quarter, once the contest had been decided, I heard drunken Watertown fans in the end zone yell mockingly before every Syracuse snap,

"Watch number six." Then Porche would come open over the middle on an underneath route and the officials would move the chains.

I was impressed by the speed of the game at this level and by the great size of some of the players. Viper linebacker Wilford Stephens, named national semi-pro defensive player of the year that season by the American Football Association (semi-pro football's national governing body), appeared to be of NFL proportions, six-foot-two and 250 at least, the size of Philadelphia Eagle Levon Kirkland. Their tackles were six-five and 350. Still, I was eager to give this a shot. I had been a good little high school player, I told myself, all-conference as a sophomore and again as a senior. I could hang with these guys.

* * *

The first stage of my own grief about the end of high school football fifteen years before had been denial—evident, I think, in my college choice. I had banked on a Division I college football career, even at five-foot-nine and 185 pounds, and when the major football schools didn't recruit me I filled out only two college applications: I was rejected by Notre Dame (which went on to win the football National Championship under Lou Holtz my freshman year) and was accepted at Loyola University in New Orleans, a school that at the time of my enrollment had no intercollegiate sports at all. So I went to Loyola where I would not think about football, only academics.

And it worked, sort of. I did well in school and began to develop an identity as something other than a linebacker. But my transformation was not complete; I had lapses. Along with some guys from my dorm, I tried my hand at intramural flag football my freshman year of college but was suspended after the first game for tackling (the supreme no-no in flag football) and never bothered to get myself reinstated. Flag football is a finesse game, a showcase for quarterbacks and the fleet of foot—"touch football was never meant to be and will never become football," writes theologian William Dean—and it merely frustrated a player like me who had only ever distinguished himself on the gridiron by the collisions he could get himself into.

The next year when I joined a different, long-standing intramural flag football team I met the guys who are, even now, my closest friends. We were a successful team and I enjoyed that, league champions who traveled to play in the state championships a couple of times, the nationals at the University of New Orleans once, but I rarely got playing time when our games were close. My friends carried me on the roster the way a hockey team carries a goon, for intimidation and brawling, though opponents who knew me at all were hardly intimidated and though we never once had a brawl. Standing on the sidelines all that time mellowed me. Once during my junior year, I even skipped a league championship game to work on a term paper for my Wordsworth seminar, leaving my friends to play the game six players against seven. They played and won, even short a player, but the guys shunned me that night at our favorite bar. "Hey, Wordsworth, could have used you today," Andre Garsaud told me, picking up his beer and walking away.

In 1994 I moved to Lincoln, Nebraska, to begin a Ph.D. in American literature and that's where I fell off the wagon. Lincoln is a heaven on earth for any college football devotee, even more so for me as a lifelong Cornhusker fan. The football fanaticism I had been bottling up was commonplace, among women as well as men. I rented an eighth-floor condo only blocks from Memorial Stadium and attended every home game over the next four seasons at student ticket prices—a span during which Nebraska won three national championships and lost only two games—and I drove across the Midwest to catch several more contests. Many autumn afternoons I concluded my daily jog down by the Ed Weir track where the team conducted practices. I watched them carefully, a sea of players one hundred strong, with a mix of admiration and envy. There were a handful of football players in my writing classes and in my mind I couldn't help but size them up physically, compare my high school self to them. Why hadn't it been me?

Amid all the football, I did manage to complete that Ph.D. Yet at work in the English Department, I could not openly declare my passion for the game, sensing that football had to remain a guilty, secret pleasure. Despite the Nebraska program's success, and the fact that legendary head coach Tom Osborne held a doctorate in educational psychology, the faculty and many of my fellow graduate students at Nebraska had at least a low-grade contempt for Cornhusker football. In 1996, the team had three players simultaneously under indictment who remained enrolled in classes and continued to compete on Saturdays, including one notorious running back who pleaded no contest to assaulting his girlfriend, and a receiver who played the whole season with a bullet lodged in his back from an off-season drive-by.

Then there was the matter of budgets and funding. Andrews Hall, for instance, which housed the English Department, could have used a serious makeover, yet it seemed that each year the athletic department was unveiling a new facility, an indoor practice field, or a million-dollar replay screen. Those of us in the department who followed the team, the quiet handful, spoke behind our hands in the department mail room about getting together to watch road games on television. We were die-hard fans but couldn't afford to compromise our public identities as intellectuals.

In August of 1996, my brother, Jimmy (he as big a Husker fan as I was), flew out to Lincoln from Kentucky to catch the Nebraska-Michigan State tilt. It was a warm, bright day and as we waited for the team to charge from the locker room tunnel, the whole stadium adrenalized, we agreed how great it would be to come out of the stands and onto the field again, if only that were possible. A couple of years later when I accepted a teaching position at Saint Lawrence University, an hour's drive from Watertown, suddenly, magically, it was.

The hot August evening my younger brother Jimmy is issued his junior high football equipment I am an hour or so late getting home from my own varsity practice. This is a big moment in the life of a boy in Martin, Tennessee—his first set of pads—but I am all self-regard. As usual I have taken the long way home, the very long way, blaring AC/DC or Journey or REO Speedwagon in the little lawn mower of a car I am driving at the time, sucking down Mountain Dew and crunching through a sour apple Blow Pop in a couple bites, mooning over cheerleaders.

Football has always been my game—my mother used to let me skip Sunday Mass as a preschooler so I could watch what I called "music football," the NFL Films Game of the Week *narrated by Jack Whitaker—but I never got the sense it meant that much to Jimmy. Relatives who mailed me a Dallas Cowboys helmet for Christmas mailed Jimmy a Tonka truck. He and I played football together some, but we were four years apart in age and not always a good match in size and ability.*

When I finally get home, I realize the game had gotten its hooks in him while I wasn't looking: through the back door's window I see my brother sitting fully padded on the couch—helmet, shoulder pads, and all—erect as a Buddhist monk.

"Please pay some attention to your little brother," my mother whispers to me once I get inside. *"He's been sitting like that for two hours just waiting for you."*

Building the Beast

This Patriot repeats the hulking face of a superhero in a comic book—thick-necked, leering with mayhem, giggling with sadism, brow furrowed not by thoughts of his tiny dinosaur brain but by anabolic steroids—an image of the decline of the public's hero from enlightenment ectomorph, spiritual with endeavor and guilt, to sadistic, hulking mesomorph, an apelike Homo Footballus, the object of our weekend attention and obsession, squatting before the goalposts of a diminished life.

>   —poet Donald Hall on the old New England Patriots
>   helmet logo in "Football: The Goalposts of Life"

I called my brother Jim in Louisville and told him about my conversation with Ashcraft. My brother's support was significant. He was someone I respected as a tremendous football fan and a former player. Like me he had grown up split at the root—in the household of egghead English professor parents stranded in a meathead Tennessee town—so he understood my conflict. And he knew what my body was capable of, having a very similar (though slightly newer) model himself. Most important, I trusted him to have my best interests at heart. He was a social worker and counseled troubled boys for a living and I liked the tone he took with me when he wanted me to see something in a situation that I was missing. When he burst one of my ego balloons, he took pains, the experience somehow not as concussive as when my wife took the same task upon herself.

He waited on the phone a long time before he said anything. I could tell he had some misgivings and was, I think, a bit sorry he couldn't be there to try out with me. I was sorry for that too.

"You're going to have to get in the gym," he told me.

"I'm on it," I told him. I really did plan to go.

"How good are these guys?" he asked me before hanging up. "I'm just afraid they're going to kill you."

* * *

The Saint Lawrence fitness facilities were housed, in those days, in a pair of smallish, windowless basement rooms beneath the gymnasium—the place was a dungeon, really. A sauna was constructed in the center of one of the rooms, which made the place also a sweatbox. I went out directly and bought weight-lifting gloves and was there every weekday morning after an early forty-minute run. The abject terror I had begun to feel about the project was a great motivator.

After a week or so on my own in the weight room, once I had reacquainted myself with the equipment and established the hours I could devote there, I decided to get smart and ask Jimmy about a weight program that would achieve the desired results. There were athletic trainers on staff at S.L.U. I might have consulted, one who'd been with the New York Rangers of the NHL, but I didn't want to go that public yet. Besides, Jimmy was something of a weight-lifting guru, having worked in a gym through high school and college and having trained and competed as a bodybuilder.

"I want to be nineteen again," I told Jimmy. "Got a program for that?"

"Well," my brother said. "What hurts *already*?"

Only my back, I told him. I had put in a lot of road miles in the previous decade, eight full twenty-six-mile marathons in ten years, and the pounding had taken a toll on my back. In my mid-twenties a doctor diagnosed sciatica, common in runners. Essentially, discs in the lower back pinch the sciatic nerve, which runs along the spine and branches into both thighs, causing a burning and stiffness. A chiropractor I consulted had my back x-rayed and discovered that because one of my legs was significantly longer than the other, my hips had rotated out of perfect alignment to compensate. He yanked and tugged at me for several weeks to correct it but I never noticed an improvement. The morning after each marathon I always arranged to have a one-hour massage, which helped with the soft tissue damage, but by the time I ran my last marathon, the 1999 Cape Cod, my back had gotten so bad my hamstrings and gluteals had become unnaturally stiff and had seized up in an attempt to protect the spine. I limped across the finish line and asked Candace just to shoot me.

"Sore back is usually a result of weak abs," Jimmy said. He suggested a lot of stretching and a strenuous abdominal workout—crunches in the hundreds every day and hanging knee-ups in a Roman chair.

"The distance running is probably counterproductive for what you want to do anyway and cutting that out would take a lot of pressure off the back," he said. Football workouts I've seen since confirm this—football is a game of short bursts and not long-distance jaunts so sprints and interval training would have been the answer. But I was afraid to drop a fourteen-year-old endorphin habit on this football whim. I'd see how things went, but for the time being I would continue to run every morning.

I told my brother I thought I could spend about forty-five minutes a day in the gym and still hold down my job and keep my marriage together. One of the great things about a professorship is the flexible schedule; I didn't meet any classes until noon that spring semester. My brother fashioned a workout for me based on a model he said was employed by the legendary Bulgarian power-lifting team: high weight, low reps.

My mesomorph metabolism, which I had always cursed as a runner, was an advantage now. I used to have to compete in the "Clydesdale" class in most of the road races I ran, but now my size meant that I didn't have to rely on the unpleasant dietary supplements ectomorphs used (creatine and the like) in order to see results quickly. I had always told runner friends and training partners who had tried to get me into the gym for supplementary workouts that I had to stay away, that if I even looked at weights I got bigger. But it was mostly accurate. Within a few weeks, I noticed how snugly my clothes were fitting in the neck and arms.

You can get too much of a good thing. Gradually my progress began to plateau and all that exercising and teaching and diaper changing got me very fatigued. Then I contracted pneumonia. I complained for a week or so that my workouts were becoming tedious and taxing, but I chalked it up to burnout. The discomfort persisted, but Candace didn't believe I was sick. As tired as she was herself and as much time as I spent working out every morning (three hours every day, counting the running and the gym and the shower after) while she got ready for work at the salon and got the baby ready for the babysitter, she couldn't spare the sympathy. Only when Jackson developed a cough and I took him to our physician did I get an "oh, by the way" diagnosis. "Yeah, you have pneumonia," our hockey-crazy Canadian physician told me.

Candace was shocked when I came home waving my prescription for an antibiotic and so guilt-wracked, she said, that I could not mention my illness in her presence. I took the antibiotic and temporarily ceased the frigid early-morning outdoor jogs, as directed. I was too weak to go to the gym for more than a week but I dared not stay away too long. May 5 was only a few months away now and everything in my life had begun to point to Watertown and that date.

● ● ●

To get to Watertown from Canton for the first night of practice, I'd take U.S. Highway 11 south, sixty miles from point to point, though the rural two-lane highway is so slow it takes between seventy-five minutes and an hour and a half to drive it. The only route north from Syracuse, it's always clogged with overland trucking, farmers' pickups, army convoys from Fort Drum.

Though it skirts the north edge of the vast and breathtaking Adirondack Park, Route 11, winding lazily past rusting barns and double-wide mobile homes, cannot rightly be called scenic. Frederick Exley characterized the cold, stony, barren country around his hometown as "Russian—almost steppe-like," and writer T. C. Boyle, who went to college in Potsdam ten miles northeast of our home in Canton, called it "the frozen skullcap of the world." Candace's parents live eight miles south of our house on Route 11 in a tiny hamlet called DeKalb Junction and on days when I would strap Jackson into the car seat and drive him out to stay a few hours with his grandparents, he always fell asleep before we got there. "The Route 11 snooze," his grandmother and I called it. I always felt bad about handing her a snoring lump, but she seemed to understand. "Nothing to look at between here and there," she'd say, shrugging her shoulders.

Later in that long season, once I had gone back to teaching and the days grew short and it began to seem like I had made the trip a million times, that snooze became a temptation for me too. But those first few weeks my anxiety kept me alert. It wasn't simply dread I felt on the way to May fifth practice. Fear had accompanied me a few months before when, after six years without dental care, I drove down to see a Watertown dentist about a decaying tooth a Canton dentist thought he would have to pull (my Watertown dentist saved it without so much as a root canal). What accompanied me to that first practice was different, more complex, dread but also tremendous curiosity.

I pulled into the fairgrounds complex that first night headed straight for Duffy Stadium, where I had attended the playoff game the previous October, assuming practices were held there too, until I saw cars and trucks parked along another football-sized practice field across the road, footballs—kicked, punted, and thrown—whizzing through the sky above them. I turned in that direction.

The night was cool, in the fifties. Spring arrives late to the North Country—my colleagues recall snowstorms on Mother's Day and during commencement—and it lingers well into June, so I had packed both long- and short-sleeved shirts just in case, along with a new pair of nylon jersey shorts and Nike Shark cleats I had purchased at the mall. I parked my Subaru as inconspicuously as one can park a station wagon at a football practice and walked toward the field. Men I took to be veteran players huddled under opened SUV hatches, music blaring from in-dash speakers, metal music of a vintage so recent I didn't recognize it.

The field was full of hopefuls; more than seventy signed up that first night. Enormous endomorph linemen throwing footballs back and forth always amuse me—as if these behemoths ever see the ball in the game (I played from May to September before I ever touched a ball). Fleeter players ran pass routes or fielded the punts to kill time. The quarterbacks hummed spirals back and forth with that feigned nonchalance.

I can honestly say I was not intimidated by the physical specimens before me. The tryout was open to the public and brought all kinds: some of the more athletic veterans wore souvenir T-shirts from Arena Football League tryout camps, but I saw one kid, probably nineteen, wearing a Scooby-Doo T-shirt and smoking a cigarette right through the workout that ensued.

I stood on the field a long time before anyone spoke to me, I'd guess fifteen minutes, like the guy at the prom no one will dance with. The turf was bad, rock hard in some places and treacherously soft in others. I followed the flying footballs, listening to the thud of punts. I feigned stretching and thought seriously of going home.

The first player to approach me was Scott Ford, the place-kicker. He was a handsome, moon-faced guy, wore a goatee like mine. He said he sold cars in Watertown and he had the firm handshake and hearty hello to prove it, though he struck me as earnest, not your average used-car dealer. He had been a minor league hockey player in Europe and then the coach of the hockey club at Syracuse University, I learned, and had grown up in Potsdam, the son of a barber. "You've got a haul," he said.

I had noticed him clowning with the other veterans before we met. Because he plays one of only two essentially "noncontact" positions on a football squad (the other being punter), and because the fickle hit-or-miss nature of his success makes him readily "scapegoatable," the kicker must feel his bond with teammates to be a tenuous one. I thought that explained Ford's jester role, one he maintained all season, and his glad-handedness with me. While I didn't yet reveal myself as a professor, I couldn't help but divulge some of my performance anxiety. "You're a big man," Ford told me. "You'll be fine."

Finally head coach George Ashcraft called us together at the 50 yard line. "Gentlemen," he began firmly (this was how he began every address he made to us). He wore a black Red and Black wind suit, a ball cap, and a whistle—every inch the football coach, pretty close to what I had imagined from our phone call. "We were nine and three last season. That's a pretty good year for most teams, but it's the first time in, what, five years that we didn't win ten games."

He looked to veteran players for confirmation, and they nodded. Ashcraft had taken the team to the playoffs in each of the previous four seasons.

"I don't know about you, but I'm back here to win an EFL championship. We beat the league champion twice last year but couldn't beat them in the playoffs when it counted." He referred of course to the Syracuse Vipers and the playoff game I'd seen. Before that, the Red and Black had lost in two consecutive New York Amateur Football League title games.

"But I like our chances this season," he continued. "We got Al Countryman back, and I got a call last night that Earnie Wash will be back from his tour in Egypt by about the third game. This is our year, gentlemen, and it starts tonight."

I have been a lifelong student of football-coach rhetoric, always partial to the sentimental, George Allen/Dick Vermeil school, and I had a good feeling about this guy. Ashcraft was a gruff man from a long line of gruff people (when I mistakenly called his father's house looking for him, I got an earful from his mother), but there was something inviting in his signature Watertown gruffness. It summoned the basest loyalty. "I've got only one disgruntled ballplayer in all my years," he told me proudly later, "and that's his own fault."

Like perhaps nothing else in his life except his thirty-year marriage, George Ashcraft's coaching job suits him. Watertown is a tough place for being such a small city—home to prisons, a major military base, and nearly six months of winter—and George Ashcraft is a tough man for a tough town.

"Pudge" to his mother, George Ashcraft was born in Carthage, New York, a village on the Black River east of Watertown, home to a handful of paper, concrete, and cheese manufacturing plants and site of a famous nineteenth-century factory fire. Ashcraft graduated from Carthage High in 1973 and right out of high school went to work in an area paper mill, hanging on in such jobs until 1999, when his was one of sixty-seven jobs eliminated in a buyout. He had played middle linebacker for the Watertown Red and Black teams of '74 and '75 before a severely broken leg cut short his career, living the next many years in a house on Washington Street across from the Watertown High field where the Red and Black played home games.

He stayed away from the organization while his children were in grade school, returning to the team as a defensive coordinator in 1989 and taking over head coaching duties in 1991. Since that time he has devoted himself full time and whole hog to the Red and Black—"I can't really afford a nine-to-five day job at this point," he told me. Inheriting a 2–9 team back in '91, Ashcraft won three games in his first year as head coach and four in his second, but he'd taken the franchise to the playoffs in eight of the last nine seasons, the only miss the '95 campaign, marred by a player eligibility scandal (something that still frustrates the coach). His overall record in eleven seasons as head coach was an impressive 73–46–1, with nearly a third of his losses coming in those first two rebuilding years.

"Before I turn it over to our general manager," Ashcraft told assembled hopefuls that night, "I want to let you know we got about seventy-five people here—that's good numbers. Hey, God love you guys for coming out. I don't have a dime to pay you, but we'll take care of you best we can."

I hadn't been sure about the money issue, whether anybody got paid. At the turn of the century in the pre-NFL era, J. B. Wise had a ringers' payroll that exceeded $15,000, serious money in those days, while local players played for a split of the till. Paying players was prohibited by adult amateur leagues, though it was the charge outmanned teams always leveled against teams that overwhelmed them. I knew that a handful of players on other, more metropolitan squads played in the Arena Football League during the winter months for decent money, playing for free in the EFL in the fall as a tune-up, but apparently here in Watertown, though the coaches and general manager were paid a couple of thousand for their efforts—about what a New York State public school teacher would earn for coaching a scholastic team—the term "semi-professional" was merely a means of distinguishing these competitors as adult amateurs not scholastically affiliated.

General manager Sam Verbeck also talked to us about money. We were one of only two EFL teams, he said, whose players didn't have to buy their own equipment, the Syracuse Vipers being the other; it seemed that at this level, as in the NFL, money was a factor in football success. But it did cost $27,000 to run an EFL franchise, he told us, and the board had secured only $8,000 in local sponsorships and advertising to that point. "So, basically, we're sucking hind tit on nineteen grand right now," Verbeck said. One of the solutions to this problem was a season-ticket drive, and each of us would be responsible for selling ten season tickets—five home games for $10, a $40 savings. And he encouraged us to drum up local business support, hit up the management at work.

Bruce Gonseth's hand shot up. "Hey Sam," he said wryly. "I work in a prison."

I sold exactly three season passes: one each to my wife and her father, the third to my closest Saint Lawrence colleague, Liz Regosin, who never actually made a game in Watertown that season. I left a stack of laminated passes with Candace at the salon but she didn't move a single unit. My colleagues made a lot of noise when I first announced my intentions about a tailgate party before a home game or a road trip to Montreal. But nothing ever worked out. I certainly didn't blame them.

Offensive coordinator Mike Britton had nothing to add that evening except hello. He looked pensive, even sullen, clutching a clipboard to his chest. He and Ashcraft were practical contemporaries, both natives of Carthage, New York, though they had attended different high schools before playing together, Britton at running back and Ashcraft at middle linebacker, on the Red and Black teams of the early seventies. By day, Britton was a middle school gym teacher, having held various coaching positions at the high school, college, and semipro level over the past twenty-five years.

Sam Verbeck rallied us for our workout once the obligatory speechmaking ceased. Verbeck was not an ex-player and didn't look like one in fatigue shorts and knee-high tube socks. By day, he was an army physician's assistant at the Fort Drum facility and so served not only as the team's chief operating officer but also as the trainer and conditioning coach. He had been involved with football at other posts, Fort Knox, Kentucky, for example, and his foster son Aaron Brown, a giant offensive tackle, was an erstwhile Red and Black star gone to start a junior college football career on Long Island. Verbeck was but one example of the contributions the base made to the current team, and its contributions to the community at large were comparable. Established around the time of the Second World War as a training facility for troops from New Jersey, New York, and Massachusetts, Camp Drum became Fort Drum and is now home to the U.S. Army's Tenth Mountain Division, an elite force trained in alpine combat, training more than fifty thousand soldiers annually, pumping as much as half a million dollars into a grateful local economy.

This first practice was known among the coaches and veterans as "Black Friday," as the initial workout of the new season was always held on the first Friday evening in May. Verbeck proceeded in a vaguely military fashion, barking nasal orders, but the veterans treated him like a substitute high school teacher, heckling him and mocking his demonstrations of the calisthenics and grass drills. Because the evening was so cool, I guess, and because of the off-season layoff, Verbeck had us stretching a long time. He put us through the paces, the grass drills I would have predicted: high knee run, butt kickers, back-pedaling, sprinting out of a stance. He also added a lot of poly-metric exercises I wasn't familiar with, bounding and skipping (something the guys really camped up, some holding a pinky out as they skipped), and something called a "Sumo walk" modeled on the Japanese wrestling tradition.

I thoroughly enjoyed myself. So many years of watching practices enviously and now I was partaking. I had thought I would not have this chance again in my life, to be sure. Still I anticipated the next day's soreness. And what's more I knew it was all prelude. As Ashcraft had said to me on the phone months before, it doesn't matter how fast you are (or in this case how limber or how well conditioned) if you can't take a hit. Those of us who had played football before knew practice really began with contact at the end of the month.

Once or twice a week the first September Candace and I are married, after I'm through with afternoon classes, I head up to the ball fields behind Canton Central School to haunt my stepson Jake's eighth-grade football practice. Conifers shade the whole field and the ground is cool to the touch, still holding morning dew though it's now four in the afternoon. A handful of fathers, would-be coaches, are there watching sons play. I watch Jake carefully, preparing a critique that no matter how presented will only hurt him. "He just wants your approval," Candace says later. I want to play so badly my guts churn.

I remember the old practice field at Martin-Westview, the smell of whatever oil they used to line the fields lingering in the burned grass, the August swelter. Fathers, done with work at the Goodyear plant or body shop, come out to take stock of the team and speak a word, once coach is done with practice, for the son who's worked all summer in the weight room. "He deserves a shot," they'll say.

My father is there too, inside whatever used Chevrolet he has driven to the gravel parking lot adjacent to the field, his nose in the Riverside Shakespeare he's brought along, or a stack of student exams, folded lengthwise and rubber-banded together. "Just marking student papers," he says cheerily as I wedge my sweat-soaked pads in the backseat. He always says "marking" and not "grading." He starts the Chevy and we disappear into the dust its tires make in the gravel.

Committed

but I remember all the bad old days
back in the world of men,
when everything was serious, mysterious, and scary,
hairier and bigger than I was
— Tony Hoagland, "Dickhead"

Empire Football League history doesn't reach back quite as far as that of the Red and Black, only thirty years or so, but it's one of which the league's board, mostly ex-players and coaches, is very proud. The EFL boasts not only two of the country's oldest semi-pro franchises (Watertown and the Glens Falls Greenjackets, established in 1928) but also a handful of former players who went on to fame in the NFL, among them defensive linemen Jerry Drake (Arizona Cardinals) and Ray Seals (Pittsburgh Steelers). The EFL, which regularly placed teams in the national Top 25 poll published by the American Football Association, would be composed in 2001 of twelve teams from four states (New York, New Jersey, Pennsylvania, and Connecticut) and one Canadian province (Quebec). Watertown joined the Greenjackets, the Syracuse Vipers, the Capitaland (Albany) Thunder, the Lake City (Plattsburgh, New York) Stars, and the Montreal Condors in the league's Northern Division, while the Connecticut Chiefs, the Orange County (New York) Bulldogs, the Broome County (Binghamton, New York) Jets, the New Jersey Ravens, the Wilkes-Barre Blaze, and the Scranton Eagles would compete in the Southern bracket. Each team was slated to play a ten-game regular-season schedule, two games against each division opponent. The top four teams in each division would then play in a single-elimination playoff tournament, the championship to be played on the home field of the Southern division champion.

League contracts, to be mailed to the league office in Endicott, New York, seemed a formality at first: one page with lines for home address, home and work phone numbers, description of football experience, position played, and the player's signature (which made one the "property" of the Watertown Red and Black football club). But Ashcraft made some to-do about them. "Once you sign it, you're mine," he told us, "you're mine." Syracuse was only seventy miles down Interstate 81 from Watertown and I gathered that over the past several seasons Red and Black players unhappy about playing time had offered their services in Syracuse, or to the Lake City Stars of Plattsburgh, New York, a hundred and fifty miles northeast. Signing this sheet made such moves a violation of league rules without the original organization's release, an attempt by the league to maintain order and prevent roster-hopping or game plan espionage. The Red and Black was forced to forfeit three games and lost a playoff spot in 1995 when it was discovered that a player on the Watertown roster had begun the season with the Central New York Express out of Syracuse, though Ashcraft later had those wins reinstated on appeal.

*   *   *

The Red and Black locker room lies beneath the grandstand of the baseball park at the Duffy fairgrounds, former home of the defunct class A Watertown Indians (a Cleveland Indians farm club), now used by the Watertown Wizards of the New York Collegiate Baseball League, a summer league for professional baseball prospects who haven't yet signed contracts and need experience with wooden bats. The cinder-block locker facilities were relatively new but dank and low-ceilinged, prone to flooding. On the season's second Friday, veterans and hopefuls lined up single file from the coaches' office waiting to sign Empire Football League contracts. The number had dwindled into the low sixties, and I saw no sign of the kid in the Scooby-Doo shirt.

From the first pungent whiff I got of the place I was anxious. I had avoided fraternities in college because I had not wanted the company of a throng of barely postadolescent, adrenalized men and I had not been in that kind of situation in a long time. All my childhood anxieties about hypermale spaces crept back—the fear of being popped by a wet towel or stuffed in a locker or given a wedgie or a swirlie (where one's head is crammed in a flushing toilet). I knew my professorhood marked me as an ideal candidate for all of these indignities.

Locker room conversation had not changed much in my time away, still aggressive, always costing someone's humiliation. The comeback for every put-down or insult in high school had been "Oh yeah? Your momma didn't complain last night." I noticed that now it was simply one's wife who hadn't complained. That was another thing: I worked at the university with people who had "spouses" or "partners" or "significant others," but apparently these guys had "old ladies." I thought again of going home.

I struck up a conversation with Matt Quay, who was ahead of me in line. "You played last year?" I asked. Yes, he told me, at center. Over the course of the season, he struck me as one of the best all-around athletes on the team. He seemed roughly my size, an inch or two taller and ten pounds heavier but sleek and athletic-looking. I suggested to my wife at the year-end team banquet that Quay and I were built similarly and she snickered at me. "You're not that tapered," she said. Quay had a tattoo of barbed wire that encircled one bicep and I detected nipple rings through his T-shirt. He'd driven an eighties-model Camaro home from practice the week before.

Matt said he had played in college, fullback at SUNY-Cortland. "I guess I just went there to play football and drink beer, and that didn't cut it for long," he told me. Now he was earning a graphic design degree from Mohawk Community College and living at home with his mom for the summer, taking a few courses online. I explained that I was a college teacher and had many students who'd stumbled down that same road early but recovered to do well. It's hard to be disciplined that first year away from parental control, I offered. I had intended to keep my profession a secret but found it difficult to do so, the job having come so much to define me. Probably I was here to shake those things up.

My football identity became the question when I reached the blank at the bottom of the player data sheet minutes later: "position to be played." Most of all I wanted to make the team, so I tried to assess team needs and make myself indispensable, but it was too soon. I hadn't observed enough to form an opinion. And I felt so removed from my playing days—what could I do anymore? I had played fullback in high school but hadn't been swift enough even then and so was switched to offensive guard in my junior season. I thought about guard but feared I would be undersized at only 230 pounds. A two-way starter in high school, I had played both outside and inside linebacker on defense before ultimately settling as a defensive end. End is where I'd felt most comfortable—I preferred the instinctive nature of that position to the deliberate, assignment-oriented offensive line positions—so I wrote that down.

I'd been kneeling beside Ashcraft's metal desk as I wrote. The coach sat reviewing the completed forms.

"What do you play?" Ashcraft asked me.

"I'll play wherever you want me," I told him. The suck-up answer, yes, but I figured the more flexible I was the more likely I was to make the team. My worst fear was that they'd simply ask me to go home.

"Hear that, Coach?" he half-yelled to Mike Britton across the room. Britton made little response. I realized I was not the sort of physical specimen over whom coaches licked their chops.

I relaxed once we were back out onto the practice field that night. We were led through our warm-up by a group of veterans this time, among them Al Countryman, to whom Ashcraft had referred in his state of the union address the week before. Countryman was a gritty billy club of a running back, at five-foot-seven and 220, thickly muscled. He shaved his head and wore eye black, which gave him a menacing, serious look, a sort of perma-squint beneath his pronounced brow. He was the heart of the team, an embodiment of the working-class image of the region, like the hero from a Springsteen song. He had the Red and Black logo—an *R* and *B* shot through with a thunderbolt—tattooed on his bicep.

Though Al was generally soft-spoken, only Ashcraft got more face time on local television. Countryman was the first person both Candace and my brother mentioned when I asked them to evaluate the talent, the only player most of my Canton friends knew by name. Everywhere we played, coaches and players alike revered him. "Al Countryman is the only guy over there with any class," Lake City Stars coach Ed McAlister would yell to our sideline late that season after a loss to the Red and Black.

Countryman's 2000 season had been cut short by an anterior cruciate ligament tear in late July against Syracuse. "I knew it was bad when he came to the sidelines," Sam Verbeck would tell me later. "He played a whole quarter after injuring it and said it felt weird but didn't hurt. There's intense pain with an ACL sprain but almost none with a complete tear." In fact, it was probably the report of the injury and its catastrophic effect on the Watertown season that first put the Red and Black on my radar—I remember it as the lead story in the sports section of the *Daily Times*. After three hours of surgery and two nights in the hospital, Countryman returned for the playoffs three months later with a large brace and a noticeable limp, neither of which he'd yet rid himself.

Now Countryman's 2001 comeback was cause for much optimism and the focus of Red and Black season previews both on television and in the newspaper. Watertown was moving to a one-back spread offense, which featured Countryman at running back, complemented by a speedy corps of receivers, and Al needed only 452 yards to become the all-time leading Red and Black rusher (surpassing, incidentally, current offensive coordinator Mike Britton). "I think physically he's one hundred percent," Ashcraft told the paper. "I know mentally he's two hundred percent. I don't have a concern about Al Countryman."

Like a lot of men in the North Country who'd heard Countryman's name on the news or read it in the paper over the past decade, I felt the urge to measure myself against his standard. Al and I were close to the same age, he a year or so younger, and I suppose I would have liked to have befriended him. One night after practice in late July, Countryman and I were stopped at the same convenience store off Route 11 in Philadelphia. He climbed out of his gray long-bed pickup to fill the tank and as I stood at the next pump filling the Subaru, we talked about home and work. He was very pleasant, but everything I told him about myself, though we'd played together for close to three months by that time, seemed news to him. I had made no impression.

A Saint Lawrence colleague once asked me if I had in fact befriended any of the guys on the team, or if they'd simply been too different from me. I knew that the decade I had spent ambling through college and graduate school Al had spent working tough jobs, most recently as a correctional officer, and playing with the Red and Black. Nine seasons before, after a year of college football at SUNY-Cortland, he had begun his semi-pro career as a defensive back and was immediately an all-league performer and a league defensive MVP (conventional wisdom was that he was a better DB than running back) before injuries to other running backs forced him into the offensive backfield in 1994, where he's starred since.

The coaches broke us into two groups the night of our second workout, linemen and everybody else. They didn't coach us— the expectation was that we were already developed players— but simply observed, took stock of talent. While the backs and receivers ran pass routes, I went with the linemen to run through the dummies and the ropes. I had always hated practice in high school—it was an exhausting event at the end of what seemed in those years an extremely long day. But with a few marathons and a few years in a real job under my belt, a couple of two-hour practices each week seemed very reasonable. I had played every down for three years in high school but didn't know how much I'd play at this level and I planned on enjoying practice this time around. Maybe practice would be the most action I'd see.

A couple of experienced linemen, Pat Nulty and Dave McNeil, led us through drills, de facto coaches. Nulty had introduced himself to me at the beginning of the evening, having noticed the S.L.U. faculty sticker on my station wagon. Familiar with George Plimpton's *Paper Lion,* he liked the idea of my project—a professor coming back to football. Forty-seven years old and a special education teacher in Carthage, Nulty had played for the Red and Black in twenty of the last twenty-four seasons, alongside Al Countryman's father, Al Sr., and Coach Britton, and had been a perennial all-league tackle in the seventies and eighties, once even an All-American. He'd taken the past couple of years off from football but was now back, at his daughter's behest, to "play until he was fifty." After his divorce, he explained, when he had his daughter only on the weekends, she'd accompany him to the Red and Black games and it became an elemental part of their bond. Now she was a freshman at Syracuse University and he wanted back in.

I liked Pat. He was something of a physical marvel, a year or two younger than our paunched offensive coordinator, a couple older than the paunched head coach, yet he was holding his own against boys half his age. He ran grass drills for an hour before every practice to get his old body ready, rubbing himself with Ben-Gay before the team gathered to stretch. To the extent that he was a player/coach, he coached like a grade-school teacher. He brought equipment from home to aid in practice, pylons made from Styrofoam swimming pool noodles, and boards measured and cut to be placed under tackling dummies while we drove them. And he encouraged us. He didn't seem the least bit alienated by what I did for a living—we had teaching in common. Over the long season, I found him very good company on the sideline.

First-team All-Empire Football League offensive guard Dave McNeil was bad cop to Nulty's good. He was ex-army, now a correctional officer, macho as all hell. He seemed mean, frankly, and at six-three and 270 he was big enough for it to matter. As we struggled to maneuver backward through the dummies, he yelled like a drill sergeant. Candace and I didn't talk much about what went on down at the fairgrounds at that point, but I did tell her about Dave.

Eventually Ashcraft made his way to where the linemen had gathered for a water break. "What do we have, twenty linemen? Twenty-one?" he began. "Everybody out here wants to be a goddamned receiver. I tell you what, I'm not going to cut any linemen," he told us. "By the first of the season last year I was down to seven linemen total, so I need the bodies." I was relieved, though I had wanted actually to earn a spot on this roster.

"You'll cut yourselves," the coach continued. "If you're playing line in this league at five-nine and two hundred twenty pounds, you're fucked." I had to wonder if he had me specifically in mind, those being my near exact dimensions, though there were smaller players in the group. He said that he'd start handing out equipment the next week. We were scheduled to hit in seventeen days.

"I got something like fifty sets of equipment," he said, "probably not enough for everybody, but if we don't give it to you, you can still come and watch."

"Yeah, and wear a skirt," McNeil added.

Once Ashcraft had moved on, Pat Nulty suggested it might be a good time to introduce ourselves and where we figured to play. At least ten of the twenty players there listed defensive end as their position. For variety, I said I'd like a shot at noseguard. "We run a four-man front," McNeil said curtly. "There is no noseguard."

"Nice to meet you too," I thought. Maybe a position switch was in order anyway, to McNeil's offensive line, where the team had been so thin the season before. Again, I had not enjoyed the offensive line so well as the defense in high school, but I wanted to be indispensable.

Rams twenty-year veteran tackle Jackie Slater said at his NFL hall of fame induction ceremony in 2001 that in all of sports the offensive lineman was the ultimate "rank and file" athlete—not a single statistic is kept regarding his performance, no yards gained, points scored, or sacks. College and professional teams had begun to count "pancake" blocks, when linemen flattened opponents, but that seemed merely compensatory. To play center, guard, or tackle requires not only brute strength (these are usually the biggest players on the field) but also extraordinary patience. While success on defense means three plays and out, success for the offensive line often means a long, sustained drive of several clock minutes and ten or more plays, the results of which most linemen never see, their heads buried in the guts or shoulder pads of their opponents. Like a tug-of-war team, these guys understand the game as a battle of attrition and continue working on an opponent's weak spot until it gives way. While fans might prefer a long pass play, o-linemen would like nothing better than to move the ball down the field methodically, perhaps even calling the same play repeatedly as they go, pounding first to one side then the other like a boxer's pair of fists.

One of the drills that evening had us bear-crawling on all fours to a cone ten yards downfield and then leaping to our feet and high-stepping hard left to the next cone, backpedaling hard left to a third marker, then sprinting to complete the square. Resting on one knee as other players completed the course, I noticed the rich grass stains in both my palms. How long had it been since I'd gone hands-first on the ground like that, even in play? I couldn't remember. "You don't like to get dirty," Candace teased me. "You've got poet hands." The first thing I did before driving home that night was stop at a service station restroom and scrub my hands clean.

It was during these first few nights of practice that I acquired my nickname; having survived a month or so, we newbies needed to be christened. They called me "Professor," "Profess" for short. Pat Nulty, whom everyone called "Nutty," must have shared what he knew about my background, and then there was the matter of the bright red faculty sticker on my car. Prior to the start of the season Candace and I had speculated about what they might call me and Professor had come up, also Doc. To most of the rest of the team I was a curiosity, like the minister in a Western, a man apart whose mysterious power was neither understood nor questioned. Guys made feeble jokes— "You gotta give the kids a lab practicum tomorrow?" Kyle Roshia asked on a day when I had to leave practice early (I reminded him I taught English, not bio). There were not a lot of university men on the roster, after all. Coach Britton had a degree in physical education, but Ashcraft hadn't been to college. Neither had Dave McNeil, who wielded my nickname derisively, as an epithet. When my feet got hung up in the ropes course or when I kicked one of Nulty's Styrofoam pool noodles out of place, he screamed it—"Come on, *Professor*!"—as though it were at once my name and an explanation for my clumsiness. I could only imagine that Dave was taking his unpleasant school experiences out on me.

Toward the end of our workout the Tuesday night of the third week, Coach Ashcraft again stopped by on a water break and sent veteran linemen to meet Sam Verbeck in the locker room and be suited up. Quay and McNeil and a kid named Brandon Payne, McNeil's complement at guard, went in first. I should go with the next group, Ashcraft told me, me and Nulty. I took this "tapping out" as the supreme vote of confidence, the sort of approval rarely meted out among men. This team needs you suited up, Ashcraft was saying, you're valuable. This meant getting at the recently reconditioned equipment early before it had been picked over. I verily floated across the parking lot and into the locker room.

The backs and receivers were on the practice field a while longer that evening working on timing patterns and establishing the numbers that would identify the various routes on the pass route tree (we linemen hadn't made nearly that much progress) and by the time they got into the locker room most of the veteran linemen had been outfitted and Verbeck was beginning to suit rookies. This did not sit well.

"Hold on a minute," Jamee Call said. "You're suiting rookies first? That's not right. There are veterans without pads out here."

We rookies stood dumb. We'd simply done what we'd been told.

Ashcraft finally suggested the rookies show up on an off night the next week to get equipped, Monday maybe. The veterans walked among the outfitted players announcing what helmet or face mask or pair of shoulder pads had belonged to them and demanding it be handed over.

Whose team is this? I was thinking. I hadn't been handed anything yet so had nothing to give back. I got in my car and drove home. But I'll admit the incident remains with me because I knew what the griping veteran players knew: the right equipment was everything. And not the right equipment in terms of fit or performance necessarily, but the right equipment in terms of appearance, fashion. Susan Faludi suggests that what matters in modern professional football, driven by TV ratings and advertising dollars, is what you look like. We semi-pro players are voracious consumers of the NFL product (professional wrestling too, in some cases) and we understood this truth. What separated us from younger fans, importantly, was buying power: we had the cash to buy the peripheral equipment our Sunday heroes wore.

Take face masks. There are, of course, functional concerns; quarterbacks need a cage that maximizes vision, running backs a mask with maximum vision as well as protection from errant fists and fingers, linemen a longer cage that protects the throat. But inasmuch as it is a sort of second face, literally a mask, the style of face mask suggests something about the man behind it also. Fifteen-year veteran linebacker Lynn Patrick, a true throwback, wore a simple, classic NOPO (industry terminology for "nose and oral protection") mask, probably the same model he'd worn his entire career, the mask itself an emblem of Patrick's longevity. Al Countryman and Bruce Gonseth purchased their own helmets online, in part to ensure quality but also because they wanted to customize the padding inside their Schutt Pro Air II helmets (the standard-issue Watertown helmet was red with white padding and black face mask but these guys wanted black padding and black vinyl chin straps). Gonseth actually bought red and black athletic tape to wear on his wrists on game days.

I'm afraid I was among the worst offenders on the team in this regard. I had been as excited about wearing pads again as about anything else. I did drive back to Watertown on the appointed night to get outfitted and was issued a solid pair of shoulder pads and a helmet that fit, but I was unhappy with the face mask, a squarish NOPO cage like Patrick's divided horizontally by two parallel bars and bisected vertically by one, the same model I had worn in high school fifteen years prior. Having watched very carefully the development of the face mask since that time I wanted something more twenty-first century. After some time on the Web, I opted for quite a long, complicated steel cage, suggesting medieval armor or a futuristic robotic visage, which I purchased from a sporting goods Web retailer for twenty dollars.

Candace felt I went a bit overboard "accessorizing" the standard hardware. Some of the things were legitimate protective equipment: a $60 cowboy collar, which rose up out of my shoulder pads to prevent my head and neck from being jammed backward (and incidentally made my shoulders look huge); $40 padded gloves for my hands (I'm a writer, for God's sake—need those digits); $20 neoprene elbow sleeves to prevent the return of the permanent scabs I had developed on my elbows during my original incarnation as a player; and a $10 concussion-proof mouthpiece to protect my thousands of dollars' worth of orthodontia (this was my mother's chief concern, as provider of that dental care).

Other purchases were a result of my keen observation of the advances in football gear. I'd worn cotton half-shirts under my shoulder pads in high school, which waterlogged quickly in the Tennessee humidity and chafed against my skin, so I purchased a $50 UnderArmor top made of a Wickaway material—black and sleeveless with a mock turtleneck collar. I also bought a girdle of the same material, which doubled as compression pants—it held my hip and thigh pads in place, snug against my thighs, and offered support and protection to the muscles of my groin and upper legs.

Then there were the purchases Candace deemed "excessive and unnecessary": the extra pair of gloves (for games), a second pair of cleats (the first pair were cheap and not sturdy enough for my liking, and I'd seen other players in snazzier pairs), black athletic socks (no good reason), and the UnderArmor all-weather top and leggings, which I wore but twice (this was a summer league). As the UPS boxes piled up on our porch Candace plotted to get my credit card out of my hands.

When I try to summon an image of my inner linebacker, for courage, I can't help but see my mother there in my mind's eye, the burning end of a long Marlboro—her brand in the good old days—poking out from her face mask. No, she wouldn't have worn a face mask—leather helmet all the way. I remember a story she tells from her Cleveland childhood of Browns quarterback Otto Graham playing the second half with a face full of stitches after taking a cleat to the mouth in the first. Maybe she was there.

My mother was my great defender when I was a boy. Right or wrong. When she caught wind that a disgruntled mother had dressed me down after a Little League game I'd umpired the summer I was fourteen, reducing me to tears, she burst out the back door in her housecoat and slippers in search of the woman (we lived across the street from the ballpark). How many kids told me later that my mother had accosted them in her pajamas, a cigarette clenched in her teeth? "Where's Rose Ennis?" she was shouting, "Where's Rose Ennis?"

When I find myself trying to describe Mom to someone, a new friend, I say she's like Sipowicz, Dennis Franz's character from NYPD Blue. *Not the mustache so much, but the lion-hearted ferocity. That's a terrible thing to say about your own mother, you're thinking, but you don't know her. Thank God she's on my team.*

Contact

Violence is the *sine qua non* of the game. Throughout the history of football, the violent spirit of the game has endured, even as other elements of the game have changed.... Commenting on football, sociologists David Reisman and Reuel Denny noted that, "Americans fear and enjoy their aggression at the same time, and thus have difficulty in pinning down the internal meanings of external violence."
— William D. Dean, *The American Spiritual Culture*

Even from the beginning in the late 19th century, football has survived despite its brutality—or, cold and sick possibility here, because of it.
— Dave Kindred, *The Sporting News*

I was in a panic the weekend before the first day of contact because I couldn't find a pair of football pants to practice in. I had overlooked practice pants in all my accessorizing, assuming that the team would provide them. None of the local sporting goods stores carried them since June was technically the off-season for football and nothing I ordered online would arrive in time for the first practice. Of course this may all have been a case of my mind diverting itself from an overwhelming concern (i.e., the arrival of full-contact practices) by focusing on inconsequential minutiae, or perhaps by omitting the pants I was sabotaging myself, giving myself an out. McNeil had said within my hearing at the last practice that he would help to make some cuts the next week and I could only assume he meant to do so by crippling those he found unfit. "Some guys just shouldn't be out here," he told Ashcraft. "I guess they just want to watch us take showers." I considered it safe to assume I was among those to whom he referred. Night and day I worried about the pants until the very Tuesday when I went to the university field house and convinced an S.L.U. football coach, one of my former students, to loan me a pair.

Verbeck established a circuit of eight different stations at the beginning of practice that night and divided the team into groups of five or six according to position. At each station the group was to perform the drill designated—squat thrusts, push-ups, and, so on—until Verbeck blew his whistle after ninety seconds or so and the group sprinted en masse to the next station. It took me a while to adjust to wearing equipment again. It added a good twenty pounds to the 230 I already moved through space, for starters. After all those miles logged running over the past decade I had become accustomed to swinging my arms forward in a particular way while I ran, but the bulky shoulder pads constrained me and I had to adjust my stride. I had never worn a face mask that extended as far below the chin as the one I was now wearing either—the cage looked imposing, as I'd hoped, but I had trouble glancing down to see my feet (Verbeck had warned me of this). And we hadn't even lined up for one play from scrimmage yet. Perhaps this was the coaching staff's rationale in easing us in, knowing we'd need to wander around the field for some time like astronauts in spacesuits, new to the moon's surface.

Toward the end of the night Coach Ashcraft, who'd been working with the defensive linemen and linebackers in one corner of the field, called the offensive linemen over to join his group. I was in that number, having finally decided that's where the team was thinnest. We'd done little more to that point than drive the blocking sled. Ashcraft had set up a hitting drill in the end zone between two tackling dummies arranged ten or so yards apart on the field. The drill pitted two offensive linemen against a defensive lineman and a linebacker stacked behind him. It's known in football circles as "Oklahoma." At the whistle, the linemen were to engage and a ballcarrier standing some distance behind the offensive linemen was to read their block and run to daylight. Ideally the offensive linemen would employ something called the combination or "combo" block, a technique more sophisticated than anything I had been asked to do in high school ball in which both offensive linemen fired out of a stance toward the defensive lineman and, according to which direction their opponent moved, one offensive lineman "slid" off that original block to the next level (the stacked linebacker).

In high school, we'd kept it simple: against a five-man front, the guard pulled on the toss sweep, for example, while on the same play against a four-man front he stayed at home and blocked the man on his nose. It's called "base" blocking. But at the semi-pro level, base blocking wouldn't get it done; defenses shifted and gambled on every down (Syracuse was particularly active on defense) and offenses couldn't count on a defender being in any particular place two plays in a row or even from the beginning of the quarterback's cadence to its end, hence the development of things like the combo technique, which allowed a blocker to adjust his assignment mid-play. Often a running play was designed to attack a general zone of the defense as opposed to a particular hole between two offensive linemen; the linemen "zone" blocked that area, their actual blocking assignments dependent upon where the defensive linemen were at the snap of the ball and where they shifted afterward, on what the pulling guards and tackles found when they arrived in that zone. In such a scheme the offensive lineman not only needs to fire quickly out of his stance toward the point of attack but also has to survey the zone as he arrives and determine precisely where to enter the breach, and to communicate this clearly to his linemates. It takes power but also body control and perhaps even some spatial acuity. Ashcraft's drill aimed to distill these split-second processes.

New players received little coaching about techniques like the combo block. Knowledge of the "chop" block, for example, where the offensive player chops the legs of a defensive lineman, felling him like so much timber, or "tracking," where the offside guard and tackle slide past their primary blocks along the line in order to move playside and cut off pursuit to the ball by linebackers and defensive backs at the secondary level, was an expectation, perhaps even a reasonable one. It was the least a developed player would have gleaned from college or progressive high school ball. I had no such knowledge, though, and thought I ought to watch a few plays before I tried my hand at the drill. I let most of the veterans go before me: Quay and Payne were a pair and McNeil teamed with returning starter Jamee Call, a 300-pound tackle who had decided to hold out most of the summer until the team resumed full contact and so had arrived for his first practice on this night. He looked like Jackie Gleason and had Ralph Kramden's patience.

When I jumped in it was alongside Pat Nulty, on his left. I figured Pat would not be annoyed by any questions I asked about how to attack the problem. The problem in this case was Tom Reid, a giant but not very athletic defensive tackle, who lumbered into the pit across from us. Reid struck me as the sort of player who was there because he was so large people wouldn't leave him alone about it. A man that big ought to play football, they'd say. But I never believed his heart was in it. He had come out several summers before and left before the season began each time. Lynn Patrick moved in behind him at linebacker but he was a secondary concern. Nulty and I didn't huddle with the ballcarrier to establish any direction; he was simply to read our block.

Reid lined up just a shade to my right, on what is called Pat's inside shoulder. At the whistle, I stepped that way and Nulty was already into him. Big as Reid was he gave little resistance and moved easily, his cleats sliding in the spring mud as Nulty pumped his thighs. I knew I needed to get off this block and slide to Patrick before the ballcarrier was through the hole. I moved off Reid and lunged at Patrick, falling weakly to the ground, grazing Patrick's knee brace on the way down. He'd broken the leg badly several years before—it was legend. Patrick locked up with the ballcarrier at the edge of the dummies. I apologized as the old linebacker helped me up. "No sweat," he said. Ashcraft did not comment at all.

Nulty and I had another go minutes later, this time against Randy Parrow, a tackle at six-foot-four and 260 pounds but much more athletic than Tom Reid, a probable starter. In the off-season, Nulty had actually worked with Parrow on technique and footwork at a local indoor soccer facility, hoping to teach the kid to beat a double team and make him an all-star. The combo block begins as a double team, two blockers against one defender, the slide to the next level merely an option in case one of the blockers handles said defender sufficiently. It took Nulty and me both to handle Parrow, who fired hard into Pat at the whistle, just as he'd been taught, jamming his hands under Nulty's shoulder pads and then spinning back toward me. He wasn't quite able to split our double team, though neither Pat nor I was able to slide off and get a helmet on the linebacker.

Nulty and I debriefed each other afterward: we thought both plays were stalemates. I guessed the second tussle was more representative of EFL competition, though I was disappointed I still hadn't really hit anybody, hadn't been hit. As my high school coach Mack Thornton might have said, you could not have cracked an egg between me and another player on that first evening.

🏈 🏈 🏈

I'd get all I wanted. Ashcraft began the Thursday practice two nights later with live kickoff coverage. "Live" is an expression you hear often on a football field—players ask if a drill or a play from scrimmage is "live," as in full speed, full contact, no holds barred, as if to ask, "Do I need to pay attention?" I couldn't believe Ashcraft would begin in this way: kickoffs often provide the game's most devastating collisions, ten defenders sprinting headlong fifty yards into a wedge of blockers who've closed ranks around the ballcarrier and begun to move slowly forward like a Roman legion. NFL kickoff coverage teams, nicknamed "suicide squads," are manned by young players out to prove their mettle and journeymen playing for the league minimum and hanging on to the dream of a career by giving up their bodies three of four times a game in what amount to low-speed car crash–type collisions. On the other hand, this drill would no doubt determine quickly who among the untested rookies could contribute to the team. Ashcraft called to the sideline for volunteers.

*   *   *

My relationship with the contact aspect of football is a curious one. In the eighth grade, I was a 130-pound cornerback for the Martin Junior High Panthers and started in our preseason exhibition against the Gleason Bulldogs. I was a budding student of the game, watched it on TV incessantly, and this had made an impression on our coach, a handsome charismatic man I was desperately eager to please. During our first defensive series, after a few snaps, I found that I could determine the upcoming play (they had only a few) according to shifts by the opposing offense. As the wingback came in motion toward me I knew he was leading the play that way, so I would yell to my teammates, "Sweep this way! Sweep!" I'd get myself into position, chopping my feet as the toss sweep came my way. Textbook. But as the ballcarrier approached I'd stand straight up and shift around like a basketball defender as the tailback ran past me into the open field. Afraid of the unknown, the contact, I couldn't force the moment to its crisis. The coach yanked me before I did too much damage.

I didn't bother to join the junior varsity team at Westview High the next year. I was instead the manager of the freshmen boys' basketball team, a humiliating job that had me washing my classmates' practice clothes. But I attended most of the varsity football games and ached to be out there. I weighed 175 by the time spring practice began at the end of my freshman year and decided that even if it meant sitting on the bench another season I had to play. The next summer we started practice with a new coach (his predecessor was fired for allegedly dating cheerleaders) and I had a clean slate.

I hustled through preseason workouts and spent all my spare time in the weight room. One August afternoon in a hitting drill much like the one Ashcraft had us running recently, something called the "nutcracker" drill (it bears little resemblance to the ballet), I lay on my back between a pair of dummies holding the ball while senior linebacker David Blake lay on his back opposite me, his head pointed toward mine. At the whistle we were to get ourselves up and turned around and run headlong at each other. Our practice field lay between two cornfields out behind the high school building and I remember that time on my back staring into the four P.M. sun seemed endless. I was terrified.

I was up quickly at the whistle's sound and sprinted toward Blake. We came together hard—either I closed my eyes or the collision was blinding, I'm not sure—and I felt Blake slide down my legs as I churned through him and past the dummies toward the rows of corn. Then the congratulatory thwack of my teammates' hands on my shoulder pads and helmet. No one was more amazed than I. Head Coach Mack Thornton, ex-Mississsppi State Bulldog and college roommate of Dallas Cowboy linebacker D. D. Lewis, leapt a blocking dummy to grab my face mask. "Well, all right, son," he said. "You're short and stocky but you'll knock the pummies out of somebody."

My mother tells me how she stopped at the grocery on her way home from work that evening and the bag boy, one of my teammates, who had never taken notice of me before, told her I'd had a good practice. When she didn't seem to understand he repeated himself. "Bobby had a really good day," he said.

After that I craved the contact. That moment between the dummies had earned me an identity in my hometown.

As a high school boy I believed there were only a few labels to be had in the first place: jock, geek, stoner, greaser. Perhaps this was more true in my football-crazy hometown than elsewhere, though I heard my stepson use startlingly familiar terminology regarding his high school friends. In any case, now I was a full-fledged jock.

I began to hear my name on the radio and see it in the paper once in a while. I became an intolerable brute around my house for several years afterward, unabashedly aggressive in almost everything. Hadn't my aggressiveness between the tackling dummies been the difference in my life? I grew my hair long in the back (the "mullet," or "short-long," as we called it in Tennessee) and wore ribbed tank T-shirts everywhere but in church. I wrote an essay for AP English that argued that Macbeth was more decisive than wimpy Hamlet because at least he'd acted, taken life by the throat. I announced in French class that the last thing I'd ever be was a wimpy teacher.

It's the violence of the game, the contact, that repulses so many of my university colleagues. It has been that way since football's late-nineteenth-century beginnings on the campuses of schools like Harvard, Princeton, Rutgers, and Columbia as a hybrid of rugby and soccer. Even then, university faculties objected to football's brutality and its dubious "amateur" status (Harvard withdrew from the Intercollegiate Foot-Ball Association, an NCAA precursor, on such grounds in 1889). The animosity between the parties seems part of the institutional culture. I wondered if the poet Donald Hall was right that half his fellow poets thought him insane to waste his time writing about sports but that the other half would murder to take his place.

Though I don't think I was ever worried that Saint Lawrence University would object officially to my playing football, I did fear personal reprisals from co-workers, the assumptions they'd undoubtedly make about me once I let it be known I was playing football. The night we were issued our equipment, I met Candace at the farmhouse of one of my new S.L.U. colleagues, a professor in the Gender Studies program who was hosting a get-together of younger faculty. When I arrived the host and several other colleagues sat cross-legged around the woodstove strumming guitars and singing tunes they'd composed about their life in Canton. A few others played cards around the kitchen table. After some prodding from the assembled guests I agreed to go to the car and get my new gear. Guests posed for pictures in my helmet and shoulder pads—men who hadn't worn either since junior high and recounted humiliations from that time, and women who had never seen football pads up close and didn't know front end from back end. "You're gonna get killed," one guy said to me, laughing.

I remember an argument I didn't get into with a fellow graduate student back in my Marquette days. We were gathered in a downtown Milwaukee bar of a Friday afternoon, as usual, and she was holding forth about her beloved Chicago Bulls, in the midst of their first NBA Championship threepeat. "There's nothing graceful about football," she said at one point, and I started to engage her when she shouted me down. That's probably just as well. I wouldn't have known at the time how to develop my argument for football's grace if I had been allowed to begin it. Lynn Swann's acrobatic catches against the Cowboys in Super Bowl X is probably where I'd have started, though Swann's grace has never been what drew me to football. Since then, I have found an argument that represents my position much better, offered by Don DeLillo's coach Emmet Creed in DeLillo's novel *End Zone:*

People stress the violence [in football]. That's the smallest part of it. Football is only brutal from a distance. In the middle of it there's a calm, a tranquility. The players accept pain. There's a sense of order even at the end of a running play with bodies strewn everywhere. When the systems interlock, there's a satisfaction to the game that can't be duplicated. There's a harmony.

I am sympathetic to people like my father who come to the game new and are puzzled—it's a game predicated on deception, feigning and faking, misdirection. And it is violent, brutal. Yet after half a lifetime of watching and playing, I am in tune with Coach Creed's "harmony."

Which brings us back to Watertown, a breezy evening that felt oddly more like autumn than early summer, and Ashcraft's call for kickoff-team volunteers. I tried to leave all my baggage behind as I trotted out to midfield to join the other volunteers, thinking it wouldn't serve me there. "Imagination, crucial for the writer," wrote Hemingway, "is death for the soldier."

Fifteen players or so had answered Ashcraft's call, mostly rookies but also veteran players who were not starters. Most of the defensive starters remained on the sideline, which seemed to disappoint Ashcraft, and he called a few out to the field. I got the feeling that a spot on one of the special teams was precisely what many of these men were after, a starting spot he could talk about at work. I suspected this of Ed Pierce, a grocery store manager about my age, and David Dummitt, a pest control specialist probably closer to forty. I couldn't believe no one had incorporated Dummitt's occupation into a nickname—the "Exterminator," or something similar ("He'll have to hit somebody first," Countryman said when I brought it up). Neither man was athletic or fierce and I couldn't imagine either had even been a starter on a high school football team.

Aligning his coverage team, Ashcraft called my name first—"Cowser, wedge buster!" he barked. I considered this another victory. The two wedge busters, lined up on either side of the kicker, are really no more than bowling balls into the receiving team's wedge of blockers, felling them like pins. To tackle the kick returner is a bonus but certainly not expected of these men. The only other thing I had to remember was to stay in my lane. Each coverage man was assigned an imaginary lane so that the team of ten scraped down the field like a giant rake. If one or two coverage men left their lanes to follow the flight of the ball, though, or were forced off course by a crushing block, huge return lanes opened for the receiving team and this often meant long gains or touchdowns. The coaches stressed discipline in this regard.

Coach Britton used practically the entire starting offense as his kick return team. He had Payne, Quay, and McNeil across the front, Call and a backup tackle five yards behind them—his offensive line. Big hitters made up the next two rows, tight ends and fullbacks, with Countryman and rookie second-string running back Erin Woodward deep to receive. Britton announced he didn't plan on running a conventional wedge return, though; research had shown that more aggressive approaches, which had the return team moving forward as the ball was kicked and then attacking a designated coverage man, were resulting in longer returns and better field position for the offense. This seemed Britton's specialty: X's and O's, research and innovation.

Dave McNeil stared me down as we took our positions. He moved awkwardly like a bear rearing on its hind legs: heaviest in the middle, swinging powerful paws. I figured he had drawn me as his blocking assignment. Maybe he'd rigged things to get that assignment, switched with someone. Like most of the other veteran players, McNeil was concerned about protecting the proud tradition of the team from what he called riffraff, such as the Scooby-Doo kid and Tom Reid, whom they eventually humiliated into quitting again. But McNeil protected the hierarchy with much greater fierceness than the other players. He admitted later he was in fact trying to eliminate me. I was his project.

Of course I harbored a host of my own prejudices about McNeil, as numerous no doubt as those he'd formed about me. Candace's ex-husband had also been a corrections officer and she offered me statistics about the rates of divorce, abuse, and alcoholism in the ranks. Conover's book *New Jack* confirmed all this for me when I'd read it that summer—dim interiors and draconian codes. Conover suggests brutal prison work had hardened even him, and everything I observed in McNeil—the quick temper, rough humor, and adolescent cronyism—suggested he was just the sadist Conover says is drawn to corrections work, or inevitably produced by it. Because McNeil had six inches and nearly fifty pounds on me, I tried to think of the moment between the dummies with David Blake and of my strengths: leg drive and low center of gravity. Leverage is everything in football—"low man wins," line coaches are always saying—and I knew McNeil would have to come down to get me.

Ashcraft announced we'd cover five or six kicks, that we should consider it part of our conditioning program. At some point I tuned him out entirely. Wind swirled around the field and whistled through the ear hole in my helmet. I heard former

NFL running back and current coach Dan Reeves say in an interview once that you couldn't teach a player to hit any more than you could teach a puppy to bite. I hoped desperately that this law had a corollary: hitting was also like riding a bike and you never really forgot how. As Scott Ford approached the ball and swung his leg the first time, I exhaled hard and moved straight toward McNeil, surrendering dutifully to my beating.

We made up the ten yards between us quickly and the impact of our collision knocked us both flat. Imagine a medieval joust. I had never brought my full adult weight to bear in this way before and, lying on my back on the ground, I had to take a moment to reorient myself. When I opened my eyes, there was a green tint to everything I saw, as if someone had spread green cellophane over my face mask. My breath was short and I sensed the onset of a killer headache. I hadn't the slightest thought of the kicked ball or making the tackle, and in this way I suppose McNeil won. Yet I felt triumphant; the battle within the war had been at least a draw. McNeil got to his feet slowly, perhaps surprised at my fortitude.

"There's no reason one of those fat guys in the front row should touch you!" Ashcraft yelled to me as I trotted back to the huddle. "Just juke and move past them, then get to the ball and hit somebody." I tried that on the second kick, feeling I had proven my mettle on the first. I ran at McNeil just as the first time but at the last moment stepped inside him and sprinted toward the center of the field. I saw Al Countryman scoop the ball off the ground and begin to run and I adjusted my course accordingly, sprinting hard downfield until felt Erin Woodward's shoulder pads in my thighs—a great block—and I went head over heels.

Though I hadn't made the tackle, I'd shown McNeil up, shaken his block, and he was riled. I was still out of breath when Scott Ford booted the third ball but did my best to shake McNeil again. I gave him a weak head-and-shoulders fake and he grabbed me under my shoulder pads, throwing me like a doll to the ground. I was not often handled with such ease and was unnerved, the way I felt after the minor car accidents of my teens. I lay on my face awhile, the freshly mown grass of the field in my face mask and mouthpiece. Coach Britton took a moment making a point to his return team regarding a missed block and it gave me some time to recover my breath. I resolved to charge McNeil again on the fourth kick and aimed for the spot between the 5 and the 4 on his chest.

I was off at Ford's kick, sprinting toward McNeil, when at the last moment he crouched hurriedly to meet me, almost as though he expected I'd try again to avoid him. Our face masks collided with more force than even on the first kick. Golfers and hitters talk about hitting the ball true with the sweet spot of the club or bat and there's an equivalent sensation in football when, because he hasn't seen you coming or engages you awkwardly, your opponent seems to absorb all the force of a collision and you float featherlike to the ground, often on top of him. This was one of those hits. McNeil got out of his helmet quickly and I saw blood form on his forehead where the impact had split the skin. His neck had been bent awkwardly as we collided and he sat on the ground trying to work the stiffness out.

"You all right?" Ford asked him as he trotted past the crouched McNeil toward the huddle.

"Just a stinger," McNeil said. "Nothing a good dick sucking won't cure."

I am five or six years old, with my dad and older sister Mary at a high school football jamboree held every year on the campus of the University of Tennessee at Martin, where Dad teaches. Eight northwest Tennessee teams have gathered to play in a sort of one-game preseason, two teams facing off in each quarter. The first quarter was under way when we arrived and I could hear the various marching bands tuning up as we made our way through the parking lot, percussion sections hammering out the sort of martial cadence I will always associate with autumn Friday nights in Tennessee.

After buying tickets, Dad walks us behind the south goal end zone toward the large grandstand. It's dark back here and we have to walk around a throng of helmeted ballplayers busy with pregame stretching. They are just sixteen or seventeen years old, these boys, but they seem enormous, full grown, and the large "C" decals on their black helmets glisten in the glow of the distant stadium lights.

"Who are they?" I ask my father.

"The Camden Lions," he tells me. Camden was a town an hour east of us, toward Nashville. Though I could not have expressed it then, I think of these boys as the very height of cool, and I never fully shake the idea.

First Team

Everything fine about being a quarterback—the embodiment of his power—was encompassed in those dozen seconds or so; giving the instructions to ten attentive men, breaking out of the huddle, walking to the line, and then pausing behind the center, dawdling amidst men poised and waiting under the trigger of his voice, cataleptic, until the deliverance of himself and them into the future.

—George Plimpton, *Paper Lion*

atertown Daily Times sportswriter Rob Oatman published a feature in the sports section one preseason Saturday about veteran Watertown quarterback Doug Black and his infant daughter Shea, the same age as my Jackson, who had been born without a right hand and had been fitted with an experimental prosthesis, one of only twenty of its kind. I had missed the piece in the paper but overheard veterans discussing it when I arrived for practice on Tuesday. "I'm done talking to the media," I heard Jamee Call say angrily.

I eventually read the article via the paper's online archive but struggled to find what had Black and his friends upset—it seemed like a feel-good piece. Shea had been born to Black's longtime girlfriend Jennifer Fox the evening of a game with Syracuse the previous season, her defect a terrible surprise not detected on the ultrasound. Doctors guessed the umbilical cord might have become wrapped around the hand late in the pregnancy and cut off circulation. Oatman's story explains how Black took the field and led the team to victory anyway. Black discusses his devastation and Ashcraft and Countryman testify to how much the experience of fatherhood has changed Black. More church, less beer. He and Fox now plan to marry. Very sweet.

This turnaround is meaningless without some understanding of the former man, though, which must have been Oatman's thinking. He refers to the turbulence of Black's relationship with Fox, how they'd broken up late in her pregnancy. No sweet without the bitter. This must have been what Black and friends objected too. Jamee Call had been open with the media to that point, he said, but not after what Oatman did to Douggie (if Countryman was the team's acknowledged leader, Call was a sort of sergeant at arms, an enforcer protecting team interests).

I joked on the sideline—to no laughs at all—that the hardest part of the transition from high school to semi-pro ball was dealing with the media scrutiny, echoing something I heard all the time on ESPN from professional athletes and coaches. It was a joke, sure, but for a team and a league as small and minor as these were, the coverage they got really was incredible. Television trucks from the two local Watertown stations (CBS and ABC affiliates) were at every practice and home game, along with sportswriters from the *Daily Times* and other regional papers, though the league champion Syracuse Vipers, in competition with Syracuse University athletics and minor league baseball and hockey franchises, got very little press. "It's the only game in town," explains Mel Busler, local sports anchor at WWNY and Watertown native who remembers attending Red and Black games with his older brother. "It's *the* summertime sports story."

John O'Donnell, who covered the team as sports editor for the *Daily Times* for twenty-five years before his retirement in 1996, recalls partaking in raucous back-of-the-bus parties with the team in the days before the paper published a Sunday edition and he was responsible for a story the next morning. Once, a bus driver had called the Red and Black head coach on a post–road game Sunday morning inquiring about the whereabouts of the bus's rear seat. But the media's coverage of the team has changed, O'Donnell says. The paper has begun to pay greater attention to Syracuse University athletics and less to the Red and Black, which has ruffled more than a few feathers at the fairgrounds, while news writers like Oatman maintain greater distance from the subjects of their stories in the interest of objectivity. I suppose players like Call take this distance for malice.

Doug Black had enjoyed a very successful tenure as the Red and Black signal caller. He directed the run-oriented veer attack at General Brown High School outside Watertown (under the direction of former Red and Black star Steve Fisher) before attending college on a basketball scholarship, but he had become a pure pocket passer since joining the Red and Black, flourishing in Britton's system, and needed only a little more than a thousand passing yards in the upcoming season to become the most prolific passer in team history. Watching him calm and still in the pocket as he threw, like Dan Marino, hurling passes out of there before a rush could get to him, you had to marvel.

If Al Countryman was the team's quiet, working-class hero, Black was more enigmatic, aloof. Black missed a lot of practice. In his defense, he had a commute of several hours to the prison along the Hudson River where he worked as a correctional officer. But I sensed that wasn't really it. He had a quarterback's confidence, even arrogance. Often he didn't run the play sent in from the sideline (a big joke among the offensive starters), and over the course of the season I noticed how he bristled when either coach offered criticism.

I remembered seeing him seated in his gold, four-door Taurus back on that initial Black Friday, pulling on his cleats, blaring radio highlights of the career of Dallas Cowboy quarterback Troy Aikman. Black had a T-shirt he was fond of wearing that had "I'm Not Prejudiced" printed on the front; on the back it read "I Hate Everybody" and all around that phrase in smaller type was every racial slur imaginable. I heard him tell black players who challenged him, truly or in jest, that he'd seen their brothers or fathers at work on the cell block and that they'd asked him to pass along a hello. He was always ragging players, white and black, who had tattoos or piercings.

"Does it bother you?" I asked them.

"That's Douggie," they'd reply, a sort of nonanswer. What could you do? He was the league's best quarterback, hands down.

I spent the first several full-contact practices watching Watertown's first-team offense in action. They were sharp, the chief reason for all the preseason optimism: a healthy Countryman in his tenth season, eight-year veteran quarterback Doug Black at the helm, an experienced line with four or five years together. That was an advantage a team had in semi-pro ball: you didn't have to give up a proven performer after four seasons like you did in high school or college. The speed at which this offense operated was impressive, a result of physical talent but also of their many years together, and I was certain I'd have to push myself to keep up athletically.

At the end of that first contact workout, Ashcraft had announced that he'd lay in the first-team defense against Black's offense and that if the defense could stop the offense in four downs, the offense would have to run wind sprints. If the offense could move downfield and score, however, the defense would have to run. On the sideline we took odds, but Doug Black ended speculation quickly on the third play, completing a beautiful post pattern to Odell Bowens who outran the secondary into the end zone. As a gesture of unity, the whole team lined up and ran a single hundred-yard sprint.

I slipped in behind Dave McNeil as the second-team left guard. Walking among the ranks as we stretched one evening, Coach Britton had said he thought that would be a good fit for me. Pat Nulty was playing second-team left tackle behind Potsdam native Shane McCargar, recruited specially by Britton to replace Sam Verbeck's foster son who'd played there the season before, and I felt comfortable with Pat at my side. I thought I'd still see the field a lot.

I tried to pick up as much as I could about playing weak-side guard and McNeil actually turned out to be quite the generous mentor, giving me five plays or so with the first unit to his ten (though I had to be aggressive about relieving him), encouraging me as I left the field. "You done good," he'd tell me, slipping his helmet back on his head. Ours was the classic bully/bullied dynamic: once I stood up to him, he softened, even embraced me. The times I missed practice, he sulked like a neglected playmate. "Where you been?" he'd say.

I learned quickly that neither friendships nor playing time came easily among that group, and how I missed my guess laying all that at Dave's feet. Offensive linemen cultivate something of a collective identity anyway, these anonymous pachyderms, and they don't take to newcomers. While coaches readily substitute defensive linemen to get fresh legs in the game and maintain pressure on the quarterback, the performance of the offensive line depends upon continuity, repetition, rhythm. They are rarely relieved in the course of a game (in Watertown's case, there had been hardly a man on the sidelines who could have been inserted along the offensive line in the previous season). Trust is crucial: the guards need to believe the center between them will pick up a linebacker who shows blitz in that A gap between them, or that the tackles on their outside shoulders won't chase a defensive end across their faces. Trust like that is developed over time, only through endless repetition.

The unit was made more insular by the fact that they'd been together four and five successful seasons and most of them were EFL all-star performers (McNeil and Call as first-teamers and Payne and Quay on the second team). Add to that the fact that Payne, Call, and Quay were all graduates of Indian River High School twenty miles north on Route 11 in Philadelphia, New York; Countryman was another Indian River alumnus— "The Indian River Pipeline," the *Daily Times* called it in a feature. It's little surprise, then, that they never invited me to their pregame go-cart extravaganza they held on Saturdays during the season at a local track.

Instead, I most often found myself standing with Nulty, or with PFC Eric Huck of Fargo, North Dakota, a fireman out at Fort Drum, new to the base. "I'm doing this to prove something to the people back home," he'd told me when we met. I figured he had his own Coach Coady—maybe we all did. Eric insisted everyone call him "Huckster" (though he spoke with a pretty serious lisp and it sounded more like "Huckshter" when he said it). He was green, guileless, like the bumpkin plowboy in a war movie who's a choirboy and a crack shot but the first one in the platoon—this you know the moment he walks on-screen—to take a bullet.

Huck was a rangy kid, six feet tall and a bit on the light side. But he seemed fit and athletic. And he hustled, the embodiment of gung ho enthusiasm, the kid who swallowed whole all that the army had fed him about being all he could be, all that his football coaches had fed him about giving it that impossible "110 percent." Actually that kind of hustle was the only way to really distinguish oneself in those early non-contact workouts and I found myself succumbing—when spirited veterans improvised a belly flop at the end of an already challenging thirty-second footwork drill a few weeks before in the dummies course, I couldn't resist adding it also.

A rather anxious person by nature, Huck talked ceaselessly but with no sense of his audience and how it received him; you didn't really have a conversation with Huck so much as he talked *at* you. I guess this made him seem friendly, though, which may explain how I got entangled. I shared my frustrations about playing time with Huck one evening. After that, he was like my shadow. "Who's your friend with the Harley-Davidson bandanna?" Candace asked me a few games into the season (Huck actually had two bandannas he alternated as do-rags under his helmet—the other was a Confederate flag). "He talks to you constantly," she said.

Most frustrating was that because of Huck's absolute lack of audience awareness polite hints of uninterest did not register with him. I've had students like this who show up in office hours because they're far from home and lonely and need you to listen, but I was paid to handle those kids. Besides, in my office, I could always invent something I had to read or write or a call I had to make. Not in this case. As Huck began talking I'd move down the sideline to escape, but he'd follow. Subtly insulting him in an attempt to shake him didn't work either, subtlety being lost on him altogether. He seemed startled sometimes when I left his side to go into the game for a few plays, but he kept talking to whoever happened to be there until I returned. I practically stopped talking to him altogether after a while, never offering more than one-word answers to his questions and sometimes offering less, only grunts and uh-huhs.

Other players were more direct with Huck—"Dude, do you ever shut up?" they'd say. Then he'd find me again. As quite a talker in my own right, I couldn't bring myself to cut him off at the knees like that. I began to think of him as a kind of karmic lodestone I'd earned with a lifetime of talking. Finally, mercifully, in August the army sent him and several others from the team to Fort Polk, Louisiana, for intensive, specialized training. The Red and Black regularly lost players to such deployments—Hurricane Andrew, Haiti, Somalia. When the contingent returned just in time for the playoffs, Huck came back to the team but he was hardly his old self. He wasn't playing much. He had been too long away. Finally he stopped coming at all.

● ● ●

It became evident how much experience would count on this team, and that I had little of value. I was okay on pass plays. Though I usually faced bigger defensive tackles, I could get low, dig in, and hold them off for the three or four seconds Black needed to get the pass away (his quick release was a trademark). But running plays were another story. I knew hustle on my part was essential, yet I found it hard to be aggressive when I wasn't certain of my assignment or how to carry it off. When we pulled right to lead a sweep, McCargar, a 300-pounder, teased that he was going to catch me from behind. Al Countryman was less forgiving if he found me in his way. Once, encircled by the defenders I hadn't managed to block, he threw the football at my back. "Shit, you run it," he said.

The team's bread-and-butter running play was the 25/26, a trap play to Countryman. I don't know how many hundreds of times we ran it in the months of June and July. When the play was called to the left (25) and I was the playside guard, I usually combo-blocked the defensive tackle with either the left tackle or the center, depending on the defender's alignment. Here I had help. My role was more crucial on the 26, when I was the offside, trapping guard and I was on my own: I fired laterally out of my stance past the center toward the six hole between the right tackle and end looking for the defensive end, whom it was my job to drive into the sideline as Countryman took the handoff from Black and cut upfield behind my block.

Body control seemed my biggest issue. I got myself down the line of scrimmage as fast as I could, prepared to deliver a knockout blow to the defensive end. As out of control as I was, though, I lunged and left my feet on nearly every play, making contact with no one on my way to the ground. Observing McNeil and Payne, I realized it wasn't necessary to knock the end off his feet with a devastating hit—which I sought to deliver on every down—only to move him out of the way and in time for Countryman to burst through the lane created. Some-times even realizing this didn't help, though. I'd reach the end of the line of scrimmage and not recognize what I found. Depending on the defensive formation and presnap shifting, the man designated for the trap might change—it wasn't al-ways the defensive end. I'd run toward the hole and past it, making contact with no one, as though I'd missed my exit on the interstate.

Pat Nulty had been away long enough that he too felt out of sync and we both approached the coaches about a playbook. Of course the starters knew the offense and got all the reps, but in order to contribute we wanted to see these plays drawn up, to understand this offense more thoroughly. Studying: I was confident I could do that. A week or so later Sam Verbeck dis-tributed a bound playbook of more than 160 pages and thirty offensive formations—the Flex / Pro Spread Plus (One/No Back) Offense. It was clearly Britton's brainchild, an offense he thought would showcase the talents of both Countryman and Doug Black, something he'd cobbled together from the exhaustive research I imagined him engaged in away from the field. If Ashcraft was the hail-fellow players' coach, Mike Britton was the "football mind," less interested in cultivating friendships with his players, less able to do so.

There was something essentially melancholy about Britton, owing perhaps to the untimely death of his father, the smartest man Britton says he ever knew, the year Mike turned twelve. It was in the days just before Christmas, and the family had moved for a time to Schenectady where his father, an erstwhile lineman for New York Telephone, had taken a new job in sales. Mike, eldest of his parents' four chil-dren, remembers imagining his father's appearance in his dreams that night. "Good-bye," his father told him, "you're the head of the family now." Mike wakened to find his father dead in his bed—a heart attack—his mother hysterical.

Football saved him. He and his brother Pat distinguished themselves first on the playgrounds of Schenectady, then, after his mother moved the family home to Carthage to reconnect with her roots, on the field at Augustinian Academy, where he and Pat starred in an eight-man version of the game, like what I'd seen in my years out in Nebraska. Pat Nulty, a few years behind Britton and ahead of George Ashcraft at Carthage Central High, remembers hearing each weekend about the exploits of the Britton boys, Mike in particular, over at Augustinian.

Britton parlayed his prep success into a football scholarship to Xavier University in Cincinnati, but when that school dropped football after his freshman year, he transferred to SUNY-Brockport, closer to home, where he took a bachelor's degree in P.E. and a teacher's certification. Rather than resume his collegiate gridiron career in Brockport, he chose to drive home to Carthage in the summers and play for the Red and Black. "Oh, he was tough," remembers Pat Nulty. "Gung ho." I chuckle at pictures of Britton I find in the archives at the *Watertown Daily Times*, the flowing hair and romantic, chivalric gaze. A perennial all-EFL selection, Britton led his teammates to that storied 1980 title, turning down a handful of NFL free-agent contracts to stay home with his two young daughters.

Pat Nulty says Britton never parlayed that toughness, that fire into successful coaching. Shortly after college, Britton took a head coaching job at Immaculate Heart Central High in Watertown, leading the talent-laden Crusaders to a 45–9–2 record in five years (the school recently enshrined Britton in its hall of fame), but he managed to win only four of twenty-two games as head coach of the Red and Black in the 1983 and 1984 seasons, and after a series of mediocre seasons in the late 1980s he was let go as head coach at Potsdam High. He's been driving the seventy miles to coach under Ashcraft ever since.

It just seemed Britton couldn't reach guys, not the grown ones anyway. At least not these grown ones. "The wisdom that spews out of these two," Bruce Gonseth used to say of Britton and Ashcraft. Before our preseason game in Vermont, Ashcraft deferred to Britton to deliver the pregame talk, and he began by invoking St. Michael. "Pray for us," we were to answer in chorus, I think, but no one did. Not Catholic enough. His address to us became increasingly maudlin and personal, Britton talking about his divorce and having fallen away from the Church, hardly mentioning the game. He stopped practice for fifteen minutes the next week to confront players who had complained on the bus, despite the rout, about their statistics. "This is a team game," Britton reminded us. "I will be happy to go down the road to coach somewhere else, if that's what you want. I would be happy to go down there, happy as a turtle," his voice trailed off. He was another Yogi Berra, a Casey Stengel, often wandering out onto sentences this way as if they were tree limbs, and find himself stuck, unable to complete metaphors he'd begun in the first clause or to find his way back to the sense he was trying to make. "Happy as a turtle curled up in a shell with another turtle," he finally said.

If I hadn't known better, I'd have guessed Britton was reluctant to release his playbook to us, the one he forever clutched to his chest. It was an impressive tome, in terms of presentation and contents but also just in terms of sheer size, not the loose-leaf binder Marcia's boyfriend stole from Greg on that *Brady Bunch* episode. I had the best of intentions about reading it; I left it on the dining room table all summer planning to read it every morning with my breakfast. But I was teaching an eight-thirty A.M. summer school class—Survey of American Literature II—and rarely had time for breakfast. I confess I didn't make the time for the playbook, either.

Jake has decided to move with his father to Alabama. Tonight. No time for discussion.

Try to think of some positive images of stepfathers in literature, film, even television. I dare you. I would have said Joe Gargery, the simple blacksmith from Great Expectations, *but he's Pip's brother-in-law, I eventually deduce, not his stepfather. Mike Brady from* The Brady Bunch *got on ridiculously well with his stepdaughters, but then that's not the half of what was make-believe about Robert Reed's portrayal of that character.*

"It's a thankless job," the marriage counselor tells me, "practically impossible. You simply can't be his father and shouldn't try to be his friend."

"What then?" I ask him. "I don't do thankless jobs, as a rule."

I hound the boy about why we can't get along better. Jake and I have managed to string two or three good weeks together here and there, shooting hoops with his buddy Jared or sneaking a late-night pizza past his mother. It lifts her spirits to see us this way, something Jake and I both want—we do have a love for her in common. But then I go back to chewing my late-night cereal so loudly it wakes him from a deep sleep upstairs, and I can't understand why he's had to befriend and bring home every delinquent in the eighth grade. A bad day sets us back so far I despair of the whole enterprise.

"Look," he finally says, "it's nothing you did. I just don't like you."

The Pretender

Drummond believed in law and order and the maintenance of the established, but this riotous savage within him would have none of it . . . somewhere behind those eyes, battling for control of their mutual body, were Freddie Drummond, the sane and conservative sociologist, and Bill Totts, the class-conscious and bellicose union workingman.

—Jack London, "South of the Slot"

The fall term at Saint Lawrence begins in the third week of August each year, marked by a formal convocation where the president welcomes new students. Faculty are required to attend the ceremony, decked out in our academic regalia (caps and gowns and robes indicating degree and field and alma mater), and to proceed to our seats in the front of the university chapel accompanied by sacred choral music. Though I groan with my colleagues every year about going, I inevitably and secretly enjoy the pomp. Rarely do faculty receive this kind of recognition for our lonely years of study, and truth be told I actually daydreamed more about moments like these as an undergraduate than about moments in front of the classroom when the real work of teaching gets done. The night the Red and Black opened its regular season home game against Albany's Capitaland Thunder at the fairgrounds, we undertook what I came to realize was a similar procession: out of the locker room, through the goalposts, and onto the field, two by two in our own regalia.

● ● ●

Saint Lawrence University, named for the mighty seaway running eighteen miles or so northwest of campus, had a reputation as something of a country club when I took the job in 1998—"tony" was the word used in an A&E *Biography* episode detailing the life of alumnus Kirk Douglas (actor Viggo Mortensen is another celebrity graduate, as are Walter Mondale's daughter Eleanor and former New York Giants punter and current television analyst Dave Jennings). Certainly the school had more resources than anywhere else I had taught or studied, fielding squash, equestrian, and both Nordic and downhill ski teams and offering more than thirty abroad programs for students.

The lowdown I got on the average S.L.U. student, called a "Larry," was that he was the wealthy product of a New England boarding school who hadn't been accepted to first-choice schools in the Ivy League and now paid Harvard-sized tuition for his S.L.U. education, somewhat grudgingly. "Larry" was able, people said, but not always willing. This characterization has proved mostly unfair. Except for a handful of hard cases, I found these students mostly sophisticated, hardworking, friendly people (visiting writers commented without fail on the social graces of the student body). Who cares if most drive better cars than the faculty?

Anyway, I knew these kids—the atmosphere at S.L.U. is like what I experienced as an undergraduate in New Orleans, if more affluent. I had gone to Loyola with the idea that I'd be a sportscaster, maybe do play-by-play as I had done in high school for the baseball team, but the pull of literature proved too strong. It had a relevance I thought sports lacked, and I found that the grace I had always wished for on the playing field could be mine on the page. I remember late September of my first college term, my independence in full bloom, sitting in a poetry class in the early afternoon watching the girls swoon to the professor's reading of Baudelaire's "Invitation to the Voyage." Forget what I'd said in high school about sissy teachers, I thought, this is heaven as I need it. I was enrolled in a master's program before I had even graduated from college.

There were practical matters, too; having more or less grown up in English departments I knew the perks of the professorial life well—flexible schedules, sabbaticals, the certain distinction that accompanies the title. I took the job at Saint Lawrence just before I turned twenty-eight, which made me twelve years younger than the next youngest member of the department, another writer who had chaired the search committee that had brought me to campus. I cannot say why they hired me, but I expect it was my enthusiasm for teaching, the primary mission of a small university like S.L.U. At a panel on teaching at liberal arts colleges offered for graduate students at Nebraska while I was there, a visiting faculty member from Occidental College told us that liberal arts schools like Saint Lawrence and Occidental want to hire Peter Pan, that teacher with an infectious, childlike enthusiasm for his discipline. I thought of Robin Williams's Mr. Keating from *Dead Poets Society*, a sentimental film I had secretly loved. I wanted to participate in the awakenings of others just coming to poems and stories, to share with them writers I loved.

"It seems your dream has come true," my father told me on a recent visit to campus, he who'd taught four or five courses a term for thirty years (so many of them freshmen writing courses) and may have had a more personal dream in mind. He's not wrong, anyway. I appreciate the autonomy of the college classroom and the chance to talk all day about poems and stories and be paid for it. I can hardly imagine doing something else. In fact, joining the football team in Watertown represents one of my few attempts to do anything else, my first real foray outside the academy's safe and familiar ivory tower in more than a decade. Even as an undergraduate I had preferred the academic cocoon, quitting Loyola's school of journalism for its English Department just about the time I realized I couldn't avoid the beat reporting and cold phone-calling required in the advanced news writing classes.

Since moving to Canton, I have done no better—performed no community service, joined no fraternal organizations like the Moose or Elks, don't even go to church. I wouldn't say our community is plagued by vicious "town and gown" hostilities, but Saint Lawrence University affluence does stand out in St. Lawrence County, the largest, least populous, and among the poorest counties in the state of New York, as do liberal leanings. I expect the North Country community has been just as leery of me as I have been of it. Yet I realized a tenure-track job and a wife who owned a local business meant I couldn't avoid the civilian population any longer. I was counting on football to change things. Archibald MacLeish claimed that during the senate hearings that confirmed him as an assistant secretary of state under FDR, it was only the fact that he'd played college football at Yale that mitigated for the Committee on Foreign Relations the fact that he was also the author of love poetry. That a man has played the game, says MacLeish, not watched but actually played, offers skeptics the guarantee that "no matter what else he may be or do, will at least *act* as though he were human."

● ● ●

One of the short stories in the anthology I happened to choose and teach in my American literature course that summer was Jack London's "South of the Slot." I was not familiar with the story before choosing it, had not read London since his "To Build a Fire" in high school, but included it to round out a day's readings in naturalism, a turn-of-the-twentieth-century literary movement applying the principles of scientific determinism to literature. It's the story of Freddie Drummond, Berkeley sociology professor, who routinely engages in what we would now call "participant/observer research" among the working classes of old San Francisco in an area south of the slotted cable car tracks, then publishes passably good textbooks about his experiences. The slot, according to London's narrator, is a metaphor for the cleft between the distinct worlds of the middle and working classes of the city during that time; Drummond is the rare man who can move between these worlds "signally well."

I had informed the six students in the class of my football project and, on the morning we discussed the London story, one particularly perceptive woman began our conversation by asking if I had picked up on the coincidence between Drummond's research and mine. It had occurred to me, in fact: like Drummond, I was an academic infiltrating the "working" class. My preliminary research had revealed class as a long-standing issue in American football: the game began in turn-of-the-century "athletic clubs" in cities like Syracuse and Watertown where men of all social classes met to enjoy sports competition, the ambitious younger men hoping to rub elbows with older, better-connected gentlemen and perhaps gain entry to more exclusive university or metropolitan clubs.

The crux of the London story is that as the professor's alias-*cum*-alter ego, labor organizer Big Bill Totts, establishes himself among his co-workers, the professor seems to recede further and further into the background of the story, until in the climax, in a scene right out of an *Incredible Hulk* comic, the professor is overtaken from within by the beastly Totts, never to be heard from again. London the naturalist seems to argue that the professor's refinement is so much bunk that beneath all human erudition lies the base, instinctual Big Bill waiting for its opportunity to emerge.

My perspective on the split I had begun to feel in myself that summer was less Darwinian, but it was there. There was the subtle physical transformation, of course: though I'd done what I could in the past, with wardrobe and eyeglasses, to look like a professor, the time I was devoting to weight lifting was beginning to undermine these efforts. My shaved head and short goatee, considered the "Foucault look" if worn by most of my slighter faculty colleagues, had children at the public swimming pool mistaking me for a professional wrestler.

I sensed deeper changes, too. I had liked to think of myself in terms of something one of my favorite writers, Tobias Wolff, had written of another, Andre Dubus: that while Dubus had made his mark with his formidable intellect, he was always also looking for something strenuous to do with his brawny body. During the two months between the end of summer school and the beginning of the fall term, though, brain was being edged out by brawn. I began to indulge in the fantasy that I was in fact a football player and not just a professor masquerading. The drive from my home to practice was long and hypnotic enough that I suppose I came to view the Subaru station wagon as something of a cocoon from which I emerged transformed twice a week upon arrival at the field house (the helmet and shoulder pads I kept in the hatchback important accoutrements of this fantasy).

It's not that football was going well necessarily; my performance produced much anxiety in me. It's that the anxiety began to occupy my every thought. What did Jack London or tenure matter anyway? For ten solid years since high school, my focus had been solely on my academic career, on arriving at the place I now found myself, in a tenure-track job. It's perhaps understandable that I began casting my gaze about for a new focus. What alarmed those who love me was that my new interests, the search for my inner linebacker, seemed regressive— these were old dreams revisited, from the glory days.

Maybe I knew all along, at some remote level, that this book project business was a ruse, that what I really wanted was to be thrown to the semi-pro briar patch. The academic life was a challenge, probably more than I had bargained for. I'd presented myself to Candace a few years before as having already arrived with my new gig, living on easy street, but the demands of the Saint Lawrence University job, the first I'd ever had when you thought about it, taxed me.

I have mostly done well teaching my three small classes per term at Saint Lawrence; student evaluations of my courses are solid, not great but good. Still, tenure would be no gimme— this was not my father's academic career—especially when you considered the amount of writing I was getting done between teaching, parenting, and generally wasting time. A couple of glasses of wine into a dinner Candace and I were sharing with a married pair of department colleagues during my second year at the university, one leaned across the table to share an anxiety she could no longer contain. "I don't think you're writing enough to get tenure," she told me. When a local sportswriter featured me, the football-playing professor, in a small article in the *Saint Lawrence Plaindealer* early that season ("You're like that squirrel on *America's Funniest Home Videos* that water-skis,"

Candace told me), the head coach from a local junior college team called to offer me a job coaching his defensive line. I daydreamed about leaving academia behind entirely for a career on the sidelines, seriously daydreamed.

"Oh yeah, great idea," Candace told me at the salon when I informed her of the coach's phone call. Her patience with my regression had grown thin. The football thing had been okay as a lark, a one-shot deal, but I was losing all perspective now. "You and your brother are otherwise reasonable people," she told me at Christmas the first year we were together, "but when you sit down to watch a football game, it's like your brains fall out the sides of your heads, both of you." Candace and I had always sparred, playfully, to the delight of my family and hers, only now her barbs seemed sharper, betraying real resentment.

At the top of her list of complaints was my inattention to the very belated wedding reception we had planned for months to host at a local restaurant on our first anniversary. We had more or less eloped the summer before—this was the second marriage for both of us and spending the money on an elaborate ceremony didn't seem prudent. Instead we arranged to celebrate our anniversary with the sort of grand reception we'd skipped on the day of the wedding, inviting a hundred guests or more. My parents and siblings and their families had arranged to stay at our home for the weekend, only now I realized our first home game versus the Capitaland Thunder fell on the night before the reception, and the game was garnering all my attention. "This is our wedding reception," she told me, "these houseguests are *your* family."

Candace flatly refused to go to the game, as did my mother. Too much going on.

"You used to love my high school games," I reminded my mom.

"Yes, well, I don't think I have the nerves for it anymore," she told me.

It had been my mother who fanned the flames of my football interest in my childhood, not my dad. For his part, my father seemed interested in football only insofar as it touched his native Texas (he grew up near Mount Vernon, home of Dallas Cowboy great Dandy Don Meredith). When we watched the Cotton Bowl, for instance, he could be counted on to provide information on the Kilgore Rangerettes, to know the distance between Austin and College Station, to sing "The Old Baylor Line." As to the game itself, however, I remember him having almost no interest, though I do remember during the years when both my brother and I were playing football—he for the junior high on Thursday nights and I for the varsity on Fridays—finding a book on my father's dresser called *How to Watch a Football Game*. Each page was laid out like a television screen, a football play illustrated and diagrammed inside it.

My mother would not have needed such a book. She grew up in the flats of Lakewood, Ohio, her brothers Joey and Eddie members of the legendary St. Ignatius Wildcats teams, which have dominated Cleveland high school football since the 1950s. Her brother Joey, as she tells it, an offensive tackle, actually had a locker at Syracuse University with his name on it—this would have been the Jim Brown/Floyd Little era—but chose instead to play at the Naval Academy. Yet her feelings for the game were mixed: that same brother, badly injured in a high school game, spent an entire school year in a body cast. She actually forbade me to play high school ball—my decision to defy her my first real stroke of independence—though no one seemed to enjoy my success more than she once it arrived. Joining Candace's boycott that weekend seems now an important show of solidarity on my mother's part, though; perhaps the two women had found in football something they could ignore together. I'm glad I didn't push it.

♦ ♦ ♦

In the end, my brother was the one person in my old life who seemed to really understand my project from day one. If my wife held me to my various commitments, if my mother had grown to fear everything but peace and quiet, at least Jimmy would still play along, and despite his own wife's protestations it was Jimmy who drove me down to the fairgrounds that Saturday night. He dropped me at the locker room two hours before kickoff then took my car to the Salmon Run Mall for something to do while I dressed and warmed up with the team. Though the game had originally appeared on the schedule as a road contest, the Thunder had been unable to secure a field in the Albany area (something they never managed all season) and the game was moved to Watertown. The boon of home field advantage—not to mention the prospect of gate and concession revenues and the $900 the team stood to save on charter coach rental—thrilled Coach Ashcraft.

An Empire League–best 1,200 fans, on average, attended Red and Black home games, at five dollars per adult ticket. They filled the fairgrounds' aluminum bleachers and sat in lawn furniture behind the end zones, coolers of beer tucked beneath the chairs. Most seemed like longtime backers, working class and middle aged. Twenty- and thirty-something men who cared anything about football were likely suited up for the Red and Black, the rest of that demographic scattered in bars around the city or the local Lake Ontario resorts, such as Alexandria Bay and Sacketts Harbor. These fans were older than that, likely remembered the last Watertown championship in 1980, perhaps attended the heartbreaking near misses of recent seasons. Perhaps they had sons and nephews and co-workers on the team. They cheered that way: loyal to longtime players, mildly enthusiastic about Watertown successes, and mildly frustrated about its failures, as though both were somehow to be expected. Just before the seven-thirty kickoff, I found my brother among them, near the top of the bleachers, dragging on a menthol cigarette and talking with a man I took to be another player's father.

It had been a relatively sultry weekend in the North Country, in the lower eighties, but the sunset was cooling things off. A large hot-air balloon lay beached on the grass behind one end zone, the name of a local auto dealer across its belly (we players also wore the dealer's name embossed on a patch on our jerseys). The PA system blared metal music as we pranced through our grass drills. The veterans, I could sense, were more serious in their preparation than they'd been the week before in our exhibition; this was an established foe that'd lost to defending-champion Syracuse by only a touchdown the week before. Ashcraft assembled us behind the grandstand for a few final instructions before the starting lineups were introduced over the PA. I fully expected when he named players on the kickoff team that I would be in that number.

When I wasn't, well, my anger surprised even me. I felt wronged, overlooked, underestimated (part of this, I'm sure, was the lather I had just moments before worked up preparing for kickoff). Hadn't I been to every practice? Hadn't I practiced with the kickoff team since the first night of contact, survived McNeil's attempt to purge me from the roster, leveled Ice Storm players in all nine kickoffs the week before? And for what? To watch from the bench now that it counted? Had my brother come all the way from Louisville for this? My wife and mother were right to stay home.

I succeeded in getting my brother's attention as the team moved through the goalposts and to the sideline for the national anthem and the kickoff, but it was difficult to explain from such a distance that I had been slighted. It was unfair to him, really; he seemed to understand that I was angry but not why, and he looked very concerned, even began to make his way out of the stands to try to get a handle on what I was gesturing about. I waved him off. I knew this was no way for a football player to behave. I had never expected to be a starter on this team anyway, had promised myself I would be a team player this time around. Ashcraft *had* placed me on the extra-point team, perhaps as a consolation prize.

Eric Huck confided that he'd taken an ephedra-based metabolism booster called Ripped Fuel a few hours before kickoff and he was idling very high. "They gotta let me off the leash, Professor," he kept telling me. Most of the forty players left on the sidelines, the also-rans, had been, like me, high school starters, even all-stars, and the bench was a new place for us, an affront. One by one, they sought me out, sensing somehow that I'd be sensitive to their situation. Albert Williams, a Fort Drum soldier who had hoped to see playing time at linebacker, asked why I wasn't a starter. "I've seen you play," he told me. "You oughtta be out there." I was sorely tempted to believe this flattery, though later in the season it became clear he'd had me confused with first-team center Matt Quay. Exterminator Dave Dummitt offered me some advice about getting in the game. "Stand next to George," he said. "Look eager." If Ashcraft wants me, I thought, he knows where I am.

Countryman completed an eight-play drive with a five-yard TD run on the opening Watertown possession. Then Doug Black scored from a yard out on the very next possession, capping a sixty-four-yard drive and giving Watertown a

14–3 lead with 9:08 to play in the half. I had been in on both extra-point plays and was flagged for jumping offsides both times. While rules allow defensive linemen to move, the offensive line must remain perfectly still for a full count before the snap, and having come to the line very tense I flinched when the Thunder players feigned their rush. "Just look at the ground until the ball moves," Pat Nulty told me. In the end the infraction only meant Scott Ford had to convert the kicks from five yards farther back, and that I was replaced at halftime.

Watertown was ahead at the break, 17–10. The excitement of the game did manage to quell momentarily my frustration about playing time. I knew this contest wasn't in hand. The score certainly didn't reflect Watertown's first-half dominance, usually an indication in my football-watching experience of the dominant team's poor execution and failure to seize opportunities. The Capitaland touchdown late in the second quarter brought them much closer than they should by all rights have been and proved they could be dangerous if not dispatched straight away. A late-third-quarter Thunder touchdown pulled them within a point, though they muffed the point after.

Then, dropping back to pass on the ensuing third-quarter drive, Doug Black stepped in a hole in the field and suffered what trainer Verbeck feared was a broken bone in his foot. We crowded around Doug as he lay on his back on the bench, Verbeck manipulating the foot and veterans filing by with condolences. Doug seemed to be sobbing, in frustration as much as pain. The season, rumored his last, had hardly begun.

Rookie backup quarterback Brad Howery was called upon to replace Black. A new Fort Drum soldier, Howery had reputedly been a college QB at Division I Wake Forest, though I was never able to confirm this; semi-pro football, I had begun to understand, is a world of semi-truths and fantasies, even in my own case, and I was wary of any such boasts I encountered. Coach Ashcraft told the *Daily Times* he was not panicked by Black's injury. "We knew that if Douggie just happened to be out, [Howery] could take the snaps and do a good job," he told reporter Parrish Johnson.

In fact, there was some panic on the sideline. Black had made every start for eight seasons—even on the bittersweet night of his daughter's birth. Howery had been a bit of a whipping boy for the first-team Watertown defense all summer (a shoulder injury he suffered in preseason practice would require winter surgery) and he often irked the starting offense because he didn't know the plays well enough yet to make the reads or adjustments or call audibles. "If you see nine guys in the box," I remember Countryman yelling at Howery in practice after the quarterback sent him into a virtual ambush, "you'd better get out of a run play!" This team, proud of its hundred and a half years of history most of all, was something of a cult of familiarity, suspicious of the contributions of fly-by-night new-blood like Howery, something I knew firsthand.

In that sense, the rest of us rookies went out with Howery to the huddle that night at the fairgrounds. He represented us well, completing both passes he attempted for a robust 62 yards, including a twenty-six-yard completion to longtime R&B great Earnie Wash, which set up Scott Ford's game-clinching field goal. Another former option quarterback, Howery proved to be a much better scrambler than the classic passer Black and improvised the offense to victory. "Backup QB Saves the Red and Black" was the *Daily Times* sports section headline Sunday morning.

I took my time undressing and showering in the dank locker room, stopping intermittently to sulk. Coach Britton must have noticed. "It's a long season, Professor," he told me. I wasn't sure if he meant to say I'd get my chance or that there was a lot more bench time ahead. Coach Ashcraft propped the door with a folding chair to let in some cool air and walked about making nice with everyone, particularly those of us who hadn't played. Outside, as my brother and I walked to my car, Jim only wanted to talk about Jesse Lamora, whose three sacks of the Thunder quarterback, including a blindside job that ended the Thunder's last-gasp scoring threat, had earned him local Channel 50's player of the game distinction. "He's a menace to society, man," my brother told me, explaining that it was Lamora's father I'd seen him sitting next to in the stands.

Me, I complained all the way home about not getting to play. "Hey, you were in there. I saw you jump offsides ... twice," my brother teased. I didn't laugh much, and I think my brother was surprised by the depth of my disappointment. "You looked buff," he offered. Back in Canton, finding the house asleep, we split a pizza on the front porch and then went to bed.

I drop into the salon frequently, with lunch in my hand or the baby on my hip, or to say good-bye before I make the drive to practice. Just to see Candace. "Speak of the devil," she always says when she catches sight of me in a huge mirror as I enter, "and the devil appears."

Clients on their way out the door all but pinch my cheeks. "We hear so much about you," they say. I'm often surprised when a client recognizes me on the street or strikes up a conversation about some fact of my life, which I had to that point considered a secret. I try hard to accept what her first husband could not: that being married to Candace means sharing her with these people.

I like being there—it's the place, I suppose, where we fell in love. But she's there so much. She doesn't prefer the salon to being home; she simply has no preference. Once at work, it seems she's in no hurry to leave.

"Where's Mommy?" I ask Jackson on the evenings we await her arrival for supper.

"Salon," he says. "Cuttin' heads off."

Carpool Mutiny

The classes melded together, unconscious of convergence, in the hobby of violence. . . . But it is not only violence or simple violence. . . . It is an organized and socially endorsed mob ritual of licensed fury . . . a fury we cannot detach from an underclass the game exploits.
   —Donald Hall, on spectators at a Detroit Lions game at Tiger Stadium

The question looming over our practice sessions the following week was whether Doug Black would be healthy enough to lead the team into battle with Syracuse, and Black wasn't there to dispel the cloud. The Thursday *Daily Times* reported that he was scheduled to begin therapy on his injured foot, ice treatments and electrolysis, that afternoon at the SPORT clinic in Watertown. "I plan on playing on it the rest of the year," he told Rob Oatman. "If I have to get surgery on it, I hope to wait until the off-season. The doctors say if it's a sprain it will gradually improve, but if it's broken it won't get better."

To make matters worse, backup Brad Howery had been called home to Virginia—a family emergency; custody hearing or something—so the coaches looked to receiver and former Watertown High quarterback Mike Lafex to fill in. Like Howery, Lafex was a fine athlete but more of a runner than a thrower. Whereas Black's eight seasons helped him make reads and get the ball away quickly to thwart a pass rush he could not elude on foot, Lafex was elusive but indecisive, scrambling willy-nilly but never throwing the ball until it was too late, frustrating receivers awaiting his passes and linemen charged with his protection. Eventually, a desperate Ashcraft put a call in to former quarterback Lee Castor, another pure passer who hadn't been with the team since 1996, to inquire about his interest in returning. Everyone's sincerest wish, though, was that Black would play. It seemed the only real hope against the Vipers.

* * *

Defending Empire Football League champions, the Vipers headed up Interstate 81 to Watertown on the twenty-eighth of July winners of two of their first three, their only defeat coming in an extra-league game against the perennial powerhouse Marlborough, Massachusetts, Shamrocks in a preseason charity bowl. This was the team I had seen dispatch Watertown from the playoffs the previous October and I had to concede their physical superiority to any team I had seen to date. Their relentless defensive pressure reminded one of the '85 Bears.

In the locker room prior to kickoff, I sensed intimidation. We were unusually quiet, our numbers low. "These guys are good," Jesse Lamora told me, he who my brother had called a societal menace only a week before. It did feel early in the year to have to face such a test. "Things aren't clicking the way they usually do by this point in the season," trainer and former player Pete Abass had told me after practice that Thursday night.

Things lightened considerably as word of Doug Black's late arrival to the field house made its way around the pregame locker room. X-rays had revealed no fracture in his foot. He brought a young boy of eight or ten with him whom I took to be his son.

"You dressing?" Eddie Pierce asked him. He stood across from Black, who had taken a seat on an aluminum folding chair in front of his locker and had begun to pull on a pair of game socks.

"What do you think?" Black snapped.

During warm-ups Bruce Gonseth did what he could to rally troops. "Whatever you need to find to motivate yourself, now would be a good time to dig it up," he barked.

Ashcraft hadn't even seen fit to have me on the extra-point platoon that week. The game was too important to risk new blood: Black would play hurt and the coach would go with players who had been there. I was disappointed again, of course—a couple of my Canton friends from my running days brought their wives to see what I had given up distance running to do with my spare time.

Candace was there too, it turns out, with her father. Neither had planned to come. They had been at the wedding reception of one of her younger sisters back in DeKalb, but she'd had some wine and gotten upset thinking about the mess with Jake. He and his father had been in Alabama a couple of weeks by then and we'd just received papers from an attorney requesting an amendment to the custody agreement, and child support. Her dad had taken her to get some air—sixty miles down Route 11 to the fairgrounds. My kind of dad.

Doug Black was effective, if slightly hobbled, early in the game. Having taken the team to midfield toward the end of the first quarter, thanks largely to Countryman's tough running, Black took a short drop and stepped toward the Red and Black sideline to avoid backside pressure from Vipers end Ronnie Johnson and threw a short outlet pass to Countryman. As he planted his sprained foot, though, it seemed to buckle under him. The pass floated, allowing Syracuse linebacker Roy Daniels to step in front for the interception and race forty-six yards down the Watertown sideline before Countryman finally caught him at the Red and Black seven. Enormous Viper fullback Leonard Hamilton scored on the next play, dragging three or four tacklers with him across the goal line. "You ain't gonna stop the bull," a Viper yelled at our bench as they gathered in the end zone to celebrate. My teammates' pregame mood made some sense now.

On the Vipers' next possession, speedy receiver Steve Scott (invited to the Washington Redskins training camp at season's end) took quarterback Duane Milton's short slant pass and outran Watertown corner Darin Phifer seventy-seven yards to the end zone. It was the simplest of plays, designed merely to get Scott matched up one-on-one with the clearly slower Red and Black corner. Veteran Phifer had played behind receivers to prevent big plays behind himself and the Vipers countered by getting the ball to Scott quickly in front of him, relying on their flanker to make people miss.

The Vipers ultimately took a 14–3 lead into the locker room, though through one half the teams seemed equal in many respects, the Red and Black even holding the advantage at offensive line and in the kicking game (no doubt at quarterback too, had Black been healthy). The Vipers' crucial advantage was in overall team speed—evidence the two big plays that led to scores—and that had clearly made the difference.

Ashcraft had little to say to us out behind the grandstand at halftime. "Two plays, gentlemen, that's the difference right now," he told us. Black's foot had tightened up toward the end of the first half and he took ice treatments during the intermission, which forced Lafex into action early in the third quarter. Black returned for one play with less than three minutes to play in the third quarter, completing a nineteen-yard pass to Earnie Wash deep in Viper territory, but despite the ice and the painkillers he told the training staff his foot just kept getting worse. Lafex took over again, turning a busted third-down pass play into an eight-yard run and a first down to the Syracuse four. Rookie Erin Woodward, a nice counterpunch to Countryman's inside running, took a toss sweep on the next play toward the home sideline and outran the Syracuse defense to the end zone to pull the Red and Black within four.

Few players in the EFL could claim to have taken the corner on the Vipers. Woodward, listed at a mere five-foot-six in the program, seemed to close the speed gap between the teams immediately. He had scored twice in the exhibition trouncing of the Ice Storm, including a fifty-yard run on an off-tackle "26" play late in the contest when he'd cut behind my lead block, but veteran players had grumbled about the proportion of his carries to Countryman's the following week so he'd been mostly shelved since. His second-half performance against the Vipers proved his mettle—he was named EFL offensive player of the week—and in later weeks Britton schemed to get him and Countryman on the field at the same time.

Woodward's running keyed the next Lafex-led scoring drive, which culminated in the second Scott Ford field goal. The Syracuse lead was but one point with eight minutes to go in the game. The fairgrounds faithful were full-throated in their support and Red and Black sideline morale was peaking; most of us were all the way onto the field when Woodward reached paydirt. Cheerleaders that we had become, the other subs and I exhorted the starters.

The game turned on what happened next. Inexplicably, Scott Ford kicked directly to Viper speedster Scott, who returned the ball straight up the middle of the field, where the kicking team, spreading out to cover the field in lanes, is most vulnerable. Like Gale Sayers in old NFL footage, Scott seemed from my vantage on the sideline to move through the Watertown coverage in an entirely different gear, a full notch faster. At midfield, he met grocery store manager Eddie Pierce, one of the veterans with whom Ashcraft had replaced me the week before.

Pierce did not look like a football player, an athlete of any kind really. He looked adolescent, though he was past thirty, and in practice seemed to shy from contact. But he talked a good game—had a fantasy league team, played rough touch on Sundays, and so forth—and over time he had ingratiated himself to Ashcraft. Confronted by Scott, he broke down into textbook tackling form, then fell backward onto the seat of his shiny black pants, clutching air as Scott sped by. Like me back in the eighth grade.

There was no one behind Pierce, and eighty-five yards and one extra point later Syracuse had extended its lead to eight once more. Pierce's nontackle was nothing less than a disgrace, and my benchmates and I agreed among ourselves that it would not have happened on our respective watches. "You kiddin' me, Professor?" said Albert Williams. I hoped I would have gotten at least a hand on Scott, slowed him down.

I saw the fans begin to fold up lawn chairs and wheel their empty coolers to their cars.

Watertown rallied. Doug Black returned and, aided by an interference call, brought the ball to the Viper one yard line. But Viper nose tackle and former national semi-pro defensive player of the year Ruben Hano-Hano penetrated the line of scrimmage on first down and dropped Lafex—in for Black, shaken up on the interference play—back at the four. Then Viper DB Eliot Reese broke up a Doug Black slant pass intended for Marcus Harrison and NFL-sized defensive tackle Scott Irons knocked a Black third-down pass at the line. Hoping to take advantage of the intense Viper penetration, Britton called a screen pass on fourth down, but the Syracuse pursuit overwhelmed Countryman, hauling him down all the way back at the eight. Team speed again.

The Vipers ran out the clock after that, handing the Red and Black their first regular season home loss since they'd begun playing at the fairgrounds six seasons earlier. Ashcraft cited the Black injury and the big plays in explaining the loss to the assembled media, scolding the Watertown offense for failing to produce points in the "red zone." The coach made passing reference to the absence at practice of key veteran leaders as contributing as well, though he did not name names. "They know who they are," he told Oatman. Mike Lafex, who in addition to going 0-for-2 at quarterback did manage to catch two Doug Black passes for twenty-one yards, was named game MVP.

Candace had come out of the stands during the excitement of the Woodward touchdown and stood behind me the rest of the game. "What kind of bad mood are you gonna be in tonight?" she asked me as she helped me out of my shoulder pads on the sideline once it was over. I told her I'd be okay, that the season was young and it was a kick to be part of such an exciting game. I took some satisfaction, too, in Pierce's screwup: maybe now Ashcraft would get the picture. I got in the car without a shower. "It's not like I need one," I told her.

🏈 🏈 🏈

Standing idle on the sideline through those first several games, I felt my peak preseason conditioning ebb. The work of six full months. While preseason practices had served as an adequate substitute to a workout in the gym, midseason practices were really only a good stretch of the legs, which, when you considered my pregame rest day on Friday and how little I was playing Saturday nights, meant I was taking four days off from exercise per week, more than I had taken at any time since high school. I needed playing time.

To be fair, I'd had my chance to impress coaches and teammates that summer, and, in short, had blown it, seen the moment of my greatness flicker. Starting right guard Brandon Payne and his bride had scheduled their wedding well before the Red and Black schedule was announced and when Ashcraft distributed copies to the players early that summer I saw Payne slump at his locker. "I'm getting married the night of the preseason game," he said. In addition to the Ice Storm exhibition, he missed both nights of practice the week we prepared to play in Vermont and as the team's third guard I was called on to fill in. I knew if I impressed, I might start that game—it was my spot to lose.

The pressure I placed on myself to perform undid me altogether and I played terribly. That Tuesday had been a bad one at home: I hadn't slept well the night before and began my day picking a senseless fight with Candace as she headed out for work about whether she would try to make it to the exhibition that weekend.

"This might be the only chance I get," I told her. "We can stay at that motel you like in Burlington."

"Too much going on," she said.

Of course the discussion might have waited, but I can always be counted on to sabotage myself in that way when I'm already anxious. The day was sweltering and I was wrung out and exhausted before I even left for Watertown.

Early in practice, scrimmaging as part of the first unit at left guard, I jumped offsides, leaving my stance on Doug Black's first "hut" instead of his second. I was thinking too much; poised in my three-point stance, most of my body weight balanced precariously on the fingers of my right hand, the sweat from my soaked shirt rolling down my forearms, I was worrying about reaching my block on a "25" play, about starting the game that weekend, about the vacation we planned to take to Key Largo between the Vermont game and the beginning of the regular season, and somewhere along the way I lost track of the snap count. "On the line," Britton had said, annoyed. "Run it again."

I made no excuses. There was no defense for that kind of mental lapse and I always resented players who tried to make one. I should have put it out of my mind, focused on the job at hand. Former Pittsburgh Steeler quarterback Terry Bradshaw says great players never think about injuries or mistakes. If I could have pulled things together on the spot I might have saved my job. But I couldn't stop thinking about my fuckup, and two plays later I did it again. This time I heard men groan on both sides of the ball. Britton slapped his playbook against his thigh. "Do we have anybody else we can get in here?"

"You're a fucking professor," Countryman said to me back in the huddle. "And you can't count to two? If you can't do the job, pack your shit and go home."

"He teaches writing, not counting," Bruce Gonseth quipped from across the ball.

Countryman peered through my face mask. He saw how this stung.

"I'm just kidding," Countryman said. "Well, not really."

Jamee Call snickered. It wasn't long before these guys lost faith in you, I could see that, and they'd lost it in me. If I asked center Matt Quay on my right to clarify an assignment or an audible the rest of that night, he just rolled his eyes. By that Saturday, they'd moved defensive lineman Adam Brown back to offensive guard in place of Payne.

Sitting in my university office the Tuesday afternoon following that Syracuse loss, shuffling papers and preparing my book satchel to head home and then to Watertown for practice, I received a phone call from an apologetic Chris LaSalle, a Red and Black tight end. "Look, Professor," Chris said, "I hate to do this to you, but Coach Britton's car is in the shop and he and Shane and I need a ride tonight. I know it's short notice." Britton had coached LaSalle at Potsdam High School years before and then invited him and his nephew Shane McCargar to join the Watertown team the previous season. The three had carpooled all summer from Potsdam, ten miles farther up Route 11 from Canton, after twenty-one year-old McCargar finished his shift at Triple A Lumber.

I told Chris a ride was no problem and that I would be by in a few minutes to pick them up. In fact, I spoke quietly into the receiver though I was alone in the office and though my football career was a secret to no one at work. The phone call *was* a problem for me somehow, a silly violation of boundaries I had tried to establish between my job and my illicit moonlight gig. I stifled the urge to say, "I thought I told you never to call me here."

What's more, I had really come to enjoy the evening drive down to practice twice a week. When you take into account the two-hour round-trip I made to and from practice twice a week, I spent as much time in my Subaru as I did on the football field that season. And driving back and forth, I listened to more radio than I'd had the chance to in ten years, since my college days in New Orleans when the Crescent City's lively FM band was my only company on daily, hour-long runs around Audubon Park. New Orleans radio had played it all—not only local heroes like Dr. John and the Meters but R&B, oldies, alternative music—and at that age I knew every lyric, could name most tunes after only a few chords. Nowadays I was lucky to recognize every other song, having failed to keep up with music's changing landscape despite promises I had made to myself to the contrary.

I tuned to talk radio, National Public Radio mostly, though sometimes on pitch-black drives home to Canton I could pick up a CBC rebroadcast of a noirish 1950s radio play or, if I searched the AM band, a ball game from as far away as Detroit. Rural northern New York's radio dial is a lonely place, and pop lyrics just don't speak to my emotional state as they had in college. I still loved music, felt that, despite all I thought was wrong with America, any country that could produce a song like Tom Petty's "The Waiting" couldn't be all bad. Only now I couldn't hear that song anywhere but on classic rock stations, whose other listeners I imagined were stuck in decades past wearing mullets and black concert tees. I wasn't ready to accept that I had moved into the "adult contemporary" phase of my life, either (the reason I was on the road to football practice in the first place?), where Phil Collins and Don Henley sang songs about second chances, thinly veiled autobiographical tunes about divorces and bankruptcies and midlife crises.

I rendezvoused with the trio at the county jail where Britton's second wife, Sue, worked as the nurse (she'd been the nurse at the middle school when they met). Britton took the seat up front next to me while Chris and Shane sat behind (uncomfortably so, as Shane goes six-five and 300) and we piled three more sets of equipment into the hatchback.

"Will we have a quarterback at practice today, coach?" Shane asked Britton once we were on the road.

"I can't say," Britton told him. The coach rode quietly up front, but the rest of us vented our frustrations.

"I want to talk about Eddie Pierce's nontackle," I said, turning back to see the faces of my teammates. The mention provoked an almost physical response from everyone in the car.

"I mean, I ought to be playing," I said.

Chris LaSalle was playing some at tight end, but certainly not as much as he'd have liked—Doug Black tended to spread the offense with three-receiver sets, leaving tight ends like Chris languishing on the sideline. Shane McCargar was actually playing with the first team, a starter on that otherwise veteran offensive line, but the Indian River boys had not warmed to him, and apparently he took their rejection of him hard. I'll admit he was a difficult guy for me to like, too, an overgrown kid who still laughed at fart jokes and was forever scratching at scabs on his legs. But we had this rejection in common.

The Massena, New York, paper ran a photo of the four of us a few weeks later, the St. Lawrence County road warriors who commuted three hundred miles a week just to play football. In the adjacent article, our veteran teammates marveled at our commitment, though, like their comments in the article about backup quarterback Howery's heroics in week one, they were mostly insincere. Jamee Call, who worked, I read in the *Daily Times,* as the wrestling coach and sports custodian at Indian River High School, had taken to calling us Britton's "boys from up north," though I had known Britton only a matter of weeks and could not rightly be called his, not at that point anyway.

From the backseat, Shane asked Britton if he might like to coach a new team based closer to home. "I've talked to a lot of guys who say they'd back us financially," Shane told Britton. "We could draw players from Potsdam, Canton, Massena, Ogdensburg. I know we've got the numbers." McCargar's manipulation of the coach was straight out of Shakespeare, *Macbeth* or *Othello.* I could see it working on Britton as we rolled along.

The coach had been involved with the Red and Black on and off for more than thirty years, stepping away intermittently to coach different high school and college programs in the area, serving on the staff of former Buffalo Bills coach Lou Saban, for instance, when Saban was hired to coach a brand-new football program at SUNY-Canton in the mid-nineties, but always finding his way back to the Red and Black sideline. Team history had become an abiding interest for Britton back in his playing days—you can feel it taking hold even in interviews he gave back then—and on the occasion of the Red and Black's centennial in 1996, he compiled a hundred-page history of the team's first century, printed and bound by the team's board of directors, a statistical almanac mostly, though the coach does offer brief narratives of each decade. He told me about his book the first time I mentioned my idea (trainer Sam Verbeck confided he was planning a book of his own, *Red, Black and Blue*). Mike remained a walking archive of team myth, lore, and statistics. "Mr. Red and Black football," sportscaster Mel Busler called him.

Only now it seemed Ashcraft had usurped Britton in this role, and Al Countryman was about to break his all-time team rushing mark. I knew it would be difficult for the coach to walk away—it would have to be someone else's idea. I could also sense his frustration with the current situation in Watertown. It was bizarre to watch him and Ashcraft coach together: Britton and his playbook standing behind the offensive huddle, tortured as an orchestra conductor mid-rehearsal, while Ashcraft stands fifty yards downfield behind his defense, bending the ear of a veteran player who'd taken a break. They already looked like adversaries.

"Why would you send in a play you know the quarterback isn't going to run?" says Britton. "The league's always been after me to get a team going up in our part of the state, to replace the old Massena Warriors."

Though this was the first I had heard of the idea, I told Chris and Shane that I might like to cast my lot with a new team. In Pat Conroy's recent memoir about his days as a member of the Clemson University basketball squad, *My Losing Season*, he says it was his time on the bench that made him a writer—all that time to daydream, in the world of basketball but not of it. I suppose I could make a similar claim, that in the participant/observer model it behooved me as the writer to observe more than to participate. But I wanted to play. On the flag football team back in college, I had done my best to accept my role on the sideline, content to let players more suited to that game lead us to victory, but even then I knew my lot was not much different from that of the average fan, who couldn't claim to have participated in any victory and was helpless in defeat. Only now I was sacrificing a great deal more to play and believed if given the chance I might really make a difference in the fortunes of the team. George Plimpton had been called a first-string writer and sixth-string quarterback. My secret vanity was that I was a much better football player than that, and I wanted the chance to prove it, even if it meant playing somewhere else.

Our opponent the following week was the Lake City Stars of Plattsburgh, New York, a team drawn from several communities around the former air force installation community just across Lake Champlain from Burlington, Vermont. When the air base was operational, the Plattsburgh Northstars had been a fierce Watertown rival. What separated the Red and Black from the Stars now were the skill players Watertown was still able to recruit from the pool of national talent that was Fort Drum, players like Woodward, Howery, Phifer, Toby Mason, and all-league receivers Marcus Harrison and Odell Bowens. The Stars had taken their share of EFL poundings but entered the game 1–1 in league play that season, just like the Red and Black, and were reportedly much improved.

With Howery still in Virginia and Lafex slated to be best man at a friend's wedding that Saturday, Ashcraft had been able to coax Lee Castor, now the father of five small children, out of retirement for the time being, to serve as Black's backup. His helmet off as he warmed his arm for the Tuesday practice, Castor resembled a scrawny surfer—the golden locks and slightly slack jaw. But he had the arm of a quarterback. He was apparently still a force in local indoor flag football leagues. When he worked with the second-team offense during the week, he aplogized repeatedly, as though unsure himself why he'd some back. "Sorry, guys," he'd say. "I'm rusty." When he took big hits from pass rushers, he simply pulled himself up smiling, his helmet slightly askew.

Castor would get his chance on Saturday. Doug Black threw six touchdown passes against Lake City, five in the first half, and was on the bench resting his foot sprain by the end of the third quarter. The game was essentially over within minutes of kickoff, before the sun had set: Black threw a thirty-three-yard touchdown to Bowens on the opening Watertown drive, then, following a fumble on the Stars' first offensive play, connected with Earnie Wash for a twenty-three-yard score. Thirteen points in fifty seconds, and the rout was on.

This was great news for second-teamers like me and Eric Huck and Chris LaSalle, who caught a first-quarter touchdown pass. Ashcraft had returned me to the starting kickoff team (though not in place of Pierce) so there were plenty of kicks to cover that night, but the blowout meant I also got to spell McNeil at left guard throughout the game. My lead blocks again sprung Erin Woodward on touchdown runs of fifty-one and twenty-one yards. I began to pity the troll-like Plattsburgh tackle playing across from me, but he asked no quarter and gave none.

The final score was 58–22. Black finished 16-for-22 for 262 yards while Lee Castor was 2-for-3 for 59 yards, including a picturesque nineteen-yard post-corner touchdown pass to Wash (a play on which Wash strained a hamstring). The margin of victory seemed to give the team room it needed to breathe after two weeks of tight games, and provided those of us disgruntled subs some time on the stage.

Candace and her father were in attendance again. Seeing me play actually piqued my wife's curiosity about the game.

"I saw you plow this huge guy—three hundred pounds. I looked it up in the program," she told me. For his part, Bill noted a tackle I'd missed on a fourth-quarter kickoff.

We joined the team at Applebee's on Arsenal Street for a complimentary postgame buffet, where Dave McNeil offered us seats next to him and his leggy bride for soggy nachos and a couple of longnecks. It was one of a string of kindnesses McNeil showed to me that fall once I had survived his personal initiation and earned my stripes. I had confided the story of Jake's leaving a few weeks before, that disastrous night of my first-string audition, and talk turned there.

"It's tough," McNeil said. "I got three kids from a previous."

I loved the way he said that—from a previous—and adopted it for my own.

That string of kindnesses included an eventual chat with Ashcraft about my playing time—I watched him stroll with the coach from the practice field to the locker room pleading my case. "He can do it," I heard him say. "Trust me."

For the most part, though, the intimidating wall of silence erected by veteran players remained intact all year. No, if I had undertaken this as a friends-making mission, it could only be considered a failure. When I had first conceived the idea, I thought of it as something of a social history, like James Agee's *Let Us Now Praise Famous Men,* but that seemed silly now. The Fort Drum guys and I got on well because we were all a long way from home, getting together to play football because the game connected us to our pasts. I was even friendly with a handful of local guys—Nulty, Dummitt, now even McNeil. But I don't believe Doug Black ever spoke to me, Jamee Call only derisively. Whom did I think I was anyway, a man who had never done a day's work, to walk onto this field and expect respect? Detroit Lions All-Pro tackle Alex Karras named a son George Plimpton Karras after the writer's stint as Detroit's sixth-string quarterback. "He's my hero," Karras said when informed of Plimpton's recent death. But I didn't see that kind of thing happening here.

Several weeks into the season, Al Countryman and I were the last two in the showers after a chilly Thursday practice. I always dragged after practice, perhaps dreading the long drive home.

We showered silently for several minutes. People gave Al a wide berth, admired him from afar. McNeil called Jamee Call Al's "shadow," but beyond that he didn't have much of an entourage.

I remained silent as long as I could stand it, but it violated everything I understood about friendliness. I remembered reading in the "controversial" *Daily Times* feature on Doug Black's daughter that Countryman and his wife were expecting as well. "How's your wife's pregnancy coming along?" I asked him.

"We lost that baby," he told me.

There had been other miscarriages, or so I'd heard. I remembered now a practice he'd missed weeks back, but I hadn't realized one absence was irregular. I waited a long time, the water running on my neck and shoulders.

"God, I'm sorry," I said.

"Hey, you didn't know," he said, then turned off the shower and went out to his locker.

I make it home early from Watertown one July evening—a light practice before our first exhibition game. It's half past eight, hardly dusk outside, but I find Candace and baby Jackson fast asleep on the couch, cheek to cheek. It's perfect, except for the huge wound I now see in the middle of the prominent forehead the boy inherited from me, big as a silver dollar, bright red and glistening with ointment. He toddled right off the porch onto the concrete, head first.

The abrasion will scab over in a couple of days, babies heal so fast, but it's worse than any wound I will bring home from the gridiron that season, and I still can't look at pictures of Jackson from that time. When new, pink skin eventually replaces the scab, we find that it glows red like a mood ring just before he screams or cries. "The mood scab," we come to call it.

"What were you doing when this happened?" I ask his mother when I wake her.

"Gee, I don't know," she says, a little hot at the question and at my manner of asking. "What were you doing?"

In Another Country

I once felt joy in being alive and I felt this mainly when I was playing basketball and I rarely if ever feel that joy anymore and it's my own damn fault and that's life. Too bad.
—David Shields, *Enough About You*

oach Ashcraft announced after the Thursday practice the following week that the team bus would leave Watertown for Montreal at noon on Saturday and return at dawn Sunday. It was understood that Red and Black players would close the topless bars on world-famous Rue Ste. Catherine in Sunday's wee hours and head home before sunrise, something of a tradition after years of easy victories (the Montreal Condors lost their first forty EFL games). Dave McNeil told me how he'd been forced to spend a week of nights sleeping in his garage astride his riding mower after participating in the previous season's postgame festivities over his wife's objections. "Totally worth it," he told me. Candace and I own a push mower so I wanted to make sure I had her permission before joining my teammates in their debauchery.

Actually I dreaded broaching with Candace the idea of my teammates and I experiencing Montreal nightlife after the game. Candace was working twelve hours a day Tuesday through Saturday at that time, more than she had ever worked in the time I had known her, making up time she'd lost during Jackson's infancy. While I was free most of the day once my summer class ended around lunchtime, I was gone three of those nights every week between five and midnight practicing and playing football, leaving her to take care of the baby alone when she got home from a long day's work. When I wasn't in Watertown playing football, I'll confess I was thinking about it, watching it on television.

I knew many guys on the team had this issue with wives and girlfriends. Many had worked out elaborate systems whereby they'd earn this game-day time off, "me time" I had overheard Jamee Call term it. *Daily Times* sports editor John O'Donnell made a joke in an article written way back in the seventies about all the bathrooms husbands had promised to paint in order to get one more chance on the field. Sadly, Candace and I hadn't come to any such arrangement—she actually preferred I not take on any home improvement projects. "Better to cut a check than cut off a finger," she'd say. So things just simmered.

Saturdays were a particular bone of contention between us. Candace felt, and probably rightly, that my game-day expectations—that I be temporarily relieved from fatherly and husbandly duties—were unrealistic. My new bride had never attended a day of high school much less a pep rally or homecoming game and had no means of relating to football preparation, reasonable or otherwise. Back in high school in Tennessee, we football players had received the royal treatment on football Fridays, moving absently through the motions of the school day without really having to engage any particular task. It made focusing on the evening's contest simple. Taking care of Jackson while Candace worked made that focus nearly impossible and I resented how tired I already felt by four P.M. when I had to begin the drive to Watertown (though, as Candace was quick to point out, I rarely played once I arrived).

She said she simply had to work Saturdays.

"That's my target clientele," she tells me. "Working professionals who can't come during the week."

"We could hire a sitter," I offer meekly.

"That would mean we pay for childcare six days a week," she says. "Who's raising this child anyway? You're his father!"

*   *   *

Even if a Watertown player got permission from his wife, there was still the matter of getting clearance from Canadian customs officials, who often posed more of a problem to the Red and Black than "old ladies" or the hapless Condors. Ashcraft warned us that even an unpaid speeding ticket might prevent us from making it across and that if we were refused entry he'd have no choice but to leave any player denied entry right there at the customs checkpoint until the bus rolled through the next morning on its way home.

The Condors played at Laberge Park in the town of Châteauguay, Quebec, just outside the city, but the visiting team dressed at a vocational high school a few miles away (the EFL required showers and locker facilities for visiting teams) and then made the short bus ride over. Doug Black and his girlfriend had spread a blanket on the school lawn and were picnicking with daughter Shea when we arrived. I saw backup quarterback Lee Castor there too, all five kids in the back of a huge, newish SUV. It was the last I ever saw of Castor, though I did hear he cut short his comeback to have a vasectomy.

The Châteauguay River, which flowed from an Adirondack lake in northern New York into the St. Lawrence River in Montreal, ran just beyond the field's north end zone, so close in fact that field goals and extra points kicked in that direction always threatened to find its waters. The playing surface, covered with waterbirds and their droppings when we got there (the park is a haven for local bird-watchers), was rough and dusty, like a baseball infield. There were no grandstands to speak of, just rickety bleachers four or five rows high. The Montreal team had long been the EFL doormat and, despite Montreal's relative size, the league's least-supported franchise, financially and otherwise. But the field met minimum Empire Football League standards—it was lighted for nighttime contests, had a scoreboard and a PA system—and the Condors players, wearing mismatched, rented or borrowed helmets and tattered jerseys, still seemed game opponents, on the verge of emergence from seasons of obscurity.

The sun was bright as we warmed up and Coach Ashcraft walked among the ranks assessing his personnel needs. As feared, many Red and Black players failed to make the trip, a whole carful held at the border because the driver, a starting defensive end, faced outstanding assault charges arising from a fistfight at a Potsdam bar where he worked as a bouncer. Britton walked quietly behind the head coach as he made his rounds, both of them headed for the spot on the field where I had myself pretzeled into position for the butterfly groin stretch.

"Cowz," Ashcraft said when he reached me, "I want to look at you at d-end."

"Yessir," I barked.

I felt my chest tighten, my breathing get ever shallower. This was the pressure that had crushed me during that awful preseason practice.

I remembered the week before my first high school start back in Tennessee the summer before my sophomore year, how I'd slept little the entire week leading up to a scrimmage at Jackson Northside High School, so excited and terrified at the prospect. Our school bus broke down on the highway probably twenty minutes from the field, near a grain silo that read "Green Acres Farm," and I remember thinking how fate had intervened and how convenient it would be if they never got that bus running, if we just stayed there at Green Acres until our parents could arrive to take us home. Once we were back on the road, scant minutes later, I fell asleep—or passed out from nervous exhaustion—against the rectangular bus window, not waking until we had arrived at the field, until it was simply too late to turn back.

I should have been more prepared for this news than I was. It was the playing time I had been bucking for all season, but the prospect of getting that time now, at the last possible moment, after almost half a season of watching from the sideline, startled me. I had come to enjoy my time on the sidelines observing, settled into my role as unofficial leader of the griping band of second-teamers convinced they should be on the field. Ashcraft's call to action would put that boast and my participant-observer status to the test.

My semi-pro career had been exclusively mop-up duty to that point. An indication of the Red and Black's general superiority, and its depth in particular, was the dominance we second-teamers showed in our limited action against the B units from other teams. I had played offensive guard against Plattsburgh and the expansion Vermont team and in both cases found myself helping a teammate double-team out-of-shape defensive tackles I could have taken myself, or pulling to crush undersized defensive ends not experienced enough to feel my kickout block coming. But tonight's action would be against Montreal's A-team, 300-pound offensive linemen, the "Montreal Wall."

The team huddled in the shadows of the goalpost prior to taking the field and Al Countryman had the last word. He must also have sensed all the ingredients of an upset brewing that evening—the literally foreign environment, the hungry opponent, the questionable morale of our weakened ranks. "We don't lose to Montreal," he said.

● ● ●

The Condors won the coin toss and elected to receive, and I was introduced immediately to playing defensive end at the semi-pro level. While ends in the run-oriented American high school game are given contain responsibility on sweeps and other wide plays run to their side and taught to patrol through the backfield on plays that flowed away, defensive ends in pass-happy semi-pro ball had rushing the passer foremost in mind. The Condors were particularly pass-happy, many offensive skill players having played together on the Châteauguay Raiders junior football team (an amateur league for Canadian men aged nineteen to twenty-two) according to Canadian rules, which allowed for only three downs per series and necessitated passing on nearly every play. From the first snap, Condors coach Wilbert Smith, an ex-NFL and CFL linebacker, sent four receivers downfield in deep and intermediate pass routes.

Inserted at right end, I found myself matched up against Montreal's enormous all-league offensive tackle Steve Pantalakis, NFL-sized at six-foot-three and more than 300 pounds, who dropped his left foot and set up to pass protect on every snap. Hand-fighting him to get at scrawny quarterback Kevin Wyeth, I was no match, too small to beat Pantalakis mano a mano and too slow and out of shape to go around the wall. Between my adrenaline and the rust I had developed through four games spent largely on the bench, I was gassed early. No amount of preseason running could simulate game intensity.

What coaches had always told me about fatigue making cowards of us all proved true; I cursed every Condor third-down conversion in that first half because it meant at least three more all-out sprints.

I did the enjoy the abandon I could bring to playing defense—"reckless abandonment," my high school teammate Jack Vincent had always called it, as though it were a charge you'd hurl at a deadbeat dad—and late in the first quarter after I had settled down, I found that on plays where Wyeth was forced out of the pocket or rolled away from me, I could get tantalizingly close to the Montreal quarterback.

On one play I had a handful of Wyeth just as he ducked out of bounds, my pinky finger hung painfully in jersey mesh—an "avulsion fracture," Sam Verbeck notified me in the locker room prior to practice the following week when I showed him the finger, where a sprained ligament brings a piece of bone along as it's torn away, the only real injury I suffered that whole year. More often I wound up face first on the dusty field just as Wyeth released a pass, carrying the dust back to the huddle on my face and in my mouthpiece. My Red and Black helmet sits on a mantel in my office now still dusted with Laberge Park soil.

As counterpoint to the CFL-style quick-strike Condor attack, the Red and Black elected to grind out yardage on the ground in the first half. Both Countryman and Erin Woodward were effective running against an overmatched Montreal defensive front, gaining 56 and 80 yards respectively on the evening. With the middle of the defense softened, Doug Black then exploited defensive backs caught cheating up to support the run defense. He threw two touchdown passes each to Kevin Simpson and Chris LaSalle and the Red and Black led 28–7 at the half.

● ● ●

Through that first half, I had been lining up on what is known as the Montreal tackle's outside shoulder, aligning my head not with his head but with the outermost number on his jersey, a technique that safeguarded against running plays off-tackle, inside of Pantalakis. But the Condors had not brought a tight end to my side or run anything but draw plays (where the offensive linemen block as though the play were a pass), had done none of the things offenses generally do to keep defenses "honest." After an Al Countryman punt pinned the Condors back at their own twenty early in the third quarter, I decided on a gamble.

On a third and long play, I moved half-again farther outside the Montreal tackle than I had been lining up and angled myself toward the quarterback. I disguised the adjustment as best I could as the Condors came to the line, hoping Pantalakis wouldn't adjust his drop to compensate. When he didn't, I found myself at the snap of the ball bearing down on Wyeth, coming from his blind side.

I felt an old enmity rise in me. Even people who know nothing of football know defensive players are supposed to hate quarterbacks, to want to kill them, eat them for lunch—it's a football given. Like so many other hang-ups, the malevolence probably dates to high school, when quarterbacks get all the attention; "Only two people really enjoy high school," claims humorist Fran Lebowitz, " the quarterback and his girlfriend." That and the fact that standing statuesque in the pocket, like the gold figure on some football trophy or the plastic groom atop a three-tier wedding cake, the quarterback is the only man exempt from the violence of an essentially violent game. It becomes the desire of every man on the defense to bring that violence to him.

Such opportunities, free shots at the quarterback, had come my way in high school a time or two, though as a left end I usually rushed directly into the quarterback's face in those days, which gave him the opportunity to get rid of the pass or sidestep me. Great pass rushers so overwhelm blockers that they can't be sidestepped or otherwise avoided, whether the quarterback knows they're coming or not, but, as I was learning all over again, I wasn't that kind of athlete. Still, by cunning, I had gained the inner sanctum of the pass pocket. I unloaded on Wyeth—somehow my knees had not given way between the line of scrimmage and the quarterback—burying my face mask in the small of his back. I felt the ball pop free, but the Montreal quarterback collapsed on top of it under the force of my tackle, recovering his own fumble.

I rose from the dust of my sack to exactly no fanfare at all. No crowd, no roar. Nothing like the fan frenzy such a play would have produced back in Tennessee. No one's even here to tape this, I thought. There were a few pats on the back from teammates, but now we had to huddle up, rush the punter, set up a return. And we had almost an entire half left to play.

The only sack I would record that season was forgotten by the end of the season, missing from a final statistical tally passed around at the postseason banquet. Still, in the privacy of my own helmet, I knew this was my moment, and it felt affirming, like that first collision with McNeil back in May. For the first time since returning to the game, I had played long and hard enough to forget myself in the melee, to play without thinking, and I remembered why I had loved it. It was rare that I could give myself up to something in that way anymore— the way I could do with writing sometimes, the way I had been with Candace when we first met. Tired as I was, I did not want the game to end.

The team held on for a 35–21 victory despite some questionable Canadian officiating, including a call that awarded the Condors a touchdown though the ballcarrier had been stopped at the Watertown ten yard line by an inadvertent whistle. I showered back at the vocational school and caught a ride back to Watertown in kicker Scott Ford's minivan, borrowed from his car lot for the evening.

As it happened, Candace's eighty-year-old paternal grandfather's sudden death of heart failure that Friday morning made the question of my staying over in Montreal moot. For the record, Candace had okayed my night out with the boys, and it was still an open question when I'd left our house that morning—I was dying to see these guys on the town, wild animals in their natural habitat. But in the end I decided not to stay: the funeral would be Monday in the small Finger Lakes village where Candace's grandparents had lived and ministered the last years of his life, and in order to make the five-hour drive with Candace and the baby on Sunday afternoon I needed to get immediately home.

I sat in a bench seat in the back of Ford's van next to wide receiver Kevin Simpson, a Cracker Barrel fry cook who had separated his shoulder in the first half and alternately snored and moaned in pain all the way home. This, not the Rue St. Catherine debauch, was probably the quintessential semi-pro football experience anyway: used-car salesman Ford racing through the Canadian night to get fry cook Simpson, spaced out on codeine that Sam Verbeck had given him, home to work a busy Sunday morning shift. This was a league of beer guts and knee braces and day jobs, after all, talent in its twilight and precious little glory.

Candace's grandfather, Reverend Scott, was buried in the veterans' cemetery in the small town of Bath the following

Monday, and I was there. I expect he might well have related to my vocational ambiguity had I known him better. An army flamethrower on Okinawa, he ran a central New York chop shop through the 1950s, then entered the Methodist seminary as part of a deal he made with God to spare the life of his only son, Candace's father, injured in an auto wreck. He and his wife attributed every good thing afterward to God's grace—the weather, their bounty of grandchildren, the new tires a local auto dealer gave them at no cost. "Now that's the Lord," they were often heard to say.

The funeral trip was the most time I had spent with my family in weeks, probably since the season had begun. I sensed things lightening with Candace, the way they can between married people when each lets go a little. During the funeral service a brother-in-law and I walked our children to a swing set the undertaker had erected for his own family behind the funeral home and I listened to Candace's father deliver the eulogy as best I could on a pair of outdoor speakers hung near the front door. "You're a good man, Bob Cowser," Candace said that evening on the drive home, out of the blue.

🏈 🏈 🏈

"What happened to you?" McNeil asked when I arrived at practice the following week. It was a wild time in Montreal, the guys told me; a few had gotten grabby and been shown the club door, though there were no arrests this time, and the Freeman bus rolled into Watertown with all its seats intact.

Ashcraft was doing all he could to hype the rematch with the 4–0 Syracuse Vipers the following week. In fact, Ashcraft was often as much a fight promoter or circus barker as he was a coach. The job required it. He chartered a spectator bus—"pep" or "spirit" bus we had called them in high school—from Watertown to Griffin Field on Onondaga Lake in Syracuse for that Saturday to bolster support, and he made incendiary comments in a *Watertown Daily Times* interview early that week. "We're the country guy compared to the metropolitan guy," he told the paper. " I think a lot gets said by that. They think they're a step above us."

Fred Exley biographer Jonathan Yardley says Watertown has always faced the world with this sort of pugnacity, born of geographic isolation and endless winters, that football has been the chief means by which the smallish city proved itself to the larger world. Claims by made by *Daily Times* sportswriter Rob Oatman that the Watertown/Vipers rivalry was on par with those between the Dallas Cowboys and Washington Redskins or between Army and Navy is certainly overstatement. Still, no love was lost between the teams. Frustrated by nearly twenty seasons since their last EFL title and pursuing a championship, any championship, before the team's core players retired, the Red and Black had played the 1998 and 1999 seasons in the less competitive New York Amateur Football League, only to lose title games both years. When the team returned to the Empire Football League in 2000, they found the first-year Vipers, rich in talent and resources, squatting on their claim.

Watertown had taken the first meeting in July 2000, 20–12, though this was the game in which Al Countryman tore his ACL and lost most of that season (messages he posted to an EFL message board suggest he considers the injury no accident and holds the Vipers responsible). The Vipers took the next game in Syracuse, 16–10; Watertown avenged that loss in September, 16–7; then the Vipers, in the playoff game I had "scouted" in October, overwhelmed the R&B 31–12 at the fairgrounds. The Syracuse team went on to that coveted league title in its inaugural season.

What was the "lot that gets said" by Ashcraft's characterization of the rivalry, anyway? The coach would have been more correct to call the mostly black Syracuse team "urban" rather than "metropolitan." His own Watertown team, save the ten or twelve players of the Fort Drum contingent, was a mostly white unit—the 2000 census reported Jefferson County, New York, as 88 percent Caucasian—and Syracuse players had called them "farmers" from the sidelines at the end of the last two victories. None among my white teammates, except perhaps Doug Black, would have owned up to the racial nature of their resentment of the Viper team, even to themselves, but the Vipers' perfectly legal if flamboyant behavior (trash talking, end zone dances, etc.), things we generally associate with flashy African-American NFL stars like Deion Sanders, drove them crazy. These were players who took to heart Lombardian (read: mid-century white, middle-class) principles of selflessness and humility, even if the latter was false. The clash was ugly, but it made for fierce football.

Ashcraft had said early in our preseason that any player who made race an issue would be asked to leave the club, as though it weren't already one. The Red and Black had had its own flare-ups over racial epithets passed among teammates early in the summer. One fight I couldn't even watch: a black player locked up with a white teammate after an extra-point attempt back in a July practice, his hand on the white player's face mask, wrenching it violently. "Come on, pussy," the white player said. "Nigger."

"We just need to play a game," was Ashcraft's analysis at the time, his explanation for the two or three fights that had erupted in a week's time. A real estate Web site describing the village of Carthage, New York, reported opaquely that Fort Drum's economic impact on the community had been very positive but that its social impact had been less so. Jonathan Yardley writes that Watertownians transformed their alliance against natural circumstances into an alliance against the rest of the world, anyone deemed an outsider, and men on the team who had attended Indian River Central School or rural schools like it might have had ten nonwhite classmates in a class of close to two hundred and made little effort to befriend black and Latino players who had joined the team from Fort Drum.

That was the biggest difference, Pat Nulty told me candidly, between the twenty-first-century Red and Black teams and the EFL Champion team of 1980: the introduction of black players from Fort Drum and the establishment of a minimum drinking age spelled the end of a camaraderie that could extend beyond the field of play. "You have factions now," Nulty told me. "Country boys from northern New York, the brothers from Fort Drum. They don't seem to want to have anything to do with each other. That's no team," he said. The EFL was no longer the small-town association it had been in 1980 and the Red and Black needed desperately the talent it culled from the men stationed at the base to compete with teams from urban centers like Syracuse, Albany, and Scranton. But accepting these men as teammates was another matter.

*   *   *

Much of Candace's extended family lived in and around Syracuse so we made a family weekend of the road trip, staying with her grandparents on Otisco Lake. Candace's surviving grandfather and uncle planned to attend the game and, after my strong showing in Quebec and a week's work with the defense, I expected to play some versus the Vipers.

This was actually her stepgrandfather, her mother's mother's second husband, Fred Fey, a semiretired septuagenarian who claimed to have installed most of the sewer line in the city of Syracuse and related to every man he met first in terms of what the guy did for a living. When Fred and I talked about football, for instance, he called my coach my "boss" out of habit. Hard work was all Fred Fey had ever known and all he respected in others and he scoffed at the young men sniffing around his granddaughters who had somehow avoided it. Candace warned me of this, but it seems I was an exception; *professor* met with his approval as a lucrative alternative to real work. Still, I hoped seeing me play might change his opinion that I was soft.

Growing up in Tennessee, every grown-up I knew talked about missing the chance to go to college as though it were a regret. But I had met many since moving to New York who did not feel that way—working-class teammates, many in Candace's family, Candace herself. I made the mistake right after we were married of suggesting a way Candace could go to college for free now that she was my spouse. It was something I wanted to do for her.

"Well, that's very sweet of you, but I'm happy doing exactly what I do," she told me. "My parents were upset I didn't go after high school, but I wanted to own a salon, so I went to cosmetology school." Maybe she'd take me up on the offer one day, she said, she'd have to see.

EFL games kicked off at seven-thirty P.M., which meant we played the first half in waning summer daylight and the second under the lights. Despite this game's importance, the bleachers around Griffin Field that evening were close to empty, seating mostly players' families. I saw no sign of Ashcraft's pep bus, no record of the game in the *Syracuse Post-Standard* the next morning.

The coach had me on kickoff team to start the game; he told the Watertown paper later in the season that there was no system with regard to special-teams substitutions until the playoffs, when he played his best athletes. Ford's opening kick pinned the Vipers deep, inside their own five, and a fumble on the ensuing snap energized the Watertown sideline and set up Doug Black and the offense first and goal on the Viper three. But when the Viper defense held, on successive inside running plays to Countryman and then an incomplete Black pass, and Watertown settled for a Scott Ford field goal, one began to worry.

Dropping to pass late in the second quarter, Vipers quarterback Duane Milton found no one open in the Red and Black zone and decided to tuck the ball and get what he could on the ground. He never saw six-foot-three, 220-pound Red and Black linebacker Derryl Green close from his flat coverage. A Drummie, Green had been a linebacker at Alabama A&M in the mid-nineties and had the sleek but powerful look of an NFL safety (Denver Bronco Steve Atwater, maybe), though he'd had a hard time cracking Ashcraft's starting lineup—blown coverages, dumb penalties.

His hit on Milton was loud and startling as a car wreck, dislocating Milton's shoulder on impact. The Viper quarterback struggled to his feet in a strange show of strength and staggered like a drunk toward the sideline, where he writhed until the ambulance arrived from the far end zone. Instinctively, I found Candace's face in the bleachers. She was videotaping intermittently, whenever she saw me run out onto the field. "Oh my God!" she mouthed.

"Nice hit," Milton would write to Green in the Red and Black Web site guestbook a few days later. "Dislocated shoulder, but I'll be back for the playoffs." He added, "I'm a pocket passer from now on." When people ask me if the semi-pro game was vicious, I tell them about this play.

The Vipers withstood the Red and Black's knockout blow, replacing Milton with towering six-foot-five backup quarterback Chris Bresnahan, a former University of New Hampshire standout who had signed with the NFL's New England Patriots out of college in 1997 as the fourth quarterback behind Pro Bowler Drew Bledsoe. The better of the two Viper passers, Bresnahan promptly moved the Vipers to the lead late in the half, again exploiting the soft coverage of Watertown corners with slant passes to Rychard Dykes and Porche and finally connecting with Johnny Anderson for a four-yard score. After the Watertown defense forced a safety on another fumbled exchange, the Viper lead was 7–5 at half.

Doug Black connected with Odell Bowens from twenty-five yards out in the third quarter, staking the Red and Black to a 12–7 lead, but Syracuse had a touchdown to answer. Scott Ford's second field goal nudged the Red and Black out in front again, 15–14, late in the period. But as the Watertown defense seemed to tire late in the game, Viper running backs Marty Clanton and Johnny Hall were able to get the corner on toss sweeps, breaking off demoralizing ten-yard gains on third and long to keep drives alive. A third Viper touchdown and extra point put the home team ahead again at 21–15.

Scott Ford added another field goal, and when the Watertown defense held on a late-fourth-quarter possession, forcing a Viper punt, Al Countryman inserted himself as the punt returner, supplanting speedy Toby Mason, who'd had some trouble with fumbling. Down only three points with three minutes remaining, it was as though Countryman trusted no one else with the team's fortunes. You could hardly blame him, or Ashcraft, who allowed the move: Al was a terrific player, past MVP of both the Empire and New York Amateur football leagues as both a defensive back and a running back. He punted, held the ball on placekicks, and returned kickoffs for the Red and Black. Whom else would you want back there?

Countryman got under the high Bresnahan punt around the Watertown thirty-five yard line, but the ball drifted on him and he had to extend his right leg to steady himself. Catching punts is difficult to begin with and now he was out of position, his body committed awkwardly in one direction. The ball fell from the deep dark of the Syracuse night, past the halo of field lights, screaming toward earth, and even before the ball slipped through Countryman's arms, rolling down his right leg and off his shoe tops, I knew he'd muffed it. A Viper gunner sprinting down in coverage dove on the ball near the Watertown sideline, practically at Ashcraft's feet. "Defense!" Ashcraft yelled. You could hear in his voice it was over.

Ashcraft actually inserted me at right defensive end for those final two meaningless minutes—Candace has the five or six plays on video. The Vipers handed the ball inside to Clanton twice and I did my best to shake their smallish tight end and get to the ballcarrier. Prior to the third-down play, Watertown defensive back Tilson Hargrove tussled with a Syracuse receiver and was ejected, the resultant penalty moving the ball inside the twenty. Johnny Hall took the ball down near the goal line on a sweep left; then Bresnahan pushed the ball over for a touchdown. After a Watertown offside penalty on the conversion, Bresnahan sneaked again for the two-point conversion, making the final 29–18.

After the game Lynn Patrick and other defenders made no bones about their frustration with the offense's production, though no one mentioned the muffed punt. Privately, Britton seethed; he had questioned Black's decision on a pass play late in the game and the quarterback had angrily rebutted him. "You see anybody open out there?" Black had barked to the sideline.

Candace's family and I stopped to eat at a favorite family hot dog stand near the field before we drove out to the Fey home for the night. "What did your boss have to say after that one?" Fred Fey asked me over a foot-long coney.

"You are two of the more stubborn people I have ever met," a marriage counselor once told my wife Candace and me, matter-of-factly.

It's a sharp autumn Sunday and we have been arguing for several minutes now, watching a Bears-Packers game. Northern New York is the first place I've lived where autumn arrives so distinctly—trees full of red and gold leaves across the loud river, the smell of woodstoves waking up in the houses on our block. A great day to be outside, but here we are, slumping into the new overstuffed sofa we could not afford.

"It's not called an after point," I insist. "It's extra point. Trust me, it's one of my only assignments—the extra-point team."

Candace last watched football in January of 1986, the last time the Bears won the Super Bowl, with her dad or some boyfriend from a Syracuse church youth group, I don't remember. At Thanksgiving, her sisters will hide the television remote from her father and me so we can't watch Turkey Day games, but Jake has been in Alabama three months now and today while the baby naps she's decided to make a newlywed's effort.

"Listen. What does P.A.T. stand for?" she asks.

"Point after touchdown," I tell her.

"Exactly. They call it the 'P.A.T.' and the 'point after'——why not 'after point' instead of 'extra point.' It sounds much cuter."

"Cuter, yeah. I don't know, Candy," I say.

Belonging

> Why are we haunted by the smell of torn earth and winter grass and the taste of time? I think I know and I think you know too. There are some things in life which have a poignance which belongs not so much to them as to the human circumstances which surround them—to the fact that they are common human experiences—experiences in common.... [Football]'s poignance is that same poignance.
> —Archibald MacLeish, "Moonlighting on Yale Field"

On the morning of September 11, 2001, I was at the changing table dressing Jackson when the second airliner crashed into the World Trade Center. "Is this instant replay or another plane?" Candace called from in front of the television. She had been watching *The Today Show* when an NBC newscaster broke in to report the crash of the first plane. We lingered in front of the set a few minutes, then both went on to work. No one had yet said anything about terrorists. We didn't realize this would become one of those "where were you?" moments, like Pearl Harbor or the assassination of JFK. Sometimes history feels exactly like getting off to work.

My teaching partner Liz Regosin and I watched CNN's coverage with the first-year students in our ten A.M. "American Identities" course. We were only a couple of weeks into the term and many of the kids were New York City natives, many others a long way from home. News anchors reiterated the same sketchy details until the towers fell before our eyes.

I wandered through the rest of my teaching day, excusing absences outside classroom doors, inviting discussion of the day's events once inside. By then you knew. Our lives were changed.

I called Coach Ashcraft at home around three P.M. to find out if he planned to practice. "I think we have to, Professor," he told me. I made the drive down, tuned to NPR from curb to curb. Because Fort Drum had been placed on high alert, the seventeen Red and Black players stationed there couldn't leave to attend practice and we had our lowest numbers of the season, fewer than twenty guys and every one a Caucasian. While we dressed, guys put aside usual discussions of pro wrestling and pieced together what we'd heard on the news. The symbolic dimension of the attack was big with my teammates—the events occurring on 9/11, the names of airlines hijacked (American and United, as in "States"). This was so early many of us were waiting for an attack on the West Coast somewhere.

At the university, I had spent the day analyzing the events in New York and Washington with students and colleagues, and heard in-depth reports from NPR on the way down, but my teammates in Watertown had no interest in that kind of thing. They wanted to retaliate. "The football player travels the straightest of lines," writes Don DeLillo in his 1972 novel *End Zone.* "His thoughts are wholesomely commonplace, his actions uncomplicated by history, enigma, holocaust or dream." Like Hemingway's Great War, here was the generation's defining event, the ultimate excuse to flex American muscle, display the emotion American men devote so much energy to bottling. I think of the rash of songs recorded in the months following by male country musicians—guys like Toby Keith and Aaron Tippin—that promised American butt kickings.

This was the moment I sensed most strongly differences between myself and the other guys on the team, the ones my colleague hinted at. I had been able to get excited about head-butting McNeil months before, perhaps because I sensed my personal safety depended on it, but I could summon no blood-thirst now. At a tender age I had imbibed what I call football coach values—God, family, country, football—and loved war-movie chauvinism. Yet my education had largely been a re-consideration of all that. A colleague in the Global Studies Department announced he would teach a course in the spring called "Why They Hate Us" in which he and students would seek reasons behind the terrorist attack, and I found my responses to the tragedy were more like his, though I was careful not to express such sentiments to my teammates; even my sister Mary thought me cold, she who drove past hundreds of abandoned cars at commuter rail stops near her home in north Jersey and prayed at Mass each Sunday for parishioners killed in the attacks.

One of the central questions I posed coming back to foot-ball had been whether someone like me who aspired to mercy and gentleness could abide such a violent game, whether I could embrace the game—its directness and brutality—without embracing the metaphoric comparisons between football and warfare that saturate our culture, without having that vio-lence bleed into other parts of my life.

Football detractors like Chicago Divintity School dean Shailer Matthews love war/football comparisons. "Football teaches virility and courage," he commented in 1905, the heart of the red-meat era, a year when seventy-three people were killed playing football, "but so does war." Oddly, though, football players and apologists for the game employ them too. "I'd go to war with him any day" is among the highest order of compliments one football player can pay another. While World War I veteran Archibald MacLeish admits football is far from war, he does claim that in both arenas men become brothers through a shared, physical struggle. Following 9/11, the media lionized Arizona Cardinals All-Pro safety Pat Tillman who, as if taking these comparisons literally, elected to forgo the final years of a multimillion-dollar football contract to join the U.S. Army's Special Forces and fight in the Middle East.

But like my fictional colleague, DeLillo's anxious professor Alan Zapalac, I draw distinctions. "Warfare is warfare," Zapalac tells *End Zone* hero Gary Harkness (who hails, coincidentally, from northern New York, a small town in the Adirondacks). "We don't need substitutes," Zapalac goes on, "because we have the real thing." I enjoy football's contact, always have, the way a schoolboy enjoys roughhousing, but it seems silly to compare the game's violence and risk to that of warfare. I just never thought of football that way, and players like Bill Romanowski and Ray Lewis notwithstanding, I doubt many football players do.

McNeil and I talk about it a little on the bus trip a few weeks later. We've stopped for provisions at a supermarket and I notice he's wearing his University of Kansas sweatshirt again. I ask if he had attended KU or visited Lawrence, a favorite destination of mine in my Nebraska days.

"I got this when I was in the military out there," he tells me.

"I bet you're happy not to be army anymore," I say.

"I tell you what, I'm glad it's Bush in there and not Clinton," he says. "Republicans know how to fight a war."

As bodies were pulled from the rubble at Ground Zero the week of the terrorist attacks, the NFL announced that its Sunday games would be canceled and area high schools and colleges followed suit, but we had heard no such news from the EFL and continued to prepare for our September 15 rematch with the 1–6 Lake City Stars. The guestbook at the league Web site was full of protests, calls for a reconsideration, but play went on as planned. Most teams had no wiggle room in rental contracts with local parks and rec commissions in charge of much-used playing fields.

The Red and Black had hardly practiced on Tuesday the eleventh, just stretched and walked through agilities, but on Thursday we did our utmost to conduct a football practice. "Here's an hour and a half where you don't have to worry about things," Ashcraft told us. At the close of the workout, Sam Verbeck distributed small American flag decals to be worn on the backs of our helmets. It was the traditional manner in which football players displayed respect to fallen coaches and players, part of the code; after coach Paul "Bear" Bryant's death, University of Alabama players wore a decal resembling Bryant's trademark houndstooth hat. I was nobody's patriot, unless you thought like Walter Lippmann that opposition was crucial to the success of democracy, and I had some issues with my government and my country. But I had worked hard to make headway with these men, to gain the modicum of acceptance I had. I wanted them to like me. Refusing the sticker in a conspicuous way would almost certainly undo that, and even neglecting to affix it to my headgear might cause a stir, so I too wore the flag.

The pregame ceremony at cozy Penfield Park in Plattsburgh held up kickoff by thirty minutes. The brother-in-law of a Plattsburgh player, a New York City firefighter, had been killed, and the team was dedicating the game that night to him and the other victims of the attacks. The community also wanted to acknowledge sacrifices made by Watertown players in the armed forces (this was an old air force base town after all). There was the invocation, the national anthem, then that awful Lee Greenwood song "God Bless the USA" crackled over the PA.

The underdog Stars rode the emotion of the week's events straight into the contest, while the Red and Black struggled early, plagued by the flatness and lack of focus that can strike a favored road team. Certainly the 9/11 events were a factor, but that alone would not have explained a similar performance against the Thunder three weeks before. Lake City had moved the ball all the way to the Watertown four yard line midway through the first quarter, and on a crucial third-and-short play Stars quarterback Craig Duprey employed a hard count to draw the Red and Black defense offsides. When Lake City offensive linemen appeared to jump instead, the Watertown defense relaxed. But officials made no call and Duprey took the snap and rolled untouched past flat-footed Watertown defenders into the end zone, staking the Stars to a stunning 7–0 lead. An upset of this magnitude would require heads-up plays just like that one.

The score seemed to awaken the sleeping Watertown giant, with Doug Black connecting on four touchdown passes in the second quarter, the first to Odell Bowens and the next three to Marcus Harrison. After that first 58–22 meeting weeks before, Stars coach Ed McCalister claimed the Red and Black had caught his team without one of its better cover cornerbacks, but it was now clear that Lake City, even with its full complement, simply lacked athletes in the secondary who could run with Watertown receivers.

I played at least a third of the snaps with the starting defense during the first half, Ashcraft having grown to trust me to spell starters Chris "The Hammer" Littel and Mike Delles at defensive end. I entered the game with confidence by this point in the season, certain of my assignment and competence, though I never seemed to make the sort of plays that would keep me in a ball game very long. "I want some pressure on the quarterback," Ashcraft would tell me, whether inserting me in the game or pulling me out.

Lake City recovered an onside kick to begin the second half, again catching the flat Red and Black team offguard. The flurry of second-quarter touchdown passes should have put the Stars away, but they roared back on the emotion of the turnover. Old football wisdom says special-teams disasters like blocked punts and kickoff-return touchdowns key upset victories. Credit Lake City coach McCalister with doing what he could from the sideline to bring about just such a play. The Red and Black team seemed distracted, searching all evening for that moment in the game when they could relax, while Lake City seemed to react in the opposite way to the week's events, relying on emotion to spark an impossible comeback. Duprey connected twice with all-league wide receiver Brian Chrietzberg for touchdowns in the third quarter and once more early in the fourth to pull within three points at 31–28.

As he'd done against the Capitaland Thunder, army sergeant Odell Bowens took the team on his back on the next drive, exhorting the offense and the sideline as he took the field, then, on a trademark post route, taking a Doug Black pass sixty-four yards for the game's final score.

Perhaps the Stars' resilience explained Mike Britton's desire to keep the ball in the air even late in the game, to keep the pedal to the floor, or maybe it was the Sun Tzu *Art of War* stuff he had cribbed from University of Florida coach Steve Spurrier, an idol, but at the very end of the game, with the Red and Black already up by ten, Britton had backup quarterback Lafex running a pass play deep in the Plattsburgh end.

"Al told Lafex not to run it, to take a knee," Ashcraft told me later. "Britton totally lost it." Somehow I missed that sideline episode, but it must have been what prompted Lake City coach McCalister's remark about Countryman's class.

According to Ashcraft, Britton quit on the spot, and when he'd reconsidered over the weekend and asked to finish out the campaign, Ashcraft took him back only on the absurd condition that he do no coaching. "He told me to stand on the sideline and keep my mouth shut the rest of the year," Britton said to me.

The final was 38–28. Black finished with 317 yards passing and five touchdowns, no rust apparent in his performance, though no passion either. On the field afterward, following the customary joint team prayer, a Stars captain wished Fort Drum soldiers Godspeed. "We know you're going to Afghanistan," he said, "and we know you're going to kick ass." Players roared. "Good luck over there," one Lake City player said as he hugged my neck. "Everybody thinks you're army," Darin Phifer chuckled as we left the field.

*   *   *

The performance in Plattsburgh had become the Red and Black's mid-season modus operandi—we played to the level of our competition, as a color analyst would say, gave just enough to beat inferior opponents. A second defeat in Syracuse marked three in a row to the Vipers, all close games. We had entered the second meeting 3–1, a game behind Syracuse in the Northern Division with a shot at home field advantage in the playoffs, but afterward found ourselves only a game above .500, all but assured of no better than second place in the division.

Only twenty-three or twenty-four players attended practices, not one of them Doug Black. They had become more or less perfunctory. The nip of fall's approach unmistakable in the air, we spent extra time at the beginning loosening up, but once we scrimmaged we took it easy on one another. Even NFL teams conduct only one or two full-contact practices during the regular season anymore, the risk of injury being too great. Most Watertown starters were already nursing injuries anyway, and all of us felt the toll of the long season in our joints and bones.

Resuming my teaching responsibilities meant an additional distraction for me. I was a bit wearier climbing into the car for the drive to Watertown for practice, had even less time for my family. There's a lot of research done on football's affect on off-field aggression—supposedly the testosterone produced in men simply *watching* football makes Super Bowl Sunday the year's worst night of domestic violence, to say nothing about the levels in a man playing the sport—but I didn't notice a major change in my own demeanor. I was simply crankier, less available to my students outside of class, just like anyone else moonlighting from his day job.

The university deployed its photographer to the fairgrounds for our rematch with the Capitaland Thunder the last weekend in August to get some shots of me on the field, to have on file in case something came of my experiment and they wanted to run a story in the alumni magazine. We exchanged e-mails that week about directions to the game and how to get the best shots—"watch the sideline," I quipped. Fortunately,

Coach Britton had me on the front line of his kick-return team and Ashcraft used me here and there as a defensive end, so the photographer did have something to shoot.

Other than a Scott Ford field goal on the game's first possession, the tough Thunder defense stymied Watertown, forcing two punts and two turnovers in the next four possessions. "It was a very sluggish game," Ashcraft would say afterward. "It was like that in our locker room. It was like that in our pregame. It was like we had a big gloom over us."

A twenty-yard Kavery Pace touchdown pass had the Thunder ahead 7–3 when the Red and Black took possession of the ball on their own twenty-five yard line with seven seconds remaining in the half. Receiver Marcus Harrison later told the *Daily Times* that Black entered the huddle and told the offense, "The name of this play is 'Make Something Happen.' We went out and did that."

Pressured up the middle on the play, Black dumped the ball to Harrison in the right flat, near the sideline. The receiver shook initial tacklers then headed across the field. As the Thunder defense converged a second time, Harrison slipped to the ground, regained his footing, then heard receiver Odell Bowens yell, "Pitch it!" Harrison claims he never saw Bowens but pitched it to the voice, and Bowens, younger brother of Miami Dolphins All-Pro defensive lineman Tim, raced the remaining sixty-six yards up the right sideline for the score, giving Watertown a 10–7 halftime lead.

While the Bowens touchdown energized the home team, the Thunder never recovered from the wacky end-of-the-half play. Thunder player/coach Paul Vasko, a forty-something car dealer, claimed Harrison was down before his lateral and refused interviews after the game. Officials ruled Harrison was never touched while on the ground and allowed the play to stand. "It was all a legal play," said Harrison. "Odell just took it to the house."

Ashcraft rotated me with speedy if undersized starting defensive ends Chris Littel and Mike Delles in the second half to get more pressure on Thunder passer Pace. The giant tackle I faced wore a face mask that resembled a chain-link fence and I was rarely in the game for a whole series before being pulled. Pace and his receivers exploited the Red and Black's weakness against the slant pass, and Adbul Akili-Duncan scored on a twenty-one-yard slant with a little more than six minutes remaining in the game, pulling the Thunder within three at 17–14.

Al Countryman was enjoying his best night of the year to that point, gaining 94 tough yards on twenty carries and scoring two fourth-quarter touchdowns. "In a big game like this, [Countryman] is going to do big things," Ashcraft later told the paper. The conversion failed, making the final Watertown 23, Capitaland 14. No one asked Black to explain his absence. Like the rest of us, he'd once again been just good enough to win.

I skipped our next game, a road trip to the scenic Adirondack town of Glens Falls, New York, to play the Greenjackets. There are football purists reading this who will say I forfeited my right to play by doing so. Maybe. I had a legitimate excuse. I had long before committed to teaching that weekend at an annual high school writers' conference that Saint Lawrence University hosts at its camp on Saranac Lake in the Adirondacks, and as an untenured faculty person I needed the money as well as the goodwill I would earn by doing it.

But then it was never a matter of guys having good excuses. Mike Lafex had missed games that season to attend a wedding, Howery for a custody hearing in Virginia, several others for work. It was that the coaches expected more, expected sacrifice. Winning required it—didn't Al Countryman work double shifts the entire off-season at the prison to ensure he'd have game and practice nights off? Home field advantage was very real in the EFL: jobs and other commitments often decimated road team rosters, and squads that traveled well, so to speak, usually wound up in the playoffs. I was sure my absence would ruin the goodwill I imagined I had begun to establish with Coach Ashcraft over the past few games, lose what playing time I had earned for myself. I stopped him after both practices that week to explain. "You gotta do what you gotta do," he told me.

It promised to be an occasion. Countryman entered play four yards shy of Coach Britton's twenty-year-old all-time Red and Black rushing record of 4,047 yards, poised to break it on perhaps on his first carry. Ashcraft suggested to me later it was this fact that had actually provoked Britton's ire back in Plattsburgh. The teams' historic rivalry was a nice stage for a record-breaking evening: themselves established in 1932, the 3–3 Greenjackets were the only other EFL team with a history as rich as Watertown's and the two had always enjoyed tight contests. "I can tell you this game won't be a laugher," Ashcraft was quoted as saying in the *Daily Times*.

I tried all week to think of a way I could be two places at once, that I might sneak off and drive from the camp to Glens Falls for the game. I had a miserable time at the camp, longing for my own game and for a once-in-a-century clash between Nebraska and Notre Dame televised that Saturday afternoon. I am afraid my high school charges sensed my distraction.

I read the next morning that Countryman did indeed break the record early in the first quarter, finishing with 42 yards on thirteen carries, as the Red and Black rolled to a 40–12 win. Doug Black's second of four touchdown passes on the night (three to Harrison, one to Wash) was also a record breaker, the one hundred twentieth of his career, though his feat received far less fanfare. A twenty-five-year-old Greenjacket player, after returning a blocked Scott Ford field goal attempt ninety yards for a touchdown, fell into cardiac arrest in the end zone and spent the night in intensive care.

"I'm glad it's over," Countryman told the paper. "It's just something that guys have been talking about for a year and a half. Now we can worry about getting the championship."

Home to Tennessee for a Thanksgiving visit during graduate school, my younger sister Ruth and I decided to catch a high school playoff game in the tiny town of Huntingdon thirty miles east. Ruth had been a football cheerleader in her high school days, married the quarterback. The hometown Mustangs were set to face the Union City Golden Tornadoes for the right to play in the class 2A state championship game in Nashville the following week. I was surprised at how the whole experience seemed a trip back in time, back not only the ten years since we were teenagers but further—cars parked half in ditches all along the road that led to the dusty little field, everyone in town pressed against the ropes that marked its boundaries, the nasal twang of the little PA announcer screaming into his mike as though he weren't wired to speakers. The zeal was religious, like a tent revival. It might have been 1950.

"You remember it this way?" I asked Ruth.

"Oh yeah," she said.

Around the same time, my dad sent me a funny short story by Texas writer Gary Gay about a high school boy in football-crazed West Texas (Friday Night Lights country) who quits the football team and spends the rest of the year explaining himself to everyone in his tiny hometown. "Know what it's like to be a heretic?" he begins. "I do, because I live in Arlis, Texas, and don't play football."

That's the way I remember Martin, Tennessee. Every boy of a certain age had to take a position one way or another on the football question. It defined him. I was lucky to have grown up with both interest and modest ability where football was concerned, but many boys my age, some the sons of former high school grid greats, had neither, yet they joined us on the field anyway to prove their mettle. We had all grown up believing the game was the only route to manhood. It's possible that what I had hoped the game would give me as a boy—local glory, the favor of pretty girls, a sense of conviction regarding my own toughness—had not changed at all in my time away.

Bitter End

Oh yeah! Life goes on
Long after the thrill of livin' is gone
> —John Cougar, "Jack and Diane"

Early in the season, Coach Ashcraft wheeled a high-end, industrial-sized, stainless steel gas grill into back of the locker room near the showers, where it sat the rest of the year. On most Thursday nights the coach and a group of veteran players hung around after practice to drink beer and fire up burgers and hot dogs. So far as I could tell everyone was welcome (if not officially invited), but most guys went on home after practice broke up at nine. My commute meant I rarely made it home before eleven P.M. even if I started back without a shower, so hanging around any later than necessary didn't usually seem prudent. The commute probably explained in part the distance I still felt existed between me and most of my teammates, though, and by the week of the rematch with Montreal late in September I realized I was running out of chances. I told Candace not to wait up.

I showered after practice that Thursday and watched Call and Countryman climb into cars and head home. Lynn Patrick stayed, though, and Eddie Pierce. Matt Quay and Jesse Lamora, Mike Lafex, who mowed the fairgrounds for the city during the week, and a safety from Canisius College in Buffalo named Kris Sullivan, whom I had gotten to know on the sideline.

Bachelors mostly with no kids to tuck in. Coach Ashcraft provided the food and beer and he was well into a second or third Budweiser by the time I got into my street clothes.

We grilled under the grandstand just outside the locker room door, huddled around the grill for warmth. I asked thirty-eight-year-old Lynn Patrick about his playing days at Buffalo State in the mid-eighties, and if he thought the end of his semi-pro career was drawing nigh. He had become the Red and Black's all-time leading tackler earlier this year and was poised to again finish among the EFL's top tacklers for the season.

"Me, I'm gonna play forever," he said.

Ashcraft had been there for Patrick's catastrophic tibia fracture years before, the worst the coach told me he'd ever seen. "I don't think anything can stop him," Ashcraft said.

Patrick told me he thought I would see a lot of playing time the next year if I stuck it out.

"It's tough for rookies," he said. "Your problem is you should have been playing defense all along."

Other than that football didn't come up much. Kris Sullivan talked about the school counselor job he had looked into up in St. Lawrence County where I lived, Patrick about the house he, an electrician by trade, was building himself out in La Fargeville.

After a burger and a few beers, I headed into the locker room toward the bathroom where I found Coach Ashcraft at the desk in the small equipment room that doubled as his office. "Cowz," he said, "I'm glad you hung around."

"Yeah, I keep hearing that tonight," I replied. He handed me a beer.

If Ashcraft's position makes him part carnival barker, he's also part zookeeper. When the EFL threatened to run background checks on team rosters a few years back, Ashcraft joked he'd lose half his team, though he was quick to point out that when his players did run afoul of the law it was usually in the off-season when they didn't have football to provide them structure.

"What I offer men is like a manly kind of rehab," he told me once. "Players at this level, you gotta trust 'em and you gotta love 'em."

"Geez," Ashcraft said now, admiring his midsection between swigs from his beer can. "I put this weight back on every season. I get up close to three hundred pounds. then I take it off again every summer. I run every day—"

"Chasing a beer truck?" Lynn Patrick yelled, headed himself for the urinals.

"See that," Ashcraft said to me. "These players love me but they don't respect me."

I know he means it. It has been hard for me to discern over the last several months exactly how Ashcraft "coached" anyway. As the organization's president, he arranged practice and game schedules, delivered pregame speeches, decided on starting lineups (with consultation from players like Call and Countryman, no doubt), talked to the media, bickered with city hall over facilities and equipment. Figurehead stuff. But I knew he didn't grade film or scout opponents and I had never observed him making defensive adjustments during games or at halftime.

"My defense is pretty simple," Ashcraft told me once. "If a guy doesn't understand what I'm running, he doesn't belong on the field." Britton sent in the offensive plays and Black ran them or didn't, but Ashcraft steered clear of that kind of decision making. After all, like Providence College basketball coach Pete Gillen, who hesitated to correct the play of NBA Olympians while an assistant coach for Dream Team II for fear they'd "buy Providence and fire me,"

Ashcraft had little authority when it counted. Without a scholarship to pull or paycheck to withhold, what leverage might a semi-pro coach apply to compel players to practice? Making people happy had to be priority number one or he'd have no team. I didn't envy him that.

Apparently Ashcraft's devotion to players and their happiness, to Doug Black in particular, had finally ruined things between himself and Coach Britton. Through the middle of the season, anticipating Black's continued absence, Britton had installed new dimensions to his offense, wrinkles that would better suit the talents of scrambling quarterback Mike Lafex, the only signal caller who attended practice anymore. When Black showed up at gametime every week, though, Ashcraft backed him. "As long as we're winning," Ashcraft told Britton, "Douggie starts." Britton's new scheme was all but scrapped. "Backing a player instead of his coaching staff," Britton said to me later. "I knew it was over then."

I asked Ashcraft about this.

"Mike can't get along with players. Simple as that," he said that night in his office. "Mike's an X's and O's guy. "But I know people."

As we finished our beers, Ashcraft asked me, "So what's this I hear about Mike's new team up north?"

"I don't know," I said, thinking on my feet as best I could. "Some of us are tired of the driving." I hadn't spoken to Britton about the matter since that afternoon in my car and I wasn't sure who had leaked the news to Ashcraft.

"I don't care what anybody says," Ashcraft told me after a moment. "You can party with me anytime."

When the coach got in his truck to drive home, the handful of players still hanging on decided we should move the party to a Coffeen Street nightclub called Mardi Gras. I rode in Quay's Camaro but I felt old and out of place once we arrived, more tired than drunk, and spent most of the evening talking to a Red and Black alum who had played against the legendary Frank Yannick–led Scranton Eagle teams of the eighties.

●　●　●

Watertown's own commemoration of the September 11 attacks preceded the game with the Montreal Condors two nights later at the fairgrounds. The infernal Lee Greenwood song again. Condor players were effusive in their condolences. "God Bless the USA," wrote one Condor player in the Red and Black Web site guestbook.

Montreal had managed to get only twenty-four players across the border that night but the Watertown performance resembled all those the team had turned in since the second loss to the Vipers, since Black had stopped attending practice: "dominant but sloppy," wrote Rob Oatman in the *Daily Times* the next day. Ashcraft had to concede that, but he did so carefully. "They haven't played their best game yet," he told Oatman. "It's a win, it's not a loss. There's nothing to get all paranoid about. But I really feel this team can be so much better than it is. Maybe it will still happen this year. I don't know." Trademark Ashcraft diplomacy: the noncritique critique, the "excuse-me" exhortation. Maybe we'll play better.

Like Lake City the previous week, the Condors jumped to an early lead on a nifty wraparound draw play to fullback Andrew Blevins from three yards out. Condor quarterback Wyeth suckered Red and Black ends Littel and Delles upfield with his drop, then slipped the ball to Blevins, who waited a count, staring straight upfield, then dashed toward the line of scrimmage, past Watertown defenders caught flat-footed or headed full speed the other way toward the empty-handed quarterback. They probably called that play four times in the opening drive alone.

The Red and Black answered on the strength of Countryman's 124 first-half rushing yards and two Black to Earnie Wash touchdown passes. Three-hundred-pound tackle Jamee Call, inserted in the backfield in one of Britton's new offensive sets, a short-yardage formation called "jumbo," also scored on a five-yard dive in the second quarter, and the home team had a 21–6 lead at halftime. The Red and Black took a 35–6 lead headed into the final period.

The Condors mounted a late comeback, however, just like the ones Watertown had held off the week before and in most other wins that season. On the strength of receiver Geoff Brown's eleven-catch, 144-yard performance and several timely draws to Blevins, Montreal scored 12 fourth-quarter points. Ashcraft had begun to platoon me with the starting defensive ends, though I was as susceptible to the draw as they were. The key was Condor tackle Pantalakis, who left his stance on the draw play the same way he did on any other, dropping his foot as if to pass protect. He offered no clues at the snap as to what the play would be, and by the time I read draw Blevins was all but behind me.

I recorded no tackles, though I did manage to add to our sloppiness by drawing an unsportsmanlike-conduct penalty late in the fourth for a late hit I gave quarterback Wyeth. On a play that called for the Montreal quarterback to roll away from me, I gave frantic chase, arriving three or four steps after Wyeth had thrown the ball away. A step or two was forgivable but not four, though I doubt officials would have made the call had Wyeth not performed his pain so well and loudly lying on the ground.

"You're like I was," Ashcraft told me when he got me to the sideline. "You're not gonna run that far without hitting somebody."

Countryman sliced through the Montreal defense as he'd done in the first meeting, though this time, with backup Erin Woodard deployed at Fort Polk in Louisiana, he got all the carries and finished with 159 yards rushing on twenty attempts.

The Red and Black, now 7–2 on the year, clinched a playoff spot with the win, and home field advantage through the first round, though the team seemed no more certain of itself than Ashcraft had been. Maybe we'd play to our enormous potential in the coming weeks, but who could say?

Watertown entered the playoffs on a five-game winning streak, the Northern Division's second-ranked club having squeaked by Glens Falls 21–14 in the regular season finale, but I dare say we didn't feel like winners. The season had grown long for a team that had started practice seventy-eight days before the ten-week season began. Doug Black had completed only eight of twenty-four passes for just over one hundred yards the previous weekend against the Greenjackets, his lack of practice time becoming increasingly obvious.

Watertown's first-round playoff opponent, the Capitaland Thunder, headed into their eleventh road contest of the year having lost all four of its meetings against playoff-bound teams, including two to the Red and Black. But the margin of defeat in the two earlier games had been a combined thirteen points, and they had destroyed the 1–9 Lake City Stars 52–16 in the final game of the regular season on the strength of three first-half touchdowns by aging third-string Thunder quarterback Len Noisette, who would get the start at Watertown.

The pregame forecast called for chilly temperatures and possible drizzle at the fairgrounds, so I broke out the leggings and long-sleeved mock turtleneck, both made of a Wickaway neoprene, which I'd bought online months back. Ashcraft didn't have me in the lineup to begin with and I figured I would need to stay warm and dry.

The Watertown offense opened strong, moving sixty-seven yards in nine plays, the last Al Countryman's five-yard up-the-gut touchdown run. In truth, the Red and Black never looked back, scoring in the second quarter on a forty-four-yard Black to Harrison touchdown pass and a Scott Ford field goal. With only twenty-six seconds left in the first half, Noisette seemed to catch the Red and Black defense headed to the locker room a play or two early, completing a forty-eight-yard touchdown strike to John Mulino, who'd gotten behind the napping defense.

But the eleven-game road schedule seemed to have taken its toll on the Thunder, so game in the two earlier meetings. Only twenty-five players made the trip from Albany, and the team played as though content for their season to end.

"We were kind of expecting a closer game after the first two, the way they went," Doug Black told the paper afterward. "I think the running game, getting going early, really helped us out."

Ashcraft placed me on the kickoff team to start the second half, at head hunter just to the right of kicker Scott Ford. As speedy kick returner Akili Duncan fielded the ball, he darted right, drawing the defense to him, then stopped, waiting for what I diagnosed right away as a reverse developing back to his left, just in front of me in my lane. The bit of razzle-dazzle was a good call. Despite the Red and Black's statistical domination, the Thunder team trailed only 17–7 and was desperate to perpetuate whatever momentum had been gained by Noisette's last-second touchdown pass the previous half. Plattsburgh's onside kick had met with great success in their second meeting with Watertown only a month before, sparking a roaring comeback.

Duncan tossed the ball back toward trailing returner Chris Brown, who planned to head back left along the visitor's sideline. But Duncan's hesitation had been fatal, the play too long in developing. I lay out, my body fully extended, and got a gloved hand on the lateral before it reached Brown, landing on my belly as a swarm of Red and Black players recovered the ball. The fairgrounds were hard, frosty. Doug Black turned that Thunder turnover, one of six Thunder giveaways and perhaps my most significant contribution of the season, into points on the next play, an eighteen-yard slant pass to Earnie Wash. The Thunder gamble had backfired and the Red and Black rout was on, 24–7.

Ashcraft emptied the bench after that, which was not altogether good news for me. McNeil decided he was finished early in the fourth quarter, so I went in at left guard and with 3:36 left led Erin Woodward on a thirty-six-yard touchdown run—the "26" play we'd been running since May. I covered the ensuing kickoff, thoroughly winded, then Ashcraft motioned for me to stay in to play very the next series at end with second-team defense. I turned a toss sweep back inside then chased down Noisette as he scrambled to throw, drawing my second roughing call of the season. It was as much continuous action as I had seen all season and I was relieved when Ashcraft pulled me after the penalty. I found McNeil on the sideline.

"I can't go," I told him, practically wheezing.

"What are you talking about, there's like a minute left," he said smiling. "Ain't this what you wanted?"

It was, yes, and back in August I was in the sort of physical shape that might have allowed me to play both ways. But that was months ago. I took the field again with the second offense to run out the clock.

Afterward Ashcraft spun the win a bit differently than had Black, crediting the team with putting everything together for the first time all season in the 44–14 win.

● ● ●

Al Countryman told assembled media at our practice the following Thursday before the divisional championship game with the Vipers that he absolutely believed the Red and Black could beat the defending champs in the third meeting between the two teams, though he realized he might be the only guy on the team who thought so. Maybe veterans understood his confidence, he said, but younger Watertown players seemed intimidated by the Vipers.

I wanted to believe a victory against the Vipers was possible, even imminent, and a win at Griffin Field Saturday night might turn our disappointing season around. But our performance thus far that season made it difficult to believe we could make it happen. I am afraid it was precisely my age and experience, rather than my relative "youth" as our captain had suggested, that made me skeptical. A true motivator, a Lou Holtz type, with a few well-placed challenges to individual players during the week and a fiery pregame pep talk, might work a bunch of high school or college kids into such a froth that they believed they could win this game (with a solid game plan, the talent was there to actually pull it off). I had been part of a high school team that upset a state-ranked opponent favored to win by 35 points and even now when I see the game film I marvel at how undersized we were, how overmatched, how impossible the win actually was.

The Red and Black players weren't kids anymore, however (Countryman himself was hinting about retirement). I fancied I could size up a situation pretty quickly and this did not look good: a lame-duck offensive coach, a quarterback who didn't practice, a game plan that hadn't been adjusted in the slightest since the last time this team handled us. Unlike high school kids who believed football was everything, that the NFL lay ahead for us, we had jobs and families and whole strings of disappointments, personal and professional, which taught us that life went on, no matter how a game turned out.

I realize it's another football heresy to think that way. Probably it was yet another dimension of what separated me from great ones like Countryman, this inviolate belief in oneself and the team and the fact that I just didn't have it. In fact I felt guilty even at the time about my negative attitude. While Sam Verbeck taped my ankles before the game, on a set of aluminum bleachers at Griffin Field near where Ashcraft had parked his enormous red and black pickup, I told him I thought we had them this time, as if my positive thoughts might will us to victory.

"Oh yeah," Verbeck said. "Oh yeah."

The city of Syracuse had recently determined the contest would be the last football game played at Griffin, presumably to make room for high school soccer games, and the city seemed to have already begun to pull up stakes: the scoreboard wasn't operational and there was to be no PA system that night either. "I've seen Pop Warner games better prepared," Ashcraft said afterward. "For this level of the game, it's just too bad."

The Vipers were loose and chatty during pregame warm-ups. Confident. They heckled us as we returned to the locker room after a warm-up. "Here comes Johnny Flex," one said of me as I headed in. ("Don't worry," I wanted to tell him, "I probably won't see the field.") My impression was confirmed early on by a Viper defense that attacked with renewed, playoff intensity. Most of Al Countryman's ten carries resembled the scene in *Dances with Wolves* when the last Crow warrior standing, his horse ankle-deep in a riverbed, finds himself surrounded by Sioux. Al ducked tacklers, took on two and three at a time, but finished with just 45 yards rushing.

The rest of the Watertown team would have all done well to play like Countryman, give a final war cry and ride headlong at the enemy. But we played more like Doug Black, who looked like something out of *Dazed and Confused,* finishing the game for 11 of 33 for just 61 yards passing, all of them on shorter, checkdown routes. There's that locker room saw about quarterbacks receiving too much blame and too much credit, and it may apply here: on a night when the Red and Black offense netted no points and only 112 total yards, Doug Black interceptions accounted for only four of the seven Watertown turnovers. Linemen Call, Quay, and Payne seemed to sleepwalk, and McNeil couldn't contain his frustration at the offensive futility, drawing a pair of unsportsmanlike-conduct flags.

At the half the Viper lead had been only 6–0, on the strength of two Trevor Barbano field goals. "The defense played the game of their life," a tearful Countryman told the paper afterward. "They kept us in it. That was the best game the defense ever played this year. And the offense couldn't step up to the challenge."

The *Daily Times* correspondent on the sideline reported "bickering" and "a lack of composure." That was mostly linebackers Gonseth and Lynn Patrick, who, once the game was decided, heckled Doug Black after an incomplete pass or an interception. "Yeah, who needs practice when you can make throws like that," Gonseth would yell. "It's frustrating," Gonseth told the paper. It made me think of NFL coach Buddy Ryan's dominant defenses and their feuds with offensive teammates who struggled (Ryan once punched colleague and offensive coordinator Kevin Gilbride on the sideline during a game). At one point, things were so chaotic that Candace's grandfather Fred Fey felt comfortable coming out of the stands to sit next to me on the team bench. No one said a word.

Ashcraft had pretty well kept a lid on that kind of thing all season—even his gag order on Britton was still secret—but the facade was giving way. "I could tell in that playoff game in Syracuse," broadcaster Mel Busler told me later. "Britton was a glorified clipboard holder. We're talking about a guy who left body parts on the field for that team for twenty-five years."

Viper Bresnahan's numbers weren't gaudy—like New York Giant Phil Simms in the 1980s, or Tampa Bay's Brad Johnson more recently, Bresnahan's defense set up him up time and again, and he needed to convert only a few opportunities to win. He completed a thirteen-yard touchdown pass to Steve Scott with less than four mintues to go in the third quarter—another slant in front of Darin Phifer—which made the Viper lead 13–0. Then, following Black's fourth and final interception, Viper noseguard Ruben Hano-Hano, inserted at fullback à la Jamee Call, scored on a one-yard plunge to put Syracuse ahead 20–0 and salt the win away.

I entered the game at that point to play defensive end, having stood (or sat) on the sideline all night. What I needed most was a men's room—my compression pants, the chill, all those water bottles on the sideline. Candace came down from the stands to get video of those last couple of series; you can hear offensive lineman Adam Brown ask her for a copy of the tape. The Vipers' second unit struggled to get in and out of the huddle, and I was in on two or three tackles on interior running plays. "You were in on every one," Coach Britton said to me as I left the field. He'd taken a fresh interest in me those last few weeks of practice, his mind turning to the idea of the new team. When he saw the extra point team sloughing in practice, he'd send me on a stunt to block it, or blitz me against his own first-team offense.

Other than the item in the paper documenting the collapse of team composure, there was no serious postmortem offered on the 2001 season, by either the media or the Red and Black coaching staff, not one that took into account the team's play on the field, a game plan, or personnel, anyway. If asked, I might have said that had the Red and Black approached the game as underdogs, done the sorts of things underdogs do to defeat stronger opponents, the sorts of things teams like Plattsburgh did when playing Watertown, and here I mean onside kicks, fake field goals, and the like, we'd have stood a better chance. Part of the team's stubbornness, though, seemed to include an inability to acknowledge weakness, acknowledge we were underdogs. And what about film of the two prior contests? Might it have helped to view it? But no one had asked.

*   *   *

Unable to find anyone else interested in going, I drove myself to Syracuse the following Saturday night to see the 11–0 Vipers take on undefeated Southern Divison Champion Scranton in the EFL Championship game, to be played at P&C Stadium, regular home to the AAA Syracuse Skychiefs, a Toronto Blue Jays farm team. I didn't count heads to verify, but when I arrived it seemed there were more uniformed players on the field than there were fans in the stands. I'd bet there weren't a hundred people in the eleven-thousand-seat ballpark.

It's hard to say where everyone was. The powerful Syracuse University football program had hosted a college game across town in the Carrier Dome earlier in the day and there were important college games on television that evening (semipro games in July had no such competition). The sparse crowd offered me some perspective on the whole enterprise anyway, the emotional mess up in Watertown. Who really cared, beyond those guys on the field? A visitor to a Scranton Eagle Web forum debating a season-long lack of attendance there apologized for his candor but suggested that no one attended because there was nothing to see. "The EFL is a nothing league," he wrote. "Football has no real minor league . . . When was the last time a Scranton Eagle went on to become famous?"

Among the handful of spectators were Ashcraft and Verbeck and their wives, whom I found right away sitting in box seats along what would have been the third-base line. The EFL held an annual meeting following the championship to tie up loose ends and plan for the next year, which general managers and head coaches from every team were required to attend or incur a fine.

Lynn Patrick had no better reason to be there than I did. I saw him and his girlfriend in the concession line while I waited to buy some nachos. "Sit with us, Professor," Patrick offered. So I did. We walked down to where the Ashcrafts and Verbecks were seated and they all greeted us warmly.

"So is it true what I hear," I asked Patrick once we got ourselves seated. "Are you done?"

"Oh, he's done . . . or I'm leaving him," his lady friend interjected, leaning forward in her seat to find my face.

The championship game was to pit strength versus strength: the Viper defense versus the Eagle offense. The Eagles were winners of eleven of the thirty-three EFL titles contested since 1969, including threepeats between 1982 and 1984 and 1986 and 1988, last claiming the title in 1999. They lost another four championship games, including one to the season before to the Vipers, 31–24. Nineteen-year veteran quarterback John Kennedy, like Countryman a legend you've never heard of, led the team to ten of those titles and holds all-time national semi-pro records for attempts, completions, yards, touchdowns, and interceptions (the better-known Jim "King" Corcoran, Pottstown, Pennsylvania, Firebirds QB made famous in Jay Acton's *The Forgettables,* is second in many of these categories).

On the strength of trademark interception and fumble returns for touchdowns, the Vipers jumped to a first-half lead. I confess I didn't pay much attention. At the half, Coach Ashcraft invited me out to the parking lot where we met Montreal Condors owner and coach Wilbert Smith, who had loaded down his trunk with potent Canadian beer, Ashcraft's favorite. Smith's Cadillac may have been one of ten cars in a gravel lot two football fields long. Built under an I-81 overpass near the train depot, the lot would have been a good location for a gangster film.

I sipped my beer as the two men caught up. They had last visited at the EFL championship the previous year outside of Scranton, a game attended by some forty-five people. "The night before," Ashcraft recalls, "sixty-five hundred people came to watch a high school game played on the very same field. I tell you what, we'd pack the fairgrounds, standing room only." I didn't doubt the coach, semi-pro football having always been a small-city ball game.

The Vipers hung on to win their second straight EFL title that night, 24–18, but I wasn't there to see it. Hoping to catch a late college game from the West Coast, I headed home at the half. The beer had me a little sleepy anyway, and it felt right to end this thing—if that's what I was doing—the way I had begun: alone in my car.

Just a kid in Tennessee, grade school–aged, I take my Nerf football out to our vaguely gridiron-shaped backyard and replay football games I've only just watched on television. All by myself. I throw passes that I then run under and catch, even tackle myself to the ground. I have friends and play touch football with them on the playground often enough and I suppose I could ask my little brother to play with me anytime I want, but truth is I prefer the imaginary, solitary games in my yard. My performances there are consistently better.

I do the play-by-play for these imaginary games too—it's not only where I get my start as a football player but probably also as a writer, narrating my own football exploits. I always imagine myself a hard-nosed, mud-flecked halfback, courageous and reliable, a boy of few words who is just fast enough to break a long touchdown run every once in a while but who's counted on mostly for the tough yard. In fact, I am neither courageous nor quiet, but it's nice to pretend. My modesty in this regard seems funny: I could be Superman if I liked, untackleable, but somehow the story I am inventing has to seem credible. I don't dare wish for too much.

An elderly next-door neighbor named Ed Hutchens, disconcerted by my little game, calls my mother and asks when I am going to be allowed to play "real" football. Isn't right for a boy to talk to himself in that way, he mutters. In due time, my mother assures him. There's no Pop Warner league in the area, so a boy has to wait until the seventh grade to play organized football. When I reach the appropriate age I do join our junior high team, a perennial county champion, but I confess I'm still playing those lonely games in our backyard long afterward, long after I know better, know enough to be embarrassed and hide the Nerf when I hear a car driving by or see old codger Ed Hutchens's face appear in the small, octagonal window of his back door.

Dream Season

I thought of the applause afterward. Some of it was, perhaps, in appreciation of the lunacy of my participation and for the fortitude it took to do it, but most of it, even if subconscious, I decided was in relief I had done as badly as I did. It verified the assumption that the average fan would have about an amateur blundering into the brutal world of professional football.... The outsider did not belong, and there was comfort in that being proved.

—George Plimpton, *Paper Lion*

Candace agreed to accompany me to the Red and Black end-of-the-year banquet, hosted a few weeks following the playoffs by the Elks Lodge in Watertown, one exit short of the fairgrounds off Interstate 81. I wanted her to have a perspective she couldn't get from the bleachers. We dropped Jackson with his grandparents in DeKalb on the way down, then, once we reached that exit, spent a good fifteen minutes searching for the lodge though it was only a mile from the exit. As much time as I'd spent in the Watertown area that fall, I hardly knew anything about the city or its geography.

I wore a suit—the only one I owned, which my mother had bought for me before my first round of job interviews at the end of graduate school—but realized upon my arrival how ridiculously overdressed I was. Some of the other guys wore sweaters, most of them jeans. I noticed conspicuous absences right away: Doug Black (no surprise, really), Al Countryman (already working double shifts in preparation for next season), Lynn Patrick, Jamee Call, Pat Nulty, Dave McNeil. I guess they had been to enough of these things, but it would have been nice to see them, Dave and Pat especially.

Verbeck and Ashcraft were in charge of the proceedings and sat at the head table while Coach Britton sat with his family at a round table toward the back. Candace and I sat with free safety Kris Sullivan, his mother, and his girlfriend from Buffalo. We talked about our son, my book project, their engagement. I guess I started drinking right away, I don't remember.

As we dined on roast beef, Ashcraft distributed plaques to players who had been named all-league, the usual suspects. Rookie Sullivan received a well-deserved honorable mention for his work in the secondary, and I admired his hardware as it was passed around our table. Then Ashcraft announced a few team honors: Countryman was again named most valuable player and Call most valuable lineman as well as the league "Iron Man" award for his two-way play. Ashcraft accepted on behalf of both. "If we had a team of Al Countrymans," he said, "we'd be all right." I laughed imagining what a team of Bob Cowsers might be like.

The last award of the night was the sportsmanship award, and I'll admit that while Ashcraft worked up to announcing the winner I imagined it might go to me. To me, the long-suffering twelfth man of the defense who had performed ably when called upon north of the border back in August, the special-teams hero whose caused fumble in the first round of the playoffs brought on a rout. To me, who had complained about playing time all season to anyone who would listen, re-corded twice as many roughing-the-passer penalties as quarterback sacks, gone AWOL for one game, even conspired to mutiny. Oh, the vanity!

The sportsmanship trophy was in fact awarded to Mike Lafex, who had quarterbacked the team through practice for three quarters of a season though he did not see game time at that position after the third week. Ashcraft was no dummy; Black's future with the team uncertain, he had to throw his backup a bone. Mike *had* been a good sport about the whole thing, though I knew he had been in conversation with Coach Britton about quarterbacking the new team "up north," should it get off the ground. A new job with the state police might have Lafex in our area and he was eager for playing time.

There was one more order of business, a lifetime achievement citation of sorts for Britton, who had chosen this of all occasions to hush all the rumors and announce once and for all the establishment of that new team. Ashcraft also gave a plaque to Britton's daughter Tracey, who had been a Red and Black ball girl throughout her childhood. Ashcraft seemed genuine in his thanks and best wishes on the new venture, and Britton was humble and pleasant in his remarks, in spite of everything. They had been friends a long time.

The party moved to a dance club in the heart of Watertown shortly thereafter. Candace counted seven drinks I consumed over the next few hours, mostly screwdrivers, but she was the designated driver and I wasn't counting. We danced while I slurped down cocktails and watched college football games over her shoulder on a wall-mounted television, high-fiving teammates as they passed. Earnie Wash and Odell Bowens, Jesse Lamora. I suspect it was the most relaxed I had ever been among these men. By the end of that season, when I pulled into the dark locker room parking lot, their hails of "Professor," exclusionary back in July, an indication of difference, had become something else. A term of endearment.

I can't explain the striptease that ensued, and won't except to say I got down only to my slacks, socks, and T-shirt. The assembled wives seemed to enjoy it, if I do say so, even mine. Sam Verbeck's wife joined me on the club's small stage at one point and slipped a dollar in my belt loop, though Verbeck found me afterward at the bar to get it back.

"Everything I know about this guy I like," Ashcraft said to Candace in a bar whisper when I introduced the two of them later.

"Me too," she said.

He asked if I planned to play the next season.

"You didn't play me much this year, Coach," I told him. "That's a lot of driving to sit the bench." I guess the liquor had me brave.

"You'll play next year," Ashcraft said. "Maybe we can do something about all that gas money."

Yes, I guessed there would be a next year. Despite what some men will tell you, this camaraderie was not the best feeling I have ever had, not by a long shot, but it was not something I was liable to find back in the department of English and perhaps something I had come to this team looking for without knowing it. I understood that getting over football the second time around would be even harder than the first. Consider the case of Pat Nulty, by all accounts a reasonable person still at it at forty-eight years old, having played in four different decades with the team. "It's a disease," my mother's brother Eddie had told her on the phone when she'd called to tell him I was playing again. Though in the beginning I had intended to play only one year, I knew now it was more a matter of deciding between two teams for the next season: the Red and Black and, well, whatever unit I thought Britton could pull together. It seems foolish to say it, but it seemed one of the more difficult decisions I have ever made.

Candace had come around, mostly. They say most American men consider the ideal romantic partner to be something of a playmate—not a Playboy Playmate, mind you (although that probably factors into the fantasy of a lot of guys), but a woman who shares their interest in perpetuating adolescence indefinitely, one who shares their interest in sports, for example. I know I sometimes wished Candace had shown more interest in football. But this was one instance in which the fact that I had not married another armchair quarterback, that Candace had not contracted the family football disease, worked to my great advantage.

When we'd talked on the drive down, she'd said it was no problem if I decided to continue playing, despite what I had promised her, and she seemed to have given the matter much thought. "I'm a football widow one way or the other," she told me. "If you weren't playing games on Saturdays, you'd be parked on the couch watching them."

She felt much more strongly about which team I ought to play for. I'd been totally taken in by Ashcraft's barroom overture—I was an easy mark. But Candace had cast a wary eye.

"You're gonna drive sixty miles each way to stand on the sideline again?" she asked me. "Do all that work to prepare? Why?"

I couldn't say. I thought about the night of the road game in Montreal, how when my big chance came, the one I'd lobbied so hard for, I had not leaped at it. It would have been easy to remain on the Watertown sideline another season, prance around in a uniform like some fantasy camper, calling myself a football player. At some level I knew the real challenge would lie in getting a team off the ground up in St. Lawrence County, putting my body and reputation on the line every down of every game.

⬤ ⬤ ⬤

Meanwhile Coach Britton was moving full steam ahead with plans for the new team, which he had decided to call the St. Lawrence Valley Trailblazers, hoping the inclusive name would aid him in pooling talent from all over the region, from the Adirondacks to the Canadian border. He held a handful of meetings around the area in early January—well-placed ones it seemed to me—in Massena, New York, home to large Alcoa and Ford plants and until the late seventies home to a semi-pro club called the Warriors, and in Gouverneur, site of a medium security prison and thus home to platoons of correctional officers. He held meetings in Canton and Potsdam too, hoping to interest kids not already suiting up with local university teams.

I attended the Canton meeting in the wood-paneled back room of the St. Lawrence Inn, a favorite hangout of Saint Lawrence University hockey fans, but I had yet to commit officially to the project. Eight prospective players showed, mostly guys with high school experience, two or three who had played in college, none of them the kind of thoroughbred I guess I had hoped to see, the kind of athlete available to the Red and Black thanks to Fort Drum. Britton had prepared a flip chart that established the history of semi-pro football in the area and argued for its viability in the future, but this wasn't really the crowd for such a presentation. These guys just wanted to play ball, wanted to size up the competition. Maybe

Mike Britton wasn't the man to make it, either; Ashcraft the carnival barker, however, would have excelled in the role. Still, all his Stengelese aside, I thought the coach represented himself well, and by the end of his publicity campaign more than fifty area men had signed up to try out.

The night before a crucial EFL owners' meeting in Albany that February, Coach Britton called me at home. It was early on a dark North Country Friday evening and Jackson and I were relaxing in front of the television while Candace made our bed upstairs. He'd been contacted by the league, he said, who told him that the Lake City Stars had elected to play the next season in the NYAFL and that their EFL franchise was for sale. All it would take was $1,300, Britton told me, much less than he expected we'd have to pay if we were paying all the fees associated with starting from scratch. The only catch was that he had to have the money the next morning or no deal. The franchise would be sold to someone else.

If you'd asked me in those first few weeks with the Red and Black who among the men would be my one lasting friend, I would not have guessed sullen Mike Britton. But when you thought about it, despite the almost twenty-year age difference, Britton and I had a lot in common—a couple of lapsed Catholic boys who had come to football on our own, without a father's urging, but who shared a lifelong love of the game with younger brothers (Mike's brother Pat had been his Red and Black teammate). We were teachers by trade, divorced men who had just begun second marriages, and we regretted every end zone dance we ever saw, mourning an old-fashioned, chivalric brand of football, one that may never have existed except in our imaginations. Most important, I identified with something gentle in Britton, perhaps what Call and Ashcraft and guys like that sensed and rejected as "soft" in both of us. Candace noticed how every time Britton left a message on our voice mail over the next few months, each of the hundred or so times, he always made a point of saying hello to her and the baby. "Hello, Jackson," I remember him saying one day. "Tell your dad he's not a half-bad ballplayer."

I knew Mike wasn't going to ask me for the money directly. I also knew how little had been raised to that point—understandably, he had instead focused his efforts on player recruiting and negotiations with the league. The local money promised during that conversation in my car back in August had just never materialized (in fact, the player who promised it reportedly planned to stay with the Red and Black) and no one had yet pounded the pavement to drum up financial support. Reluctant as I had been to jump on board this project in the first place, I was doubly skittish about making a financial commitment, getting caught up with what I knew might become a financial tar baby.

And yet missing this boat would likely mean the end of the Trailblazer dream and consequently of my semi-pro career—Candace wasn't going to put up with me driving back and forth from Watertown again. Considering my experience with football and this league and the flexibility of my schedule, and considering our relative financial wherewithal, I figured I was probably more suited to this community venture than any other likely to come along (I knew I wasn't cut out to coach Little League). I told Britton I would give this some thought, that I might be able to get my hands on half that money, but that I'd have to discuss it with Candace first. "Sure," he said. "No problem."

I hung up with him and climbed the stairs to talk to Candace, Jackson on my hip. I guess I expected her to put the kibosh on the plan straightaway, make it easy for me. The only money available to me would come through Candace, via the salon's coffers, and I didn't think she was likely to agree. I never actually asked her for the money, just explained Britton's predicament.

"Well, here we go," she said after a moment, stretching the fitted sheet over the bed's corner. "This should be interesting."

"So you'll do it," I said, a little stunned.

"It's a tax write-off, right?" she said. "And I figure you'd spend that much in gas driving back and forth to Watertown." She knew where her interest lay in this matter, you had to give her that.

I called Britton back with our answer, and while he drove into Canton from his home out in Parishville to get the money, a twenty-minute trip, Candace drove the mile to the salon and back to fetch the checkbook. We sat solemnly on the couch until the coach arrived.

"Are you sure this is okay?" I kept saying.

"Don't be an idiot," she said.

While Candace wrote the coach a check, Britton thanked us profusely, said our money was only the beginning but that the team was now on its way. After he left, I suggested Candace and I look into buying a limo. It's the kind of thing football owners do, I told her.

Epilogue:
Boys from Up North

For he that today sheds his blood with me
Shall be my brother . . .
And gentlemen . . . now a-bed
Shall think . . . their manhoods cheap while any speaks
That fought with us.
   —King Henry to his outnumbered forces at Agincourt,
      from Shakespeare's *Henry V* (Act 4, scene 3)

The St. Lawrence Valley Semi-Pro Football Club, nicknamed the Trailblazers and decked out in the orange and green of the University of Miami, lost all ten games in its inaugural 2002 season. Beyond the flashy uniforms, wrote one cheeky *Watertown Daily Times* reporter, we bore no resemblance whatsoever to the defending NCAA national champion Hurricanes. I played every humiliating down, all the playing time I wanted and then some. I remember during some of those games praying for a chopper to drop a ladder and airlift me right out of the huddle.

We lost our first grudge match with the Red and Black on a hot July night at the Duffy fairgrounds in the third week of the season, 46–6, though we had trailed only 13–0 at the half thanks to gutty, emotional performances by a host of ex-Watertown players—Howery, our quarterback, Phifer, Woodward, and McCargar, to name a few.

Though they were largely the same group, the Watertown offensive linemen seemed much bigger that night than when I'd played with them, padded now, as Donald Hall would say, "into anonymity." From their three-point stances at the line, their face masks taken in the aggregate appeared like the grille on a Mack truck, which rumbled up and down the fairgrounds gridiron that night without regard for Trailblazers lying in its path. Our ex-teammates in Watertown had never bared their teeth in the media—Ashcraft was too shrewd to allow it—but we heard they hooted at our struggles among themselves, mocked us in practice, and they let us traitors have it that night.

Late in that game, once the matter had been decided, I wound up under the large, cleated foot of Jamee Call, pulling on a trap play. I had stunted at the snap, the "A" gap between the center and guard, and been knocked flat to the ground by center Adam Brown, a hard blow under my shoulder pads. Call stepped right on me, his sharp metal cleat running the length of my shin bone, gouging a gully two inches long and an inch wide in my leg, so deep it hardly bled at first. There was an official's time-out while Britton and the trainer helped me to the bench.

"Is that bone?" I asked about the bleach-white matter I saw at the bottom of the groove in my leg. The trainer, a local EMT who'd volunteered for the night, was pouring a searing disinfectant in the wound, torn flesh shriveling in the bath.

"Muscle," said the trainer.

I reentered the game right away and once the wound in my shin began to bleed it bled the bandage right off my leg. Between plays in the game's final minutes, Jamee Call pointed to where the crimson gauze had fallen in the grass.

"Take care of that fucking thing," he said. "God knows what diseases you guys from up north are carrying."

🏈 🏈 🏈

We were outscored 499–19 on the season (our 49.9 points allowed per game is the eighth worst in semi-pro history), held scoreless seven times (two games shy of the national semi-pro record), and finished 160th out of 178 teams in the American Football Association's final eastern region rankings. I couldn't imagine what those eighteen teams ranked below us must have been like—maybe that team of Bob Cowsers I had tried to envision at the Red and Black banquet the season before.

My four-year-old nephew Ian is fond of the Disney movie *Little Giants,* the story of the O'Shea brothers (played by Rick Moranis and Ed O'Neill) who manifest a lifelong personal rivalry when they agree to coach rival Pop Warner teams (Ian, clearly a carrier of the family football disease, is so fond of the film that he called his infant brother "Coach O'Shea" for several days after the baby was born). I've often thought, watching the movie since, that if Ashcraft and the Red and Black were O'Neill and his testosterone-juiced Cowboys, then Britton and the first-year Trailblazers were Moranis and his Giants, motley misfits with hearts of gold. In *Little Giants,* Moranis's misfits beat O'Neill's machine with a bit of fourth-quarter trickery—it's the kind of lesson you'd like your kids to learn. In real life, though, at least in real-life football, much as I hate to admit it, nice guys usually do finish last.

Maybe Mike Britton's kindness was the team's undoing in its first season, not that you could really fault a man for kindness. Like Moranis's good-hearted coach, he accepted all comers to our team and was sparing in his criticism of them, though you had to wonder if some of these marginally educated, marginally employed guys had ever seen a football game before, much less played in one. My personal favorite Trailblazer player was John "Knuckles" Sneed, a Cleveland, Ohio, native and disabled Gulf War vet who was also the veteran of two marriages and two tours in prison (one for assault and the other in the federal pen for money laundering) before he found his way to us.

It's not like the St. Lawrence Valley offered us a tremendous talent pool or the EFL offered new teams additional advantages like the ones NFL expansion teams now enjoy, such as additional first-round draft choices or supplemental draft picks. Several places in America could legitimately boast the best scholastic football—western Pennsylvania; Odessa, Texas; Massillon, Ohio. My hometown of Martin, Tennessee, population roughly eight thousand, has at the time of this writing two natives playing in the NFL, both prepped by Coach Coady: offensive linemen Chad Clifton of the Packers and Will Ofenheusle of the Jets. St. Lawrence County, New York, for all its hockey prowess, just isn't a football breeding ground. The Saint Lawrence University football team was winless for the third straight season in 2002 and the SUNY-Canton squad managed only one victory, then scrapped the football program at the end of the next year. Even when I had watched Jake and his friends play touch football in our yard, I could tell they had missed something crucial about the game growing up, about its essential violence.

Then again the Trailblazers' first season may have been a matter of karma: maybe any project undertaken out of spite (that other thing I shared with Mike Britton) is doomed. Perhaps Jamee Call was right that we splitters got what we deserved, though the Watertown coaching staff divorce that spawned our team was common in the semi-pro ranks—the nucleus of the Vermont Ice Storm team had split from the Lake City Stars, for instance, which itself split a few years later to form the Green Mountain Gladiators, and the Montreal Condors of 2001 split into two teams after the season.

If we had any victories that first year they were moral ones, which coaches like Vince Lombardi would argue don't actually exist. Foremost, we had a team on the field for all ten games (a winless EFL expansion team from Wilkes-Barre, Pennsylvania, had folded mid-season the previous year). Our closest game, in terms of the final score, was our first, a 21–0 loss to the eventual league champion Orange County Bulldogs (before we had figured out how bad we were, I told the paper). We had received equipment only two weeks prior, and, unable to afford a team bus, the twenty-one players had carpooled the four hundred miles to Monroe, New York, for the contest. At the end of that first season, I was named by the EFL coaches to the all-league defensive team, an honorable mention selection at linebacker.

The Watertown Red and Black struggled in the year following Coach Britton's departure as well, losing four of its first six games (the only two victories in those first six coming against the expansion Trailblazers) and finishing 4–5–1, falling hard to the Glens Falls Greenjackets in the first round of the play-offs. Their regular season losses included a 62–0 drubbing at the hands of those same Greenjackets, a taste of their own medicine, and the team's first ever loss to Montreal.

America's oldest rebounded strongly in the 2003 season, though, adding to their roster Ruben Hano-Hano and a handful of other members of the defunct Vipers franchise en route to an 8–1 regular season record, a Northern Division title and a berth in the league championship, played before three thousand fans at the Alex Duffy fairgrounds (as Ashcraft had promised two seasons before), the first championship game held there since 1980. Coach Britton and I watched them lose that championship 30–6 to the Glens Falls Greenjackets, who, in their seventy-fifth anniversary season, ended twenty-six years of their own title-game frustration.

George Ashcraft was named to the American Football Association Semi-Pro Football Hall of Fame at a ceremony in Canton, Ohio, in the summer of 2002, inducted as the coach who returned the oldest semi-pro club in the country to prominence; Coach Britton joined him in the hall the next year, as a player. Ashcraft remains the Red and Black head coach today with an all-time record of 99–56–2. As Al Countryman rides into the sunset of retirement, Ashcraft *is* the organization's public image, its most enthusiastic booster.

Countryman moved back to safety in the 2003 campaign to make room for younger talent at running back, announcing early in the year that it would be his last. His presence in the secondary improved the Red and Black defense immeasurably and he emerged as the most physical player on the league's nastiest defense. His performance in the 2003 EFL championship game—it seemed to Britton and me that he made every Watertown tackle in the first half—suggested he still had a few more years in him, but he and his wife had welcomed a healthy daughter into the world early in 2003 (they did not name her Roberta Cowser Countryman, as far as I know) and perhaps he is giving up the game to get on with his life. "There's a thought," Candace said when I told her.

Though I may sometimes begrudge him his successes, and his unanimous esteem among his semi-pro peers, I would be a fool to deny Countryman either. He seems a hall of fame shoo-in, and someday hence I will accept that it was my privilege to play with and against him. "When Al Countryman came out for the team eleven years ago, he didn't think he was big enough to play," Ashcraft told the crowd in a pre-championship game ceremony during which Countryman's #22 jersey was retired. "He not only proved he was big enough, but he proved he was the best ever." Countryman retired with 5,541 yards rushing and forty-five touchdowns scored, but no league titles.

Doug Black began the 2002 season as the Watertown quarterback but went AWOL after Ashcraft benched him during an opening-game loss in Syracuse. He missed the next month, and three more losses, replaced in the meantime by Todd Kiechle, a kid Countryman had coached in JV ball at Indian River High in Philadelphia, New York. Ashcraft, Black's longtime apologist, told the media that Kiechle would be his quarterback, that if Black returned to the team he'd be the backup. But when Black did return mid-season, just in time for the Trailblazer rematch, with the team's season on the line at 1–5, Ashcraft started him, and he led the Red and Black to a 27–0 win against us that night and to two wins and a tie in their final four games.

Black and longtime girlfriend Elizabeth Fox were married early in the summer of 2003 and he began the 2003 campaign as the Red and Black starter (all the veterans had returned at Countryman's call for a final championship push) but went down in week three with a broken foot, an aggravation of that old injury suffered against the Vipers two seasons before. He did not play again until the EFL title game, relieving Kiechle once Ashcraft and his staff had abandoned the run. But like Unitas in relief of Morrall in Super Bowl III against the Jets, Black seemed old, gimpy, finishing 18 of 30 for 159 yards and a touchdown. Too little, too late.

Lynn Patrick wasn't done with Red and Black football after all, despite what his lady friend had told me at the 2001 championship game. In fact, I heard he changed jobs and girl-friends by the time I saw him again, but he was still playing when the Trailblazers met the Red and Black in 2003. Dave McNeil played one more season after I left, the difficult 2002 campaign, then hung up his cleats. "Retirement's good," he told me when I saw him behind the end zone at the championship game at Watertown. "It was hard, but it feels good now." Ashcraft was sore that McNeil had made such a clean break. "He ought to come around more often," the coach said to me.

I saw several other former teammates at that game. Pat Nulty, who'd more than a year before offered me the title of this book, told me about a woman he was seeing in Boston, beautiful judging from the photo he carries, and how he was working two jobs to save money and planned to join her there if he could bring himself to leave his dead mother's house in Adams. Bruce Gonseth, who'd been transferred by the Depart-ment of Corrections downstate to Newburgh, home of the Orange County Bulldogs, was on the Red and Black sideline. I asked him about playing for the Bulldogs. "I've been ap-proached," he told me, "but my loyalty is here."

I had to wonder if that was a dig. Despite all the losing, though, I have no real regrets about my choice to leave America's oldest semi-pro team for the newest. On Sunday mornings after our most humiliating defeats, Coach Britton would leave mes-sages on our voice mail thinking it was a conventional answer-ing machine, messages intended to coax me from under the bedclothes. "I hope you're out of bed, Professor," he'd say, "it was only a football game." It's true, some days I didn't want to get up. I hurt, and I hated trying to explain our losses to people I saw in the grocery. Stress had Britton himself under a doctor's care for most of that first season and ultimately cost him his gall bladder. For my part, I tried to return a favor and remind him several times that this team had to be about more than winning games.

Our twenty-player core became a close-knit group of men, bound by what MacLeish had called "this magnificent, wild, extravagant, and often dangerous game." "The fewer the number, the greater share of glory," I told them before our first game, a line I cribbed from the St. Crispin's Day speech in Shakespeare's *Henry V.* The Trailblazer team lost a total of fifteen games over two seasons before picking up its first-ever win against the winless, expansion Green Mountain Gladiators on a warm, rainy August night in Burlington, a 20–0 shutout, and I am pleased to say I was still on the active roster, a starter at noseguard.

Somehow I became a leader among these men, their captain. It was something I had never been in my life—my high school coach had called me "a leader in the wrong direction"—and it was a mantle I wore uneasily. Still, I was proud. The boys called me "Bobby," a name out of my childhood, the name my wife and mother called me. I guess I represented a figure of some authority as an EFL veteran and college professor, but I had to laugh when I heard one of the younger guys, bless his heart, refer to me as a "no-nonsense family man." What do you mean, I wanted to say, it's all nonsense. All of it. A game.

Appendix A

Watertown Red & Black Schedule 2001

July 14	Vermont Ice Storm (Exhibition) @ Colchester, VT	W (58–7)
July 21	Capitaland Thunder (Albany, NY)	W (20–16)
July 28	Syracuse Vipers	L (13–21)
August 4	Lake City Stars (Plattsburgh, NY)	W (55–28)
August 11	Montreal Condors @ Chateauguay, QC	W (35–21)
August 18	Syracuse Vipers @ Syracuse, NY	L (18–29)
August 25	Capitaland Thunder	W (23–14)
September 1	BYE (Labor Day)	
September 8	Glens Falls (NY) Greenjackets	W (40–12)
September 15	Lake City Stars @ Plattsburgh, NY	W (38–28)
September 22	Montreal Condors	W (35–18)
September 29	Glens Falls Greenjackets @ Glens Falls, NY	W (21–14)
October 6	Capitaland Thunder (Playoff/First Round)	W (44–14)
October 13	Syracuse Vipers @ Syracuse, NY (Northern Division Championship)	L (0–20)

Appendix B

Watertown Red & Black Roster 2001

No.	Name	Height	Weight	Position
10	Scott Ford	5'10	200	Kicker
11	Lee Castor	6'1	190	QB
12	Brad Howery	6'0	200	QB
13	Willie Griffin	6'1	185	WR
14	Mike Lafex	6'1	190	WR/RB/QB
17	Marcus Harrison	5'10	170	WR
18	Derryl Green	6'3	200	SS/OLB
19	Kris Sullivan	5'11	210	DB
21	Toby Mason	5'8	185	DB
22	Al Countryman	5'7	220	RB/P
23	Trent Clark	5'10	190	DB
24	Josh Aubertine	5'10	185	RB
25	Kyle Roshia	6'1	185	DB
26	Fred Brodie	5'6	170	RB
29	Tilson Hargrove	6'0	180	DB
30	Casey Arrowood	5'10	180	K
31	Bruce Gonseth	5'10	235	LB
34	Erin Woodward	5'6	175	RB
37	Doug Black	6'1	200	QB
40	Mariam Williams	6'1	210	TE
41	Chris Littell	5'8	205	DE
43	Ed Pierce	5'11	200	LB
45	Jeff Booth	5'8	200	DE
48	Walter Canales	5'11	205	DE/FB

49	Darrin Phifer	6'1	205	DB
50	Brian Gokey	5'10	210	LB
51	Lynn Patrick	6'0	230	LB
52	David Dummitt	5'10	210	LB
53	Jesse Lamora	6'2	220	LB
54	Dave McNeil	6'3	270	G
58	Mike Delles	6'0	210	DE
61	Bob Cowser	5'9	220	DE
62	Francis Bartlett	6'0	240	T
64	Mark Bowman	6'3	290	T
65	Matt Quay	5'11	240	C
67	Brandon Payne	5'9	220	G
71	Pat Nulty	6'5	250	T
73	Jamee Call	6'0	295	T
76	Shane McCargar	6'6	305	T
82	Malon Augustave	6'1	175	WR
83	Odell Bowens	6'1	185	WR
84	Earnie Wash	6'1	180	WR
86	Kevin Simpson	6'0	165	WR
87	Chris LaSalle	6'2	200	TE
90	Marvin Hayes	6'0	225	DT
91	Bob Alexander	6'0	230	DE
92	Randy Parrow	6'4	260	DT
93	Adam Brown	6'2	285	DT
94	Johnnie Hall	5'9	260	DT
95	Bill Jones	6'5	230	OLB

Head Coach: George Ashcraft
Offensive Coordinator: Mike Britton
Trainers: Sam Verbeck/Pete Abass

Appendix C

American Football Association Final Rankings
(October 2001)

1.	Kane County (IL) Eagles	Mid-Continental Football League
2.	Scranton (PA) Eagles	Empire Football League
3.	Wichita Falls (TX) Drillers	North American Football League
4.	Puget Sound (WA) Jets	Northwest Football League
5.	Racine (WI) Raiders	Mid-Continental Football League
6.	Chicago (IL) Lawmen	Tri-State Football League
7.	Chippewa Valley (WI) Predators	Great Plains Football League
8.	Minnesota Lumberjacks	Mid-America Football League
9.	Prince William (VA) Lumberjacks	Mason-Dixon Football League
10.	Bowling Green (KY) Blitz	Ohio Valley Football League
11.	Southern Maine Raging Bulls	New England Football League
12.	Watertown (NY) Red & Black	Empire Football League
13.	New Mexico Razorbacks	New Mexico Football League
14.	West Virginia Wham!	Mid-Ohio Football League
15.	Inglewood (CA) Blackhawks	California Football League
16.	Cleveland (OH) Lions	Mid-Continental Football League
17.	Michigan Twisters	Lakeshore Football League
18.	Gastonia (NC) Gladiators	Independent
19.	Space Coast (FL) Panthers	Southern States Football League
20.	Minnesota Maulers	Mid-America Football League

Works Consulted and Suggestions for Further Reading

I would have said when I began this project that there was no canon of great football literature, taking as gospel the old saw about the magnitude of writing about a game being in inverse proportion to the size of ball used to play it. I would have been wrong, though. There are many good football books, a fact I enjoyed discovering throughout the writing of my book, including Frederick Exley's *A Fan's Notes,* George Plimpton's *Paper Lion,* Jay Acton's *The Forgettables,* Don DeLillo's *End Zone,* Buzz Bissinger's *Friday Night Lights,* and *The Courting of Marcus Dupree* by Willie Morris, to name just a handful. I am indebted to them all.

I have also consulted several histories of the game, including Robert W. Peterson's *Pigskin: The Early Years of Pro Football* and Marc Maltby's *The Origins and Development of Early Pro Football.* I looked carefully at non-football books like Susan Faludi's *Stiffed* and Ted Conover's *New Jack,* Bill McKibben's *Long Distance* and Sam Fussell's *Muscle.* All were of great use to me. John B. Johnson, Jr., and the sportswriters at the *Watertown Daily Times* have also been helpful, and I have relied greatly upon their extensive coverage of the Red and Black.

Acknowledgments

The first game ball, as it were, goes to my wife, Candace, whose support in this proves the cliché that love can surpass all understanding. And one each to my best friend, Chris Williamson, and father-in-law, Bill Scott, who though never on the field were my teammates in spirit. (Not that spirit, Bill. Nice try.)

I want to thank Morgan Entrekin and Daniel Maurer at Grove/Atlantic and the first readers of this material: Ted Cotton (mentor in all things), Joel Peckham, Liz Regosin, Paul Graham, Don Kennison, and especially Marie Harris. Your attention has made the difference. Thanks to David Shields, Alan Cheuse, Lee Gutkind, and Robin Hemley for early encouragement, and to Suzanne Gluck and everyone at the William Morris Agency for their crucial confidence. I would have given up years ago without the abiding support of longtime writer friends like Chauna Craig, Susan Atefat-Peckham, Paul Eggers, Natalia Singer, Mary Hussmann, Albert Glover, Dinty Moore, Lee Martin, and Gerry Shapiro, or without early teachers Cheryl Boyte, Larry Lorenz, and Ray Schroth, S.J. I want to thank them all here.

Acknowledgments

Special thanks also to Jon Gregg and Louise Von Weise, George Pearlman, Gary Clark, Kathy Black, and everyone at the Vermont Studio Center in Johnson, where most of this was written, for the gift of a clean, well-lighted room of my own in which to do this work, and for food (Mark Hallet) and friendships (Jill Osier and so many more) as well.

Tom Coburn and Kim Mooney, formerly of the Dean's Office at Saint Lawrence University, always said they believed in me and in this idea and proved it with a Bradberry fellowship and faculty development grant monies. Thanks also to Grant Cornwell and Margaret Bass, our current deans, who blessed me with a timely sabbatical. My colleagues in the English department, particularly our chair Kerry Grant and administrative assistant Charlotte Ward, bent over backward to accommodate my writing and football these last few years and I am deeply grateful. I learned much from my time with students like Chris and Josh Exoo, Bill Bradley, Colin Sullivan, Eileen Fenn, Bridgette Holmes, Lauren Boivin, Jess Baker, and Cate Doucette.

On the homefront, I must thank my parents, from whom all blessings flow so far as I can tell. And my sisters, Mary and Ruth, who complained about all the football on the family TV then married men as sports-crazed as my brother and I ever were (good choices both). My mother-in-law JoAnne Scott, and Jackson's army of seven aunts (Renee, Jessie, and Christa especially) provided timely babysitting and for that Jackson and I thank them heartily. My brother-in-law Pete, while he never made the *Road Rules* cast, did give me a trailer-hitch cover in the shape of a football.

Thanks to the Cloce and Fadden families who kept us in cars and kept them in good repair, and to John and Neta

Acknowledgments

Taylor-Post who provided bicycles just in case. We are also indebted to the Moses family, for candles and legal counsel.

A special thanks to Gregg and Molly at the Doggybag Deli in Canton who kept the horseradish sandwiches coming during my sabbatical, no questions asked.

Finally, I should thank my Red and Black and Trailblazer teammates and coaches Mike Britton and George Ashcraft for their cooperation and support. I may be a young man but I believe I know what a rare opportunity this has been, to take a dream from the mantel and toss it around again. Replacing it there, now that will be the hard part.

Canton, New York
February 2004